Institutional Design

Recent Economic Thought Series

Editors:

Warren J. Samuels
Michigan State University
East Lansing, Michigan, USA

William Darity, Jr.
University of North Carolina
Chapel Hill, North Carolina, USA

Other books in the series:

Mercuro, N.
Taking Property and Just Compensation
de Marchi, N.
Post-Popperian Methodology of Economics
Gapinski, J.
The Economics of Saving
Darity, W.
Labor Economics: Problems in Analyzing Labor Markets
Caldwell, B. and Boehm, S.
Austrian Economics: Tensions and Directions
Tool, Marc R.
Institutional Economics: Theory, Method, Policy
Babe, Robert E.
Information and Communication in Economics
Magnusson, Lars
Mercantilist Economics
Garston, Neil
Bureaucracy: Three Paradigms
Friedman, James W.
Problems of Coordination in Economic Activity
Magnusson, Lars
Evolutionary and Neo-Schumpeterian Approaches to Economics
Reisman, D.
Economic Thought and Political Theory
Burley, P. and Foster, J.
Economics and Thermodynamics: New Perspectives on Economic Analysis
Brennan, H.G. and Waterman, A.C.
Economics and Religion: Are They Distinct?
Klein, Philip A.
The Role of Economic Theory
Semmler, Willi
Business Cycles: Theory and Empirics
Little, Daniel
On the Reliability of Economic Models: Essays in the Philosophy of Economics

Institutional Design

edited by

David L. Weimer
University of Rochester
and
Lingnan College, Hong Kong

Kluwer Academic Publishers

Boston / Dordrecht / London

Distributors for North America:
Kluwer Academic Publishers
101 Philip Drive
Assinippi Park
Norwell, Massachusetts 02061 USA

Distributors for all other countries:
Kluwer Academic Publishers Group
Distribution Centre
Post Office Box 322
3300 AH Dordrecht, THE NETHERLANDS

Library of Congress Cataloging-in-Publication Data
Institutional design / edited by David L. Weimer.
p. cm.—(Recent economic thought series)
Includes index.
ISBN 0-7923-9503-4
1. Policy sciences. 2. Institution building. I. Weimer, David Leo. II. Series.
H97.I54 1995
363-dc20 94-33744
CIP

Printed on acid-free paper.

Printed in United States of America

CONTENTS

Contributing Authors

Jeffrey S. Banks
Department of Economics
University of Rochester
Rochester, NY 14627

Randall L. Calvert
Department of Political Science
University of Rochester
Rochester, NY 14627

Patrick Croskery
Department of Philosophy
Virginia Polytechnic Institute and State University
Blacksburg, VA 24061-0126

Johan A. de Bruijn
School of Systems Engineering, Policy Analysis and Management
Delft University of Technology
Jaffalaan 5, 2628 BX Delft
The Netherlands

Timothy Frye
Department of Political Science
Columbia University
New York, NY 10027

Stephen H. Linder
School of Public Health
University of Texas
Houston, TX 77225

B. Guy Peters
Department of Political Science
University of Pittsburgh
Pittsburgh, PA 15260

Ernst F. ten Heuvelhof
School of Systems Engineering, Policy Analysis and Management
Delft University of Technology
Jaffalaan 5, 2628 BX Delft
The Netherlands

David L. Weimer
Public Policy Analysis Program
University of Rochester
Rochester, NY 14627

Kenneth B. Woodside
Department of Political Studies
University of Guelph
Guelph, Ontario
Canada N1G 2W1

PREFACE

Policy scientists have long been concerned with understanding the basic tools, or instruments, that governments can use to accomplish their goals. The initial interest in inductively developing comprehensive lists of generic instruments to provide "menus" for policy analysts soon gave way to efforts to discover more parsimonious, but still useful, specifications of the elementary components out of which instruments can be assembled. Moving from a generic instrument to a fully specified policy alternative, however, requires the designer to go much beyond the elementary components. For example, a simple Pigovian tax to internalize an externality requires at least specification of the base to which the tax will be applied, its rate, and the administrative apparatus through which it will be collected. Rather than directly specifying some of these details, such as the base and rate, the designer may instead set the rules by which they will be specified. The creation of these specifications and rules can be thought of as institutional design. My hope that policy analysts can learn how to formulate more effective policy alternatives by better understanding institutional design was the initial impetus for this volume.

One soon discovers, however, that the project touches on many broader issues in the social sciences. The feasibility and effectiveness of policies depend on the political, economic, and social contexts in which they are embedded. These contexts provide an environment of existing institutions that offer opportunities and barriers to institutional design. A fundamental understanding of institutional design requires theories of institutions and institutional change. With a resurgence of interest in institutions among social scientists in recent years, there are many possible sources of theory.

The contributors to this volume draw from the variety of sources to identify implications for understanding institutional design. Though the result is not as big a step toward practical application as I had originally hoped, I think that it is appropriately a much more cautious step that offers something of value both to policy analysts and to students of institutions.

Many thanks to Jeffrey Banks, Randall Calvert, Stanley Engerman, James Johnson, and Andy Rutten for stimulating discussion and valuable comments at various stages of this project. I also wish to thank Warren Samuels and Zachary Rolnik for their encouragement.

David L. Weimer
University of Rochester
and
Lingnan College

1 INSTITUTIONAL DESIGN: OVERVIEW

David L. Weimer

1.0. Introduction

Administrators at private universities wish to send new alumni off with a sense that their alma mater truly values them specifically and undergraduate education generally. The turnout of professors at departmental diploma ceremonies sends a visible signal about their interest in the new graduates. Yet attendance at these ceremonies may involve inconvenience or perhaps even substantial opportunity costs. The two departments with which I am most familiar at my university deal with this public goods problem in very different ways. The political science department has developed a strong norm that usually turns out the entire faculty for the diploma ceremony year after year. The economics department has not had an attendance norm in recent years. Several years ago, prompted by several graduations with embarrassingly small faculty turnouts, the chair of the economics department increased attendance substantially by introducing a financial incentive system: each professor contributes a sum of money to an interest-bearing departmental account in September; those who attend the diploma ceremony share equally in the money accumulated in the account.

The problem of faculty attendance at diploma ceremonies was thus solved in two very different ways. One relies on mutual expectations and implicit rules about appropriate behavior; the other, on an explicit system of financial incentives. One can be thought of as the incorporation of an older academic norm into a broader departmental culture; the other, as a targeted response to a specific departmental problem. One continues to operate with the exercise of minimal hierarchical authority; the other requires the exercise of hierarchical authority for its maintenance. Yet despite these differences, each is an institutional design in the sense that it has become a persistent and anticipated set of rules and incentives that affect the behavior of individuals.

Though most social institutions appear to be the result of gradual evolution rather than sudden invention, political and economic institutions often result from purposeful design. In what ways does social science research inform the process of institutional design? The chapters in this volume attempt to answer this question.

2.0. The Agenda of Institutional Research

Recent years have witnessed a revival of interest among diverse groups of political scientists (including, for example, Shepsle, 1979; Riker, 1980; Hardin, 1982; Shepsle and Weingast, 1984; March and Olsen, 1989; Ostrom, 1986, 1990; Knight, 1992; Miller, 1992; Baumgartner and Jones, 1993; Weaver and Rockman, 1993; Calvert, 1993) and economists (including, for example, Schotter, 1981; Williamson, 1985; Sugden, 1986; Hodgson, 1988; Bromley, 1989; Eggertsson, 1990; Kreps, 1990; North, 1990) in the role of institutions in society. Unlike the largely descriptive studies of institutions that were prominent in the social sciences during the first half of the century, a time before the neoclassical paradigm gained dominance in economics and behavioralism shifted the research agendas in political science and sociology, the current wave of interest in institutions has a stronger analytical flavor. The central questions of the current research project include the consequences of alternative institutional forms on the behavior of individuals and the outcomes of collective decisions, the mechanisms that enable institutions to constrain behavior, and the logic of the processes through which institutions change.

2.1. Comparative Institutional Analysis

Most of the research that attempts to compare alternative institutional arrangements views institutions as fairly stable sets of commonly recognized formal and informal rules that coordinate or constrain the behavior of individuals in social interactions. Conventions, such as driving on the right side of the road, and norms, such as leaving gratuities for service at restaurants, are examples of relatively simple institutions that could be reasonably well described by a small set of rules. Families, economic organizations for producing goods, political bodies for making and implementing authoritative decisions, and constitutions enumerating authorities, rights, and responsibilities within polities combine large numbers of rules into complex bundles.

The interrelationships among institutions adds to the complexity. For example, the viability of various forms of economic organization depends on the particular system of property rights that is in effect, which in turn depends greatly on the specification and enforcement of civil and criminal laws. The importance of these interrelationships is extremely evident in the efforts of postcommunist countries to create market economies (Litwack, 1991; Riker and Weimer, 1993). One cannot hope to take account of these interrelationships in a formal and comprehensive way. Indeed, attempts to do so may rob the concept of institution of its usefulness. To paraphrase Aaron Wildavsky, if institutions are everything, then maybe they are nothing (Wildavsky, 1973).

Comparative institutional analysis attempts to get around these problems by assessing the consequences of specific institutional features holding other things equal. It is thus akin to the comparative statics done in partial equilibrium contexts in microeconomics. Theoretical work has dealt with such topics as the effects of organizational design on corruption (Rose-Ackerman, 1978) and the political control of administrative agencies (McCubbins, Noll, and Weingast, 1989). Empirical work involving cross-national comparisons includes studies of the effects of constitutional provisions on political behavior (Powell, 1989), the economic consequences of the independence of central banks (Alesina, 1988), and the effects of budgetary rules on deficits (von Hagen, 1992). Other studies compare budgetary restraints across states (von Hagen, 1991), test hypotheses about the role of committees in Congress (Krehbiel, 1991), and assess the importance of ownership structure on the performance of enterprises (Boardman and Vining, 1989; Vining and Boardman, 1992).

Elinor Ostrom (1990) provides an exemplary comparative institutional study. By focusing on a specific type of widely occurring institution, the governance structure of common property resources, she is able to make comparisons across a large number of detailed case studies conducted by herself and others. This empirical base allows her to identify design features that appear to limit overexploitation and underinvestment sufficiently for the resource to be long-enduring. Such features include a clear specification of the resource in terms of its relevant dimensions, a clear definition of the group of users, a congruence between use rules and local conditions, inclusive collective-choice rules for changing use rules, provisions for monitoring, and the application of graduated sanctions against those who violate use rules. Though Ostrom evaluates the design features in terms of longevity rather than efficiency, and though her largely inductively derived hypotheses about design deserve further testing, her work suggests a promising avenue for making empirical research relevant to institutional design.

2.2. The Puzzle of Institutional Constraint

Why is it that people allow themselves to be constrained by institutions? Monitoring and sanctioning may be sufficiently strong so that individuals find it in their self-interest to comply. As enforcement is usually costly to those who carry it out, however, this answer raises yet another question: What are the incentives of enforcers to enforce? Indeed, reliance on enforcement by successively higher levels of institutions raises the possibility of a complete unraveling when no institution remains to constrain the most superior. Further, individuals often comply despite facing such small risks of detection and sanction that compliance does not appear to be in their immediate self-interest, and those who have the capacity to change institutions may refrain from making changes in rules that would give themselves immediate advantage.

The puzzle of institutional constraint is perhaps best illustrated by considering a legislature that makes decisions by majority rule voting. If the legislature makes decisions over two or more policy dimensions, then in all but trivial cases of preference patterns there exists no alternative that cannot be defeated by some other alternative (Plott, 1967; McKelvey, 1976). The predicted result is that, even if legislators have stable preferences, the legislature will not produce stable policy choices. Stability can be induced by rules that structure authority within legislatures so as to place restrictions on agenda setting (Shepsle, 1979). A blunt way to achieve stability is to vest absolute control of the agenda in a single member. Stability may also be achieved in less dictatorial ways through rules that give jurisdiction for making proposals for changes in specific policy dimensions to separate committees. But if a legislature imposes such rules on itself by majority rule vote, it can suspend or change the rules by a majority rule vote when committees withhold proposals that would be favored by a majority. Only the willingness of the majority to allow itself to be constrained by the structure enables the structure to induce an equilibrium policy choice.

A "general equilibrium" theory of institutions would explain why it is in the self-interest of individuals to adhere to and to enforce the rules that are the subject of partial equilibrium analysis. It would thus be general in the sense that it does not rely on exogenous enforcement. It would be a rational choice theory of institutions because it assumes that all actors pursue their self-interests.

Modeling social interactions as repeated games provides a framework for a general theory. One begins by modeling a social interaction with a stage game that exhibits problems of cooperation or coordination in the sense that players would prefer some possible outcome to those that are equilibria. One then considers a repeated game made up of successive plays of the stage game. Depending on the payoffs in the stage game and the discount rates of the players, it is often possible to find equilibrium strategies for the players that yield the preferred outcomes that were not equilibria in the stage game.

A number of scholars have followed this approach to explain conventions and norms (Lewis, 1969; Ullmann-Margalit, 1977; Taylor, 1982; Axelrod, 1984). Andrew Schotter (1981) extends it to institutions more generally. He defines institutions as regularities in recurrent social situations such that the regularities are common knowledge among the participants, each participant expects that everyone else will conform to the regularities, and it is in everyone's interest to conform to the regularities if everyone else conforms to them. In other words, institutions can be interpreted as equilibria in repeated games.

The study of the medieval institution of the "law merchant" by Paul Milgrom, Douglass North, and Barry Weingast (1990) suggests how this theory might be connected to empirical research. They consider a repeated cooperation game in which randomly selected pairs of traders decide whether or not to enter into and comply with contracts. They show that recording contracts with a private judge, or law merchant, who makes judgments about noncompliance and keeps records of outstanding judgments can be part of an equilibrium involving contracting and compliance. Trade involving the law merchant can thus be understood as a self-sustaining institution.

A major complication of the general theory of institutions is the existence of multiple equilibria. Repeated games generally have multiple equilibria; indeed, the so-called folk theorem indicates that there are often an infinite number of them. On the one hand, the absence of a unique prediction makes empirical testing difficult. On the other hand, the existence of multiple equilibria leaves open a role for leaders (Miller, 1992): they may solve the coordination problem that players face in reaching an equilibrium by focusing their attention on a particular one.

2.3. The Puzzle of Institutional Change

If institutions are stable sets of rules, then how do institutions change? Change itself undercuts the stability on which people base their expectations. Yet failure to change in the face of changing circumstances may result in institutions whose rules constrain behavior in ways that are not socially desirable. As institutional design is nothing more than purposeful institutional change, a deep understanding of design requires a conceptual solution to the puzzle of change amidst stability.

Economists writing about institutional change have generally viewed it as a response to opportunities for Pareto efficient improvements. For example, Douglass North (1990: 83) sees institutional change as "overwhelmingly an incremental" process through which entrepreneurs operating within existing rules respond to changes in relative prices and preferences. From his perspective, institutional change enhances efficiency ex ante. It may be inefficient ex post, however, if entrepreneurs employ incorrect models of the world in making changes (1990: 104). The technically inefficient institutions that result may persist for two reasons. First, they may have induced investments that make moving to more technically efficient institutional forms economically inefficient — the so-called path dependence. Second, the interests favored by the institution may have sufficient bargaining power to block moves to more efficient institutions that favor them less. Implicit in this second reason is the assumption that transaction costs prevent those who would gain from the change from adequately compensating those with blocking power who would lose.

Jack Knight (1992) sees institutional change as inherently political. In his view institutions reflect the bargaining power of the relevant interests. They are the byproduct of conflict over social outcomes rather than the result of efforts to control inefficiency (1992: 40). In contrast to North's perspective, Knight's view allows for the possibility of institutional changes that are socially inefficient ex ante. One critical test of the theories of North and Knight could exploit their different predictions of how inefficient institutional changes could occur: without miscalculation for Knight, only with miscalculation for North. Another critical test could focus on efficient changes: Knight's theory could be rejected in favor of North's theory if we frequently found cases of efficient changes that went against the interests of those who enjoyed advantages in bargaining power.

If Knight's view that institutional changes favor those who enjoy relative advantages in bargaining power is correct, then, absent exogenous changes in bargaining power, the bargaining process should lead to growing asymmetries in bargaining power over time — a prediction that does not seem to be consistent with the broad historical record of modern liberal democracies. A social choice theorist might offer an alternative story of institutional change in which persistent losers occasionally succeed in destabilizing institutions giving unfavorable policy outcomes by introducing new policy dimensions that disrupt structurally induced equilibria (Riker, 1986). The introduction of slavery as a salient issue in the United States prior to the Civil War may be a dramatic example of such destabilization (Riker, 1982).

One of the most extensively investigated types of institutional change is the creation of property rights. An economic theory of the origins of property rights, set out by Harold Demsetz (1967), argues that property rights have value, and thus those involved have an incentive to create them, when changes in relative prices create scarcity and significant externalities. William Riker and Itai Sened (1991) set out a political theory of property rights by requiring that, in addition to scarcity, potential rights holders desire the rights, rule makers desire to recognize the rights, and those constrained by the rights respect them. Though a number of authors of detailed case studies see a bottom-up origin of property rights as suggested by the economic theory (Umbeck, 1981; Libecap, 1989), a detailed investigation of the privatization of Native American lands by Fred S. McChesney (1990) provides strong support for the political theory. McChesney finds that each of the major changes in federal policy toward the privatization of tribal lands was in the bureaucratic interest of the Bureau of Indian Affairs. Because property rights are substantively important but relatively simple institutions, studies like McChesney's are likely to offer the best empirical prospects for testing theories of institutional change.

3.0. Public Policy and Institutional Design

A growing interest in institutional policy analysis parallels the resurgence of institutional research in the social sciences. The actual analysis of institutional performance has often been limited to the consideration of specific procedural values such as fairness (Gormley, 1987). By incorporating substantive values into institutional policy analysis, it can appropriately play a more prominent role. Indeed, some observers see the design and assessment of institutions as the fundamental task of policy analysis (Brandl, 1988).

Yet some care must be taken not to define institutional design too broadly if it is to be a useful concept for policy analysis. The elements of lists of generic policy instruments (Hood, 1986; Weimer and Vining, 1989) that form the raw materials for policy design can usually be interpreted as rules and thus as institutions. Some restrictions are thus needed to make institutional design a proper subset of policy design. One possibility is to consider institutional design as the creation of relatively stable sets of interrelated rules and incentives that constitute coherent procedures intended to achieve substantive goals.

The distinction between policy design and institutional design that this definition seeks to capture is perhaps best conveyed by example. Consider the policy problem of unneeded military bases (Weimer, 1992). Before 1976, policy design was direct: the Defense Department identified bases it wished to close, gradually reduced activity levels at these bases, then simply closed them. Base closings came to a halt in 1976 when Congress made an institutional change requiring that closings be subjected to the provisions of the National Environmental Protection Act, including the preparation of environmental impact statements.

By 1988 several members of Congress were concerned about the cost of unneeded bases. They realized that representatives would fight hard against closing bases in their districts. So rather than proposing the closure of specific bases, they created a process for closing bases under Public Law 100–526: First, it gave a commission authority to apply military and cost criteria to create a list of proposed closings. Second, it exempted listed closings from the environmental impact statements that previously gave opponents an opportunity for stopping closures through court challenges. Third, it fixed the agenda for voting on the list by setting the rules such that if the Secretary of Defense accepted the list in its entirety, then Congress would accept it as well absent a joint resolution of rejection within a specified period of time. The first round of the process set in motion the closure of eighty-six bases.

One element of this institutional design that may be of more general application is the notion of fixing the agenda behind a "veil of ignorance." Members of Congress were willing to support the process before they knew for certain whether bases in their districts would be closed. Ironically, it may be easier to reach a consensus about procedural rules when the distributional outcomes of the rules are uncertain.

Consider one additional example of institutional design. Many horse races in North America are "claiming races." Those who enter horses must be willing to sell them at a specified claim price. (Claims are made before the race but revealed and executed after the race.) Tracks induce some owners to enter horses worth more than the claim price by setting purses sufficiently high so that the expected purse winnings exceed the differences between the values of the horses and the claim price. The entry of some horses worth more than the claim price creates an incentive for third parties to monitor the quality of horses. The monitoring makes it less attractive for owners to hold horses back in a series of races to obtain inflated odds in a subsequent race. Thus, claiming reassures bettors that the public information about horses is accurate.

The claiming race suggests a general concept for institutional design: create value to induce third-party monitoring (Weimer, 1992). It has a long history of application ranging from bounty hunting to deposits on beverage containers. One can imagine more unusual applications in situations in which individuals hold private information. For example, a one-time tax on the value of a natural resource would distort production decisions less than the severance taxes usually employed. The government, however, rarely has sufficient information to estimate the value reliably. One approach to valuation would be to require the owner to state the value of the resource that would be the sale price to anyone who wished to purchase it. Third parties would have an incentive to gather information about resources to take advantage of underestimation by owners. The threat of purchase by third parties would discourage owners from grossly underestimating values.

These examples suggest how approaching public policy problems from the perspective of institutional design can potentially lead to promising policy alternatives that might otherwise be overlooked. Adding design concepts of the sort proposed in the examples to the capital stock of ideas commonly shared by policy analysts is one way to develop an institutional design perspective. Candidate concepts can be drawn from a variety of fields (Weimer, 1992). Neoinstitutional economics and the rational choice theory of institutions are potentially rich hunting grounds.

3.1. Implications of Neoinstitutional Economics for Design

Neoinstitutional economics explicitly considers situational constraints, informational asymmetries, and the nature of interactions among economic actors while preserving the core assumptions of neoclassical economics:

stable preferences, rational choice by individuals, and comparable equilibria (Eggertsson, 1990). It has developed in recent years along two tracks: agency theory and transaction cost theory.

Agency theory sees organizations as bundles of explicit and implicit contracts defining the relationship between principals and the agents who take actions on their behalf. The basic elements of the theory can be found in the explanation of the existence of the firm offered by Armen Alchian and Harold Demsetz (1972). At about the same time, Stephen Ross (1973) introduced formal techniques for modeling principal-agent relationships. The application of agency theory was later broadened by Michael Jensen and William Meckling (1976), who focused on the effect of different structures of property rights on organizational efficiency. Bengt Holmstrom and Jean Tirole (1989) and David E.M. Sappington (1991) provide general overviews of the agency theory literature.

Agency theory is primarily concerned with the situations of asymmetrical information between principals and agents. Typically, agents have information, or can take actions, that are hidden from principals. In contrast to the older theory of teams, principals and agents are assumed to have different preferences over outcomes. The theory assumes that principals and agents design the most efficient contracts that are compatible with their individual incentives. It also assumes that contracts are complete and enforceable with respect to mutually observable actions and outcomes.

In Chapter 2, Jeffrey S. Banks distills propositions about institutional design from the formal literature on agency theory. He makes clear why principals and agents have a positive demand for enforcement and monitoring of contracts by third parties. He also identifies the characteristics of optimal contracts in several general contexts. Though these propositions are still a step away from direct application to practical problems of design, they provide a solid foundation for thinking about structuring incentives within institutions.

Transaction cost theory, which originated in Ronald Coase's (1937) explanation for the existence of firms and has been most thoroughly developed by Oliver Williamson (1985), shares with agency theory a focus on contracts. Unlike agency theory, however, it allows for the possibility that contracts may be incomplete, because all contingencies cannot be anticipated, and imperfectly enforceable, because detecting and punishing noncompliance is costly. Douglas Heckathorn and Steven Maser (1987) usefully divide transaction costs into the investments that parties make in preparation for contracting, the resources they expend in bargaining over the terms of contracts, and the risks of noncompliance and forced renegotiation they face after contracts are made.

The problem of credible commitment has a central role in transaction cost theory. Though especially difficult for governments because of their ability to change the formal rules (Rodrik and Zeckhauser, 1988; North and Weingast, 1989), the problem of finding ways of making credible commitments about future behavior is pervasive at all levels of organization. In Chapter 3, Timothy Frye considers this problem from the perspective of traders on Russia's commodity exchanges who cannot rely on the government for the effective enforcement of contracts. After explicating the design deficiencies of the commodity exchanges with respect to credible commitment, he analyzes the measures, such as the exchange of economic hostages and the hiring of private enforcers, that traders take to reduce their contracting risks.

3.2. Implications of the Rational Choice Theory of Institutions for Design

The possible equilibria in repeated games depend on a number of parameters: the payoffs to the players for various strategy combinations in the stage game, which determine the equilibria in the stage game and hence the credible punishment paths in the repeated game; the discount rates of players, which depend on players' marginal rates of time preference, the probability that they will play the stage game in subsequent periods, and the frequency of interaction among specific sets of players; and the information available to players about the types of other players. In Chapter 4, Randall L. Calvert develops propositions for institutional design by considering the consequences of changes in these parameters on the range of possible equilibria. He brings the propositions a step closer to application by giving examples of ways that designers can change the parameters. He also discusses ways that particular equilibria might be made more salient and therefore more likely to result.

In Chapter 5, Patrick Croskery looks specifically at the possibilities for institutional design through the introduction of conventions and norms. He follows the rational choice theory of institutions by interpreting conventions as equilibria in repeated coordination games and norms as equilibria in repeated cooperation games. He develops some design propositions directly from this perspective and others by considering the consequences of cognitive limitations that result when information and calculation are costly.

In Chapter 6, Kenneth B. Woodside explores the structure, evolution, and effectiveness of the institutions created to resolve trade disputes that arise under the Canada–United States Free Trade Agreement. One of the most interesting aspects of the dispute resolution panels has been the development of a norm of consensus so that panelists rarely split along national lines. Woodside finds that the norm has increased the legitimacy of the panels, which in turn has had some favorable effects on the domestic agencies that file complaints.

3.3. Values and the Process of Design

The discussion in this chapter has so far taken an instrumental view of institutional design: it is a means for achieving substantive values. In Chapter 7, Stephen H. Linder and B. Guy Peters contrast this view, which they call the "decisional tradition," with the "dialogical tradition" that emphasizes process values such as collective association and critical discourse in determination of ends as well as means. They explicate the differences between these two traditions in terms of the conceptions of rationality and morality that underlie them, and the implications of these differences for thinking about the process of design and the role of the designer.

3.4. Design in a Complex World

Society consists of numerous institutions with complex interrelationships. As previously discussed, the comparative statics approach to the study of institutions achieves tractability by limiting attention to a single institution or particular institutional feature. The narrowing of perspective makes it possible for analysts to formulate and test logically consistent hypotheses. It may not produce useful predictions for policy purposes, however, because the assumption of "other things equal" rarely holds in a fluid world. Put crudely, the confidence gained in terms of internal validity, which is so important for knowing what has been learned, may be purchased at the expense of reductions in external validity, the basis for applying what has been learned to policy problems.

Network theory attempts to take greater account of the complexity of the real world by focusing on corporate actors rather than individuals. In Chapter 8, Johan A. de Bruijn and Ernst F. ten Heuvelhof explore the implications of network theory for policy implementation. The strategies they identify for managing and restructuring networks can be thought of as institutional design at the macro level. Emphasizing the uncertainty facing actors in the network, they pay particular attention to ways that networks can be restructured to generate information useful for governance.

4.0. Conclusion

Social scientists are now pursuing the study of institutions from a variety of perspectives. The chapters in this volume demonstrate that some tentative propositions about institutional design can already be drawn from this growing body of research. As research on institutions accumulates, the potential for creating a body of useful knowledge on design should grow. Full realization of this potential, however, requires social scientists who are willing to think about the policy implications of their work and policy analysts who are familiar with the various research approaches. I will consider this volume to have been a success if it contributes to either of these cross-fertilizations.

References

Alchian, Armen and Harold Demetz. (1972). "Production, Information Costs, and Economic Organization." *American Economic Review* 62(5): 777–795.

Alesina, Alberto. (1988). "Macroeconomics and Politics." In Stanley Fisher (ed.), *NEBR Macroeconomic Annual* (pp. 13–52). Cambridge, MA: MIT Press.

Axelrod, Robert. (1984). *The Evolution of Cooperation*. New York: Basic Books.

Baumgartner, Frank R. and Bryan D. Jones. (1993). *Agendas and Instability in American Politics*. Chicago: University of Chicago Press.

Boardman, Anthony E. and Aidan R. Vining. (1989). "Ownership and Performance in Competitive Environments: A Comparison of the Performance of Private, Mixed, and State-Owned Enterprises." *Journal of Law and Economics* 32(1): 1–33.

Brandl, John. (1988). "On Politics and Policy Analysis as the Design and Assessment of Institutions." *Journal of Policy Analysis and Management* 7(3): 419–424.

Bromley, Daniel W. (1989). *Economic Interests and Institutions: The Conceptual Foundations of Public Policy*. New York: Basil Blackwell.

Calvert, Randall L. (1993). "Communication in Institutions: Efficiency in a Repeated Prisoner's Dilemma with Hidden Information." In William A. Barnett, Melvin J. Hinich, and Norman J. Schofield (eds.), *Political Economy: Institutions, Competition, and Representation* (pp. 197–222). New York: Cambridge University Press.

Coase, Ronald. (1937). "The Nature of the Firm." *Economica* 4 (November): 386–405.

Demsetz, Harold. (1967). "Toward a Theory of Property Rights." *American Economic Review* 57(1): 347–359.

Eggertsson, Thrainn. (1990). *Economic Behavior and Institutions*. New York: Cambridge University Press.

Gormley, William T., Jr. (1987). "Institutional Policy Analysis: A Critical Review." *Journal of Policy Analysis and Management* 6(2): 153–169.

Hardin, Russell. (1982). *Collective Action*. Baltimore: Johns Hopkins Press.

Heckathorn, Douglas D. and Steven M. Maser. (1987). "Bargaining and the Sources of Transaction Costs: The Case of Government Regulation." *Journal of Law, Economics, and Organization* 3(1): 69–98.

Hodgson, Geoffrey. (1988). *Economics and Institutions: A Manifesto for a Modern Institutional Economics*. Philadelphia: University of Pennsylvania Press.

Holmstrom, Bengt and Jean Tirole. (1989). "The Theory of the Firm." In Richard Schmalensee and Robert D. Willig (eds.), *Handbook of Industrial Organization*, Vol. 1 (pp. 61–133). New York: North-Holland.

Hood, Christopher C. (1986). *The Tools of Government*. Chatham, NJ: Chatham House Publishers.

Jensen, Michael C. and William H. Meckling. (1976). "Theory of the Firm: Managerial Behavior, Agency Costs and Ownership Structure," *Journal of Financial Economics* 3(4): 305–360.

Knight, Jack. (1992). *Institutions and Social Conflict*. New York: Cambridge University Press.

Krehbiel, Keith. (1991). *Information and Legislative Organization*. Ann Arbor: University of Michigan Press.

Kreps, David M. (1990). "Corporate Culture and Economic Theory." In James E. Alt and Kenneth A. Shepsle (eds.), *Perspectives on Positive Political Economy* (pp. 90–143). New York: Cambridge University Press.

Lewis, David K. (1969). *Convention: A Philosophical Study*. Cambridge, MA: Harvard University Press.

Libecap, Gary D. (1989). *Contracting for Property Rights*. New York: Cambridge University Press.

Litwack, John M. (1991). "Legality and Market Reform in Soviet-Type Economies." *Journal of Economic Perspectives* 5(4): 77–89.

March, James G. and Johan P. Olsen. (1989). *Rediscovering Institutions: The Organizational Basis of Politics*. New York: Free Press.

McChesney, Fred S. (1990). "Government as a Definer of Property Rights: Indian Lands, Ethnic Externalities, and Bureaucratic Budgets." *Journal of Legal Studies* 19(2): 297–335.

McCubbins, Matthew D., Roger G. Noll and Barry R. Weingast. (1989). "Structure and Process, Politics and Policy: Administrative Arrangements and the Political Control of Agencies." *Virginia Law Review* 75(2): 431–498.

McKelvey, Richard D. (1976). "Intransitivities in Multidimensional Voting Models and Some Implications for Agenda Control." *Journal of Economic Theory* 12(3): 472–482.

Milgrom, Paul R., Douglass C. North, and Barry Weingast. (1990). "The Role of Institutions in the Revival of Trade: The Law Merchant, Private Judges, and the Champagne Fairs." *Economics and Politics* 2(1): 1–23.

Miller, Gary J. (1992). *Managerial Dilemmas: The Political Economy of Hierarchy*. New York: Cambridge University Press.

North, Douglass C. (1990). *Institutions, Institutional Change and Economic Performance*. New York: Cambridge University Press.

North, Douglass. C. and Barry R. Weingast. (1989). "Constitutions and Credible Commitments: The Evolution of the Institutions of Public Choice in 17th Century England." *Journal of Economic History* 59(4): 803–832.

Ostrom, Elinor. (1986). "An Agenda for the Study of Institutions." *Public Choice* 48(1): 3–25.

———. (1990). *Governing the Commons: The Evolution of Institutions for Collective Action*. New York: Cambridge University Press.

Plott, Charles. (1967). "A Notion of Equilibrium and Its Possibility Under Majority Rule." *American Economic Review* 57(4): 787–806.

Powell, G. Bingham, Jr. (1989). "Constitutional Design and Citizen Electoral Control." *Journal of Theoretical Politics* 1(2): 107–130.

Riker, William H. (1980). "Implications from the Disequilibrium of Majority Rule for the Study of Institutions." *American Political Science Review* 74(2): 432–446.

———. (1982). *Liberalism Against Populism*. San Francisco: Freeman.

———. (1986). *The Art of Political Manipulation*. New Haven, CT: Yale University Press.

Riker, William H. and Itai Sened. (1991). "A Political Theory of the Origin of Property Rights: Airport Slots." *American Journal of Political Science* 35(4): 951–969.

Riker, William H. and David L. Weimer. (1993). "The Economic and Political Liberalization of Socialism: The Fundamental Problem of Property Rights." *Social Philosophy and Policy* 10(2): 79–102.

Rodrik, Dani and Richard Zeckhauser. (1988). "The Dilemma of Government Responsiveness." *Journal of Policy Analysis and Management* 7(4): 601–620.

Rose-Ackerman, Susan. (1978). *Corruption: A Study in Political Economy*. New York: Academic Press.

Ross, Stephen A. (1973). "The Economic Theory of Agency: The Principal's Problem." *American Economic Review* 63(2): 134–139.

Sappington, David E.M. (1991). "Incentives in Principal-Agent Relationships." *Journal of Economic Perspectives* 5(2): 45–66.

Schotter, Andrew. (1981). *The Economic Theory of Social Institutions*. New York: Cambridge University Press.

Sened, Itai. (1991). "Contemporary Theory of Institutions in Perspective." *Journal of Theoretical Politics* 3(4): 379–402.

Shepsle, Kenneth A. (1979). "Institutional Arrangements and Equilibrium in Multidimensional Voting Models." *American Journal of Political Science* 23(1): 27–69.

Shepsle, Kenneth A. and Barry R. Weingast. (1984). "When Do Rules of Procedure Matter?" *Journal of Politics* 46(1): 206–221.

Sugden, Robert. (1986). *The Economics of Rights, Co-operation, and Welfare*. New York: Basil Blackwell.

Taylor, Michael. (1982). *Community, Anarchy and Liberty*. New York: Cambridge University Press.

Ullmann-Margalit, Edna. (1977). *The Emergence of Norms*. Oxford: Clarendon Press.

Umbeck, John R. (1981). *A Theory of Property Rights with Applications to the California Gold Rush*. Ames: Iowa State University Press.

Vining, Aidan R. and Anthony E. Boardman. (1992). "Ownership Versus Competition: Efficiency in Public Enterprise." *Public Choice* 73(2): 205–239.

von Hagen, Jügen. (1991). "A Note on the Empirical Effectiveness of Formal Fiscal Restraints." *Journal of Public Economics* 44(2): 199–210.

———. (1992). "Budgetary Procedures and Fiscal Performance in the European Community." Indiana Center for Global Business, Indiana University, Discussion Paper No. 91 (May).

Weaver, R. Kent and Bert A. Rockman (eds.). (1993). *Do Institutions Matter? Government Capabilities in the United States and Abroad*. Washington, DC: Brookings Institution.

Weimer, David L. (1992). "Claiming Races, Broiler Contracts, Heresthetics, and Habits: Ten Concepts for Policy Design." *Policy Sciences* 25(2): 135–159.

———. (1992). "The Craft of Policy Design: Can It Be More Than Art?" *Policy Studies Review* 11(3/4): 370–388.

Weimer, David L. and Aidan R. Vining. (1989). *Policy Analysis: Concepts and Practice*. Englewood Cliffs, NJ: Prentice-Hall.

Wildavsky, Aaron. (1973). "If Planning Is Everything, Maybe It's Nothing." *Policy Sciences* 4(2): 127–153.

Williamson, Oliver E. (1985). *The Economic Institutions of Capitalism*. New York: Free Press.

2 THE DESIGN OF INSTITUTIONS: AN AGENCY THEORY PERSPECTIVE

JEFFREY S. BANKS

1.0. Introduction

Agency theory provides a systematic analysis of bilateral or multilateral exchange of goods and services in the presence of various factors that bring into question the neoclassical assumption of costless transactions. These factors include most prominently various forms of asymmetric information, wherein one party to an exchange has better information about the consequences of such an exchange than does another. The goal of agency theory is to identify efficient organizational responses to these complicating factors; the intent of this chapter is to survey some of the principle results from this literature and view these as fundamental building blocks in the efficient design of institutions.

As with most neoclassical economic theories, agency theory begins with the presumption that in many (if not most) activities there exist returns to specialization, either through economies of scale or through differential abilities and hence the comparative advantages of certain individuals producing certain goods and services. In such an environment, then, individuals can be seen as acting as *agents* on behalf of others: a lawyer acts on behalf of her client; a worker acts on behalf of the firm;

and government bureaucrats act on behalf of their political overseers. And along with such a relationship comes the possibility that the agent will have "better" information concerning the extent or cause of the realized benefits emanating from the relationship: thus the lawyer is privy to additional information concerning a client's case (for example, the likelihood of a favorable settlement); the worker knows to what extent his productivity is due to his own efforts rather than external factors; and the bureaucrat is more aware of the effectiveness of certain regulations. These asymmetries of information typically inhibit traditional vehicles such as "complete markets" and "perfect competition" from generating Pareto efficient outcomes in the exchange of these goods and services. The question addressed by agency theory is: To what extent can the beneficial returns to specialization be captured in the presence of these asymmetries? In particular, can the parties to an agreement *themselves* organize their relationship so as to capture these benefits?

Posing the question in this manner illuminates the fundamental behavioral assumption in agency theory—namely, that the parties to an exchange or agreement attempt to design their relationship in such a way as to best overcome these complicating factors. Thus, agency theory employs the notion of efficiency as a *positive*, rather than normative, concept. Further, the fact that in certain circumstances these complicating factors cannot be completely tamed implies the "correct" efficiency criterion is not the usual notion of classical efficiency (or "first-best" outcomes) but rather *incentive* efficiency (or "second-best" outcomes). As we shall see below, the principle difference between these two concepts is that the latter is determined with an eye toward the incentives of the individual actors to behave in their own best interests. Hence the worker cannot in general be *forced* to act in a manner acceptable to the firm, nor can the lawyer or bureaucrat be forced to reveal her information, but rather each needs to be provided with the incentives to do so. Thus second-best outcomes differ from first-best outcomes when the latter are inconsistent with individual utility maximization given the structure of the relationship. One of the primary goals of this literature is to identify the manner in which first-best and second-best solutions differ, specifically to see what sort of biases occur when arrangements take into consideration this "implementation" issue.

Efforts to achieve incentive efficiency can be thought of as the design of contracts between principals and agents to minimize "agency costs," which include "the cost of structuring, monitoring, and bonding a set of contracts among agents with conflicting interests, plus the residual loss incurred because the cost of full enforcement of contracts exceeds the benefits" (Jensen and Meckling, 1976: 305). The relative importance of these costs in any particular situation depends on the degree and nature of information asymmetry between principals and agents, as well as the degree of divergence in their preferences.

The specific plan of this chapter is to explore, from an agency theory perspective, how one particular kind of asymmetric information—namely, *hidden actions*—influences the efficient design of institutions. I begin by outlining the underlying structure of the principal-agent relationship in Section 2; in doing so I emphasize the issue of *commitment* by the parties to an agreement. Section 3 examines efficient outcomes in the presence of differing attitudes toward risk and shows how efficiency requires certain tradeoffs between desired outcomes. Section 4 extends this analysis by positing the existence of outside signals that can mitigate the need for such tradeoffs and demonstrates the optimality of "comparative performance evaluations" when the principal is interacting simultaneously with a number of different agents. Finally, Section 5 considers the problem of team production, where a number of agents work together to produce a collective output and the issue concerns their ability to construct efficient arrangements among themselves.

Before proceeding, two caveats deserve mention. The first is that I make no attempt to be exhaustive with respect to research on the issues of commitment and hidden action or on agency theory more generally. This chapter is not meant to be a survey; indeed, almost all of the theoretical results discussed below can be found in two papers—Holmstrom (1979) and Holmstrom (1982).[1] Rather, my purpose here is to describe a set of common problems addressed by agency theory, as well as identify solutions to these problems when they exist. Second, while most of agency theory (and hence this chapter) is framed in the language of explicit *contracts* or *sharing rules* between two parties to an exchange of goods or services, this by no means should be taken to imply that agency theory is silent in situations where these explicit arrangements are not allowed or not feasible. Rather, such arrangements can be found as *implicit* agreements among the parties as well, where admittedly such agreements might require a more elaborate method of enforcement. The point here, though, is that formal structure of agency-type analysis should not be viewed as necessarily a restriction on the scope or reach of the theory with respect to other, less formal, interpersonal relationships.

2.0. The Basic Model and the Problem of Commitment[2]

An individual, whom I refer to as the *agent*, influences a technology determining the benefits of another, the *principal*, where we let $A = [\underline{a}, \bar{a}] \subset R$ denote the set of possible *actions* the agent might adopt.

Common interpretations of these roles include the agent as worker and principal as owner of a firm, the agent as tenant farmer and the principal as the landlord, the agent as the seller and the principal the buyer of some good, and the agent as owner of a regulated monopoly and the principal as regulator. The agent's action is typically thought of as measuring the "effort" undertaken on the principal's behalf; hence in the above roles the action taken by the worker would be toward the production of some good for the firm, the effort taken by the tenant farmer in growing the crops on the landlord's land, the work involved in producing a high-quality good for the buyer, or the effort taken by the regulated monopoly to control costs. In this sense, then, while the principal may be able to *infer* which action the agent will take in certain circumstances, we will assume throughout that the principal will not be able to *observe* the agent's action (or, at least, not *verify* the action; see below); she can only observe the value or benefits arising from such actions.

These benefits, which for simplicity we think of as dollar profits, are written as a function $\pi(a)$, where $a \in A$ is the action performed by the agent and where π is increasing and concave in a; thus $\pi' = \delta\pi/\delta a > 0$ and $\pi'' = \delta^2\pi/\delta a^2 < 0$. Therefore, all else equal, the principal prefers the agent take a higher action to a lower action. On the other hand, higher actions impose greater costs on the agent in the sense that, for example, more effort allocated to production takes more time or exertion. Let $c(a)$ denote the cost to the agent of taking the action a, where $c' > 0$ and $c'' > 0$. This cost should not be interpreted as an *accounting cost*—that is, some cost incurred by the agent (for example, from the purchase of parts or equipment) that would already be incorporated into the determination of the profits π—but rather as an *opportunity cost* incurred by the agent due to his provision of effort on the principal's behalf as opposed to some alternative use. Finally, we assume that the preferences for the principal over profits are such that the utility from money income of m is simply equal to m, whereas the preferences of the agent over money income and the action she adopts are represented by $m - c(a)$.

The fundamental problem is one of a divergence of preferences: while the principal prefers the agent to adopt a high action, thereby generating increased profits, the agent prefers low actions in order to keep his costs down. Further, this problem is potentially exacerbated by the inability of the principal to actually observe, and hence condition on, the agent's chosen action. The goal of the theory is to identify mutually beneficial arrangements—in particular, ways of sharing the principal's benefits—so that this divergence does not significantly inhibit the participants from capturing the gains from their interaction.

It is the agent who is the producer of the good in question, whereas it is the principal who values the good. Suppose for the moment we adopt the scenario of the principal as buyer and the agent as seller of some good, where the timing of events are that first the agent produces the good (selects an action $a \in A$), and then the principal and agent bargain or negotiate to determine a price, (the amount the principal will pay the agent in exchange for the good). Suppose further that the bargaining over price is characterized by the parties "splitting the difference," in the sense that if the benefits are π the price paid to the agent is equal to $\pi/2$.[3] If the agent anticipates this bargaining outcome, he identifies his optimal action by solving

$$\underset{a \in A}{\text{maximize}}\ \pi(a)/2 - c(a) \tag{1}$$

to obtain a solution $\hat{a}$ characterized by $\pi'(\hat{a})/2 = c'(\hat{a})$. The resulting utility payoffs for the principal and agent are then $\pi(\hat{a})/2$ and $\pi(\hat{a})/2 - c(\hat{a})$, respectively.

The claim, however, is that this outcome (the action $\hat{a}$ and the distribution of profits $\pi(\hat{a})/2$ to each) is not an *efficient* outcome, in the sense that there exists another action and distribution of profits that makes both participants better off. To see this, suppose that for any realized level of profits π we give the principal a fixed amount $\pi(\hat{a})/2$ and allocate the rest of the profits to the agent. In this instance, the agent would solve

$$\underset{a \in A}{\text{maximize}}\ \pi(a) - \pi(\hat{a})/2 - c(a), \tag{2}$$

generating an action a^* defined by

$$\pi'(a^*) = c'(a^*), \tag{3}$$

where simple calculations reveal that a^* will be greater than $\hat{a}$. Further, the agent must be strictly better off in this second scenario (in solving (2)) than in the first, since under (2) one option available to the agent is to simply select $a = \hat{a}$, giving exactly the same payoff as in (1). As a^* is greater than $\hat{a}$ (or more specifically because a^* is not equal to $\hat{a}$) and a^* is unique, then it must be that the agent prefers the second scenario to the first. But then the action a^*, along with the distribution $\pi(\hat{a})/2$ to the principal and $\pi(a^*) - \pi(\hat{a})/2$ to the agent, makes the agent strictly better off, while the principal is no worse off; that is, we have achieved a Pareto improvement over the original solution.[4]

Now to identify the set of *efficient* outcomes, we solve the following program:

$$\underset{a,s}{\text{maximize}}\ \pi(a) - s \tag{4}$$

subject to

$$s - c(a) \geq \bar{U}, \tag{5}$$

where the parameter s is the *share* of profits going to the agent. That is, we maximize the principal's payoff subject to the constraint that the agent's payoff is at least equal to some level $\bar{U}$; by varying the level of $\bar{U}$ we map out the Pareto frontier with respect to the principal's and agent's utility.[5] As both parties' payoffs are increasing in income, the constraint (5) will be binding; substituting this constraint into the maximand and solving, we get $\pi'(\tilde{a}) = c'(\tilde{a})$, or $(\tilde{a}) = a^*$; and then the distribution of profits is such that $s = \bar{U} + c(a^*)$. Reexamining equation (3), we see that the defining characteristic of the efficient action a^* is that the marginal benefit in terms of increasing the profits to the principal are set equal to the marginal cost of the agent providing a slightly higher action, because at such an action level the total value of the interaction (principal profits less agent cost) is maximized. Therefore when we vary $\bar{U}$ we see that efficiency requires the agent's action to be equal to a^*, with then *any* distribution of the resulting profits being consistent with efficiency. In particular, the characterization of the efficient action choice by the agent can be solved independently from the question of how the resulting profits should be distributed; this separation result will continue to hold in later sections as well.

The source of the inefficiency in the original scenario is now obvious: the incentives for the agent to take action are not coincident with the collective incentives to take action. Specifically, while the bargaining process envisioned in the original solution is certainly fair and equitable once the agent's action has been chosen and hence the costs to the agent are *sunk*, at the margin the benefits accruing to the agent from an increase in action are only one-half of what they should be from the social perspective.

As we saw above, one reasonable way to implement an efficient solution is to adopt a particularly simple *sharing rule*—a distribution of realized profits as a function of those profits, wherein the principal receives a fixed amount, with the remainder going to the agent. This then gives the agent the incentive to adopt the efficient action because his preferences are now aligned with the social preferences. On the other hand, what this sharing rule requires is that the parties be able to somehow *commit* to this rule ex ante—that is, agree not to renege the agreed-to sharing rule. For example, the principal has an incentive to renege on the efficient sharing rule above *once the agent has taken his action* because a "split the difference" bargaining solution at this point would give the principal a higher payoff. Of course, if the agent correctly anticipated that the principal would act in this manner, his optimal action would no longer be the efficient action, and we would be back in the original scenario with a resulting inefficient outcome. Alternatively, we can view this problem as one of inducing a demand *on the part of both participants* for some third-party enforcement mechanism for the sharing rule. That is, if the application of the sharing rule is not in the hands of the principal and agent but rather is controlled by some outside party with the ability to enforce any agree-upon sharing rule, the problem of commitment is effectively nullified. This then gives us our first principle of efficient institutional design:

> *Proposition 1*: There exists a demand for third-party enforcement of agreements, in the sense that both the principal and the agent are made better of with such enforcement.

One obvious candidate for an enforcement mechanism is the ability to write contracts that are enforceable by the courts; alternative mechanisms, however, might also be used.[6] The key to any such enforcement mechanism is that the information on which the sharing rule is based—here the monetary profits—are *verifiable* by the mechanism. For example, the courts must have the ability to identify the level of profits so as to be able to ascertain when an agreement has been broken. More generally, what Proposition 1 demonstrates is how the principal and agent have an incentive to design their relationship so as to include other parties in the structure of their interaction.

Finally, there exists one interesting scenario in which such commitment is actually *not* required: suppose we consider the case of the principal as the firm, and the agent as the sole worker for the firm. The sharing rule described above that implements an efficient outcome—namely, the firm receiving a fixed amount of the profits and the worker capturing the residual—is in effect equivalent to the firm *selling itself* to the worker for this fixed amount, so that now the worker's preferences are perfectly aligned with profit maximization of the part of the firm. Thus if the agent has sufficient assets to make such a purchase, or sufficient access to capital markets, and the benefits of the principal are in some sense *transferable*, then an efficient solution can be implemented without the need for commitment.

3.0. Hidden Actions and Risk Sharing

In the previous section profits, or the monetary benefits accruing to the principal, were assumed to be a deterministic function of the agent's action; therefore, since π was assumed to be an increasing function of the agent's action, knowledge of profits was in some sense synonymous with knowledge of the agent's action. Now suppose that such a precise inference is not possible, in that profits are a function not only of the agent's action but also of a random variable θ; thus we write profits as $\pi(a,\theta)$, where for every value of θ the function π is increasing in the agent's action. In particular, the presumption is that θ occurs after the choice of action, so that the agent cannot condition his action on the realization of θ. Further, as before the principal only observes the resulting profits, not the action chosen by the agent. Therefore, from the principal's perspective a certain level of observed profits might be due to (say) a "high" action by the agent together with a "low" realization of θ, or due to a "low" action paired with a "high" θ; the problem for the principal then is to disentangle these effects. As in Section 2 a sharing rule $s(\pi)$ specifies the payment from the principal to the agent as a function of realized profits. Finally, there exists some "third-party" mechanism (the courts) able to enforce any sharing rule agreed to by the principal and agent.

We assume as before that the principal's utility payoff from income m is simply equal to m, so that in particular the principal is *risk-neutral* with respect to income: a distribution of income with an expected amount of $\bar{m}$ and receiving $\bar{m}$ with certainty give the same utility to the principal. On the other hand, the agent may be either risk neutral or *risk averse*, where the latter has the outcome of $\bar{m}$ with certainty preferred to the distribution of income with expectation $\bar{m}$. In contrast to those of the previous section, results in the current section depend critically on which of these two holds.[7] In general, the preferences of the agent over income and actions are now represented by $U(m, a) = u(m) - c(a)$, where $u' > 0$ and $u'' \leq 0$, and where $u'' < 0$ denotes the agent being risk averse.

This interaction between principal and agent is the quintessential instance of a *moral hazard* problem, in that an individual performing a task for another has divergent preferences from the latter, and where the behavior of the former is only imperfectly observable. The term *moral hazard* originates in the insurance literature, where it was noted that, for example, an automobile owner who was fully insured against any accidents (whose income in all eventualities was constant) has no incentive to take care in driving. Therefore, in the absence of perfect information concerning the care exhibited by the driver, an optimal insurance contract must have the driver bearing some of the risk involved in order to provide the "correct" incentives for taking care.

As discussed in the introduction, our immediate goal is to identify efficient arrangements between the principal and the agent, the premise being that any inefficient outcome will not persist as the participants have a joint interest in adopting more efficient outcomes. Let $F(.)$ denote the distribution of the random variable θ on R, and $f(.)$ the associated density. In the current scenario efficient outcomes are then characterized by the following program:

$$\underset{a,s(.)}{\text{maximize}} \int [\pi(a,\theta) - s(\pi(a,\theta))]dF(\theta) \tag{6}$$

subject to

$$\int U(s(\pi(a,\theta)), a)dF(\theta) \geq \bar{U}. \tag{7}$$

That is, we maximize the principal's (expected) net profits with respect to actions by the agent and sharing rules, subject to a constraint placing a lower bound on the agent's (expected) utility. Equations (6) and (7) are analogous to equations (4) and (5) above, respectively, the only difference being the presence of a random term in the former. Thus, any solution to (6) and (7) gives what is known as a *classically efficient* (or "first-best") solution to the problem—that is, an action and a sharing rule $<a^*, s^*(\pi)>$ such that there does not exist another pair $<\hat{a}, \hat{s}(\pi)>$ giving one of the participants a strictly higher payoff while giving the other participant no lower payoff.

It is easily shown that if the agent is risk averse, any classically efficient arrangement must have the principal bearing *all* of the risk involved in the randomness of the profits—that is, the sharing rule will be *constant*: $s(\pi) = \bar{s}$ for all π. To see this, take any action $\hat{a}$, and any sharing rule $\hat{s}(\pi)$ that is nonconstant. Because the agent is risk averse, a Pareto improving arrangement would be one in which the action $\hat{a}$ is still adopted, but the agent receives a constant share $\bar{s}$ equal to the *expected* share generated by the original sharing rule $\hat{s}(\pi)$. Because the agent is assumed risk averse, the agent is now strictly better off, while the risk-neutral principal is no worse off.

Therefore classical efficiency and risk aversion require that the agent bear none of the risk involved in the process. Yet under any such arrangement it is clear that a utility-maximizing agent would select the lowest possible action in response, just as in the auto insurance example described above. In this sense any solution to (6) and (7) may fail to be *implementable*; that is, given the sharing rule $s^*(\pi)$ the optimal choice of action by the agent may differ from a^*. Therefore, in order to identify arrangements that are consistent with the agent acting in a utility-maximizing manner, we need to add the following *incentive compatibility* constraint to the program:

$$a^* \text{ maximizes } \int U(s^*(\pi(a,\theta)),\ a)dF(\theta). \tag{8}$$

That is, when faced with the sharing rule $s^*(.)$, the agent selects a^* as his utility maximizing choice of action. Including constraint (8), then, gives what are known as *incentive efficient* (or "second-best") solutions, in contrast to the classically efficient ("first-best") solutions above.[8]

Note that if the agent were in fact risk neutral, so that for instance $u(m) = m$, then a classically efficient solution could be implemented by a sharing rule of the form $s(\pi) = \alpha + \pi$, which is identical to that used in Section 2 above. With such a sharing rule the incentives of the agent are again perfectly aligned with the collective incentives, and hence the agent will adopt the classically efficient action. Yet under risk aversion, if an incentive-efficient sharing rule has the agent taking any but the least costly action, it must be the case that the sharing rule is nonconstant and hence the agent is bearing some risk, for which he must be compensated through the sharing rule. At the other extreme, consider the action a^* in the classically efficient solution. At a^* the marginal benefit derived by the principal is equal to the marginal cost of providing enough income to the agent to satisfy the utility constraint (7). Hence lowering this action by a small amount will have a zero first-order effect on the principal's net benefit. On the other hand, attempting to implement a^* would require the agent to bear a positive risk burden that must be compensated for by the principal. Hence, by lowering this action a nonnegligible gain can be had by lessening this risk burden. The incentive efficient solution will thus exhibit a trade off between having a nonconstant sharing rule in order to provide incentives for the agent to take costly actions, and having to pay the agent to bear such risks. Therefore, subject to some technical conditions,[9] we have the following:

> *Proposition 2:*[10] With a risk-averse agent, an incentive efficient solution will have a nonconstant sharing rule; and the action implemented will be lower than that in a classically efficient solution.

In words, an incentive efficient solution differs from a classically efficient solution in two respects: the agent bears some risk; and the action implemented is less than socially optimal.

The next section will explore institutional responses to the message contained in Proposition 2. Before doing so, however, it is useful to get a feel for the structure of an incentive-efficient sharing rule. Suppose we suppress the random variable θ, and treat profit as itself a random variable with distribution $G(\pi;\ a)$ and density $g(\pi;\ a)$ parameterized by the agent's action and induced by the relationship $\pi = \pi(a,\ \theta)$.[11] The condition that profits be increasing in the agent's action ($\delta\pi/\delta a > 0$) is seen to translate into $\delta G/\delta a < 0$—that is, an increase in action shifts the distribution of profits "to the right" in the sense of first-order stochastic dominance.

For simplicity, suppose there are only two actions available to the agent, $A = \{a_L, a_H\}$, with $a_L < a_H$. Clearly, if the principal wishes to implement the action a_L, all that is required is a constant sharing rule $s(\pi) = \bar{s}$ because as above the agent would then have the incentive to take the lowest possible action, in this case a_L. If, on the other hand, the principal wishes to implement the action a_H, then we have the following translated versions of equations' (6), (7), and (8):

$$\underset{s(.)}{\text{maximize}} \int [\pi - s(\pi)] g(\pi; a_H) d\pi \tag{6'}$$

subject to

$$\int u(s(\pi)) g(\pi; a_H) d\pi - c(a_H) \geq \bar{U} \tag{7'}$$

$$\int u(s(\pi)) g(\pi; a_H) d\pi - c(a_H) \geq \int u(s(\pi)) g(\pi; a_L) d\pi - c(a_L). \tag{8'}$$

Equation (8′), the incentive constraint, just says that given the sharing rule $s(.)$ the agent prefers to take the action a_H rather than a_L. Point-wise optimization of this program, with Lagrange multipliers λ and μ on (7′) and (8′), respectively, gives a first-order condition of the form

$$\frac{1}{u'(s(\pi))} = \lambda + \mu\left[1 - \frac{g_L(\pi)}{g_H(\pi)}\right] \tag{9}$$

where $g_j(\pi) = g_j(\pi; a_j)$, $j = L, H$.

Classical efficiency would require $\mu = 0$, and hence a constant sharing rule; therefore (9) shows how the incentive efficient rule differs from the classically efficient rule in making the agent's share of profits vary with the realization of profits. Further, as (9) demonstrates, the crucial determinant in this optimal sharing rule is the *likelihood ratio* $g_L(\pi)/g_H(\pi)$, describing the relative likelihood of a profit level being generated by a low action as opposed to a high action. In particular, the optimal sharing rule exhibits features of *statistical inference* problem on the part of the principal, in the following sense: suppose the principal viewed the action chosen by the agent as a random variable, with some positive prior probability assigned to each of a_L and a_H. Then if the principal were to observe a profit π such that $g_L(\pi) > g_H(\pi)$, or equivalently $g_L(\pi)/g_H(\pi) > 1$, then according to Bayes's rule the principal's posterior belief would put greater weight on a_L than did the prior belief; and conversely for π such that $g_L(\pi) < g_H(\pi)$. But then the optimal sharing rule, characterized by (8), can be thought of as paying more to the agent when the principal is "more certain" the action is a_H.

Therefore, in general the optimal sharing rule will not be monotonic in realized profits π, but rather monotonic in the likelihood ratio: as $g_L(\pi)/g_H(\pi)$ increases, the share of profits to the agent decreases (recall we are assuming here that the agent is risk averse, so $u'' < 0$). On the other hand, if this ratio is itself decreasing in π, in which case we say the profit densities in the two-action case satisfy the *monotone likelihood ratio property* (MLRP), then the optimal sharing rule *will be* increasing in π.[12] Returning to the "continuous action" model, the analogous equation to (9) is

$$\frac{1}{u'(s(\pi))} = \lambda + \mu\left[\frac{g_a(\pi;\, a)}{g(\pi;\, a)}\right], \tag{10}$$

where $g_a = \delta g/\delta a$, and MLRP for this case is then that $g_a(\pi;\, a)/g(\pi;\, a)$ be increasing.

Of course, this statistical inference problem posited for the principal does not actually occur because the principal can infer precisely what action the agent will take from knowledge of the sharing rule (and the agent's preferences). Yet viewing the principal's problem in this manner is instructive in providing intuition about the structure of the optimal sharing rule, as well as additional results pertaining to the value of outside information, to which we now turn.

4.0. The Value of Additional Information

Suppose we now extend the analysis of the previous section by allowing the principal to observe an outside signal, which we denote by the variable y, which could be incorporated into the sharing rule. Thus, we can write the sharing rule as a function $s(\pi,\, y)$, and the presumption is that the outside signal y is verifiable by our third-party mechanism in the same way that π is. The idea here is that y might provide some additional information pertaining to the random variable θ, and hence the principal might be able to better disaggregate the effect on profits of the action adopted by the agent from the noise term θ. For example, a CEO's compensation might be based not only on the profits of the company but also on market conditions, which would presumably be correlated with θ. The question addressed in this section is: When would it be optimal to include the signal y in the sharing rule?

Let us continue to suppress the random variable θ, and let $g(\pi,y;\, a)$ denote the joint density of profits π and the outside signal y. Now in the previous section we saw how the likelihood ratio $g_a(\pi,y;\, a)/g(\pi,y;\, a)$

plays a central role in determining the optimal sharing rule, in that this term captures the notion of a realized profit level being "more likely" to have come from a higher action by the agent. Therefore, one would reasonably imagine that if the outside signal y effects this ratio, it should be included in the optimal sharing rule. On the other hand if $g_a(\pi,y; a)/g(\pi,y; a)$ is equal to some function $k(\pi, a)$—that is, independent of y—then y plays no role in this inference problem. It can be shown that the latter is ture if and only if the following holds:

$$g(\pi,y; a) = h(\pi, y)k(\pi, a) \text{ for all } (\pi, y). \tag{11}$$

In terms of the principal's statistical inference problem equation (11) would say that π is a *sufficient statistic* for (π, y) with respect to the "random variable" a, and hence π carries all of the relevant information about the agent's action. Therefore, we have that there exists an incentive compatible sharing rule $s(\pi, y)$ that Pareto dominates the incentive efficient sharing rule $s(\pi)$ based only on profits if and only if (11) does not hold; and hence if y generates *any* information over and above that found in π, then it should be included in an optimal sharing rule.

This result has two immediate implications for the efficient design of institutions. To see the first implication, suppose that the function $g(.)$ can be written as

$$g(\pi,y; a) = k(y, a)h(\pi, a). \tag{12}$$

If (12) holds then π and y are statistically independent, and we can think of y as a signal based on the direct monitoring of the agent's action. Thus as long as $k(.)$ depends *at all* on the agent's action, $g(.)$ cannot be written as in (11) and hence a sharing rule based on profits alone would be sub-optimal. In this sense, then, *any* amount of information generated by direct or indirect monitoring of the agent's performance should be included in an optimal sharing arrangement. Therefore we have

> *Proposition 3:*[13] There exists a demand for monitoring the actions of the agent, in that any additional information about such actions leads to a Pareto improving sharing rule.

Of course, this result does not address the issue of *how much* the participants would be willing to pay for such monitoring, yet it does demonstrate how such a demand can and does arise. In particular, if some other individuals have access to "better" information about the agent's action than does the principal, Pareto improvements may well be generated by coopting these individuals and making them a part of the arrangement. Thus, as with Proposition 1 above, we see how the search for efficiently designed interactions between the principal and agent can lead to the inclusion of outside parties into the process. On the other hand, it is also clear that the principal *herself* will wish to monitor the behavior of the agent to the greatest extent possible, for any efficiency gains due to such monitoring can be immediately captured by the principal through the sharing rule. This is in contrast to the use of outside parties as monitors, where the latter must be given the incentive to perform such tasks.

Elaborating on this role of principal-as-monitor, suppose that there were a number of different potential principals with which the agent could interact, with each receiving the same value from the agent's output. If the agent were limited to interacting with only one of the principals, then efficiency would dictate that he interact with the principal that is the "best" at monitoring his actions because such a principal generates the highest total net wealth for the two parties. Alternatively, if the agent were given the opportunity to *choose* the principal, we would predict that he would choose the best monitor because by so doing he achieves a higher utility payoff (as long as he receives a portion of the increased net wealth in the resulting sharing rule). In general, then, we would expect that the existing relationships between principals and agents would involve those principals who have an advantage at monitoring their agents' behavior.

The second implication for institutional design plays off of the first and is found when the principal deals with more than one agent simultaneously. Suppose in particular that the principal employs n agents, where agent i generates profits for the principal according to $\pi_i = \pi_i(a_i, \theta_i)$. If the random variables $\{\theta_i\}$ are not independent, then from the above discussion we see that the profits generated by *other* agents can provide valuable information concerning the actions of any one agent. The reason again is that such information can be used to better separate out the effects on realized profits of the random term and the agent's action, thereby approaching the model found in Section 2. In general, then, we have the following:

> *Proposition 4:*[14] An agent's optimal sharing rule will be based solely on his own performance if and only if the random effects among the agents are independent.

Indeed, depending on the shape of the profit functions and the distribution of random terms, these optimal sharing rules can take on particularly simple forms. Suppose for example that $\pi_i(a_i, \theta_i) = a_i + \theta_i$, so that the production technologies are common among the agents and profits are additively separable and linear in its two arguments. Second, assume

$\theta_i = \eta + \epsilon_i$, $i = 1, \ldots, n$, so that the randomness in an agent's realized output can be attributed to a "common" shock, η, found in all agents' production, and an "idiosyncratic" shock, ϵ_i, found only in the production of agent i. Finally, assume that η and the ϵ_i's are independent and normally distributed and where the ϵ_i's have a common variance. Then it turns out that an optimal sharing rule for agent i can be written solely as a function of π_i and the *average* level of realized profits, $(\sum_j \pi_j)/n$. This follows because (with normal distributions) the average or mean is a sufficient statistic for all of the relevant information from the other agents' performance. Therefore, in this environment the informational content of other agents' outputs concerning the actions of any one agent can be summarized in particularly simple fashion.

Note that this dependence on others' profits is not based on the notion that competition among the agents enhances their performance, for any such incentives could have been put into an agent's original sharing rule in the first place. Rather, it is because others' profits can provide information about the exogenous determinants of any one agent's profits that such "comparative performance evaluations" are deemed optimal by the participants. This is in contrast to the literature on "tournaments," where such comparative evaluations *do* play a role in providing agents with incentives to take better actions. For example, Lazear and Rosen (1981) demonstrate that rank-order tournaments, in which an agent's payment is a function of the position of the agent's output in the rank ordering of all agent's outputs, can in certain circumstances lead to efficiency improvements over the optimal *linear* sharing rules for the agents separately, and this even when the random terms $\{\theta_i\}$ are independent. Of course, given the above analysis it is clear that these improvements come about due to the fact that linear sharing rules (rules of the form $s(\pi) = \alpha + \beta\pi$) need not be optimal in the single-agent case (in particular with risk-averse agents) and hence rank-order tournaments can in principle provide incentives that make each agent's sharing rule look more like the incentive efficient single-agent sharing rules described in Section 3.

5.0. Team Production

Thus far we have considered scenarios in which, while there may exist other agents whose performance can influence the payments to any one agent, the profits generated by any one agent are a function only of that agent's actions and not those of the others. In this section we move to the opposite extreme and analyze an n-agent environment in which the actions of the agents generate a single output, and hence generate a single profit. For simplicity we will return to the deterministic model of Section 2, so that there will be no randomness in the relationship between actions and profits. Yet as before, any sharing rule can be based only on the realized level of profit and not on individual agent's actions, and so whereas in the single-agent model with randomness the agent's action was confounded by the presence of this random term, here an agent's action is confounded by the presence of other agents' actions. Thus an agent has the potential ability to "free ride" on the efforts of the others, in that the sharing rule cannot distinguish those agents who selected relatively high actions from those who did not. Finally, we begin by presuming the absence of the principal, and so the relevant issue concerns the ability of the agents to distribute any realized profits among themselves efficiently.

So let $a_i \epsilon A$ denote an action taken by agent i, and $\pi(a) = \pi(a_1, \ldots, a_n)$ be the profit associated with the action profile $a = (a_1, \ldots, a_n)$, where $\pi_i' = \partial\pi/\partial a_i > 0$, $\pi_i'' = \partial^2\pi/\partial a_i^2 < 0$. As in Section 2 agent i bears a cost $c_i(a_i)$ when adopting the action a_i, and has preferences over money and actions represented by $m_i - c_i(a_i)$. We can as before identify the classically efficient action profile $a^* = (a_1^*, \ldots, a_n^*)$ by solving

$$\underset{a}{\text{maximize}}\ \pi(a) = \sum_{i=1}^{n} c_i(a_i), \tag{13}$$

which gives as first-order conditions

$$\pi_i'(a^*) = c_i'(a_i^*),\ i = 1, \ldots, n. \tag{14}$$

As in Section 2, the efficient action profile is characterized by maximizing the total value of the interaction—that is, by setting the marginal increase in profits equal to the marginal cost of doing so.

A sharing rule describes the relationship between the payments made to each of the n agents and the profits generated by their actions. Let $s_i(\pi)$ denote the share of the profits π going to any one agent suppose in addition we require the sharing rule to be *balanced*:

$$\sum_{i=1}^{n} s_i\ (\pi) = \pi \text{ for all } \pi. \tag{15}$$

That is, a balanced sharing rule distributes all of the profits to the agents, regardless of the level of realized profits.[15] The rationale for such a requirement is that, in contrast to the commitment issue discussed in Section 2 in which one party to an agreement had an incentive to renege, when a sharing rule is *not* balanced the individual profit shares add up to less than the total profits and hence *all* parties to the agreement have an incentive to renegotiate. Because, as in Section 2, efficiency constrains only the action choices by the agents and not the distribution of profits, the set of classically efficient and balanced solutions consist of all pairs $\langle a^*, s^*(\pi)\rangle$ satisfying (14) and (15).

In terms of incentive efficiency, each of the agents realizes that profits, and hence his resulting monetary payment, are a function of all agents' actions, and therefore the optimality of any action will in general depend on the agent's conjecture about how other agents will behave. Thus we can think of the agents as being involved in a *noncooperative game*, with strategy sets given by the set of available actions and payoffs given by the agents' resulting profit shares less the cost of action. Suppose we use the *Nash equilibrium* concept as our behavioral model of how agents play this game, where an action profile $\hat{a} = (\hat{a}_1, \ldots, \hat{a}_n)$ constitutes a Nash equilibrium if for each $i = 1, \ldots, n$, it is the case that

$$s_i(\pi(\hat{a})) - c_i(\hat{a}_i) \geq s_i(\pi(a_i, \hat{a}_{-i})) - c_i(a_i) \text{ for all } a_i \in A \qquad (16)$$

where $\hat{a}_{-i} = (\hat{a}_1, \ldots, \hat{a}_{i-1}, \hat{a}_{i+1}, \ldots, \hat{a}_n)$. That is, given the action choices by all other agents, agent i selects his action to maximize his share of the resulting profits less the costs of action. Assuming that the sharing rule is differentiable, then, we see that at any interior Nash equilibrium (16) implies

$$s_i'(\pi(\hat{a}))\pi_i'(\hat{a}) = c_i'(\hat{a}_i),\ i = 1, \ldots, n, \qquad (17)$$

where $s_i' = \delta s/\delta\pi$. Equation (17) simply says that at a Nash equilibrium agent i's action is chosen to equate the marginal increase in the profits accruing to i with the marginal cost of doing so; contrast this with equation (14)—that is, the equation defining the efficient action profile, which equates the marginal increase in *total* profits with marginal cost. Equation (17) is thus our incentive compatibility constraint, and we say that a solution $\langle a^*, s^*(\pi)\rangle$ is incentive efficient if it satisfies (14) and (17).

Inspection of equations (14) and (17) immediately implies that if $\hat{a} = a^*$—that is, if the sharing rule is such that the Nash equilibrium action profile is equal to the classically efficient action profile—it must be the case that

$$s_i'(\pi(a^*)) = 1 \text{ for all } i. \qquad (18)$$

That is, the sharing rule equates the marginal increase of each agent's profits with the marginal increase in total profits, thereby aligning individual and group incentives. But from the requirement that the sharing rule be balanced, we have that

$$\sum_{i=1}^{n} s_i'(\pi) = 1 \text{ for all } \pi, \tag{19}$$

where (19) comes from simply differentiating both sides of equation (15) with respect to π. It is readily apparent that equations (18) and (19) are inconsistent, since (19) requires s_i' be less than 1 for some i at all profit levels but (18) requires s_i' be equal to 1 at some profit level for all i. Thus we have shown

> *Proposition 5*:[16] Any balanced sharing rule will not be incentive efficient, in that the equilibrium actions will be less than is socially optimal.

Proposition 5 demonstrates the existence of a fundamental tension between providing the "correct" incentives for the individuals to act in a socially efficient manner and the notion that all profits should remain within the group of agents. Therefore structures such as partnerships, cooperatives, and the like, which collectively share in all the gains from production or exchange, will invariably fall prey to free-rider types of problems wherein actions taken by the members are below the socially efficient levels.

This inefficiency in team production is at the core of numerous models describing hierarchical relationships, the most well-known in economics being Alchian and Demsetz's (1972) theory of the firm.[17] They see the natural response to such inefficiencies as being the introduction of a supervisor whose charge is to monitor the behavior of the agents in order to mitigate any free riding. To give this supervisor the appropriate incentives to perform such monitoring activities, she is made the residual claimant on the team's profits, so that her interest is in maximizing the team's profits net of the shares going to the agents. As in the previous sections, we see here how the goal of efficient interactions implies the expansion of the set of interested parties. More important, *this supervisor can be seen as playing the role of the principal in the preceding sections*, in that the principal was the individual receiving the profits over and above those accruing to the agents as in Sections 2 and 3, and has the proper incentives to perform the monitoring tasks described in Section 4. In this sense, then, agency theory applied to the problem of team production endogenizes or creates the role of the principal as the structural or organizational superior of the agents.

6.0. Conclusion

The purpose of this chapter was to describe some of the features inherent in individuals' attempts to capture the economic gains from specialization. Employing the concept of efficiency as our model for how these individuals agree on the rules governing their interaction, we have seen how a relatively simple problem—namely, the production of a good by one person for the benefit of another—can have as solutions complex arrangements involving various degrees of commitment and third-party enforcement, risk-sharing, monitoring, and comparative performance evaluations. The cause of such complexities is found in the inability of the participants to identify or verify certain types of information, where this information is valuable in determining the optimal methods of exchange. Agency theory thus provides answers to questions involving the efficient design of social institutions in those domains where market forces, with their attendant efficiency-inducing properties, are absent.

Notes

1. Hart and Holmstrom (1986) provide a thorough review of the literature on agency theory.

2. To keep the analysis simple, unless otherwise stated all parameters will be single dimensional, all functions will be twice-continuously differentiable, and all solutions will be interior.

3. This can be shown to be equal to the Nash bargaining solution, as well as the unique subgame perfect equilibrium outcome of an "alternating offer" bargaining game.

4. This inefficiency result would hold as well if the parties first negotiated a price, and then the agent produced the good: in this case the principal can foresee the agent taking the least-cost action $a = \underline{a}$, and hence the principal and agent would receive $\pi(\underline{a})/2$ and $\pi(\underline{a})/2 - c(\underline{a})$, respectively.

5. An equivalent formulation maximizes the *agent's* payoff subject to a constraint on the *principal's* payoff.

6. In Chapter 4 of this volume, Randall Calvert demonstrates how repeated interaction of individuals can provide an *endogenous* enforcement mechanism—that is, one generated by the behavior of the individuals themselves.

7. Allowing the agent to be risk averse would not qualitatively change the results in Section 2 (as there existed no uncertainty and hence no risk) but would render the intuition somewhat less transparent.

8. This problem did not arise in the model of Section 2 because without the random term the sharing rule can be thought of as a function of the agent's action directly; and whenever this is so, a sharing rule can be designed to essentially "force" the agent to adopt the appropriate action. See Harris and Raviv (1979) for more on forcing contracts.

9. Most important, that we can substitute the agent's first-order necessary condition

for an optimum for constraint (7); see Grossman and Hart (1983) and Rogerson (1985) for conditions under which such a substitution is legitimate.

10. See Holmstrom (1979).

11. This technique was first suggested by Mirrlees (1976).

12. This concept of MLRP was introduced into the economics literature by Migrom (1981).

13. See Holmstrom (1979).

14. Holmstrom (1982). The proof of this result requires profits from agent i to be monotone in θ_i.

15. Note that we have implicitly assumed balance in the sharing rules of the previous sections, because all of the profits went to either the principal or the agent.

16. See Holmstrom (1982).

17. See Miller (1992) for a broad discussion of team production inefficiencies, as well as potential solutions, in a variety of different environments.

References

Alchian, Armen and Harold Demsetz. (1972). "Production, Information Costs, and Economic Organization." *American Economic Review* 62(5): 777–795.

Grossman, Sanford and Oliver Hart. (1983). "An Analysis of the Principal-Agent Problem." *Econometrica* 51(1): 7–45.

Harris, Milton and Arthur Raviv. (1979). "Optimal Incentive Contracts with Imperfect Information." *Journal of Economic Theory* 20(2): 231–259.

Hart, Oliver and Bengt Holmstrom. (1986). "The Theory of Contracts." In T. Bewley (ed.) *Advances in Economic Theory* (pp. 77–155). New York: Cambridge University Press.

Holmstrom, Bengt. (1979). "Moral Hazard and Observability." *Bell Journal of Economics* 9(2): 74–91.

———. (1982). "Moral Hazard in Teams." *Bell Journal of Economics* 13(2): 324–340.

Jensen, Michael and William Meckling. (1976). "Theory of the Firm: Managerial Behavior, Agency Costs and Ownership Structure." *Journal of Financial Economics* 3(4): 305–360.

Lazear, Edward and Sherwin Rosen. (1981). "Rank Order Tournaments as Optimum Labor Contracts." *Journal of Political Economy* 89(5): 841–864.

Milgrom, Paul. (1981). "Good News and Bad News: Representation Theorems and Applications." *Bell Journal of Economics* 12(2): 380–391.

Miller, Gary J. (1992). *Managerial Dilemmas: The Political Economy of Hierarchy*. New York: Cambridge University Press.

Mirlees, James. (1976). "The Optimal Structure of Authority and Incentives within an Organization." *Bell Journal of Economics* 7(1): 105–131.

Rogerson, William. (1985). "The First-Order Approach to Principal-Agent Problems." *Econometrica* 53(2): 1357–1368.

3 CAVEAT EMPTOR: INSTITUTIONS, CONTRACTS AND COMMODITY EXCHANGES IN RUSSIA[1]

Timothy Frye

1.0. Introduction

The design of institutions to create trust between trading partners who have incentives to cheat is a critical aspect of economic development. Without credible guarantees for contract enforcement from third parties, such as the state, trading partners face a dilemma. They would benefit by trusting their partners and exchanging their goods, but in the absence of institutions to punish traders who break contracts, they have stronger incentives to cheat. As each party can foresee this logic, mutually beneficial trades will not be made, and societies will experience slow economic growth and social conflict.

Traders in diverse historical settings have devised many institutions to support exchange. Anthropologists emphasize the importance of blood ties and community pressures in mitigating economic disputes. Economists argue that social coalitions, private judges, and organizational forms, such as the firm, reduce opportunism. Political scientists typically stress the state as an enforcer of contracts.

The success of these institutional structures in enhancing contract compliance has great implications for economic growth. Institutions that enforce contracts and resolve disputes at low cost increase efficiency. Douglass North and Robert Thomas cite the efficiency of state enforcement in Europe as the motor for the rise of the Western world (North and Thomas, 1973). The existence of the state as a reliable enforcer of contracts is, however, far from the rule. From the Champaigne Fairs of medieval Europe, to frontier communities of the American west, to many sectors of developing countries, trade under conditions of weak enforcement by the state is common (Clay, 1992; Greif, 1992; Milgrom, North, and Weingast, 1990). This problem is also central to reform in Russia because the state lacks adequate resources to act as a reliable third-party enforcer of contracts. How can institutions be designed to support exchange given the precarious nature of contract enforcement?

I examine this question through a case study of commodity exchanges in Russia.[2] After a theoretical discussion of contract enforcement, I describe the rise and decline of commodity exchanges in Russia during the last four years. I then argue that the institutional design of Russian commodity exchanges hindered contract compliance by making it difficult to identify dishonest trading partners, by inhibiting repeat trading, and by providing weak dispute resolution procedures. All trading partners on the commodity exchange recognized the benefits of institutions that provide the collective good of contract enforcement, but the cost to individuals of creating such institutions were prohibitive.

I then discuss the theoretical aspects of various types of third-party contract enforcement including private arbitration, state enforcement, and private enforcement, as well as other institutions that brokers have relied on to support trade on the commodity exchanges. In addition to private and public enforcement agents, economic hostages, relational contracting, and vertical integration have supported trade with varying degrees of success. Each of these institutional arrangements pose interesting theoretical questions about exchange and the prospects for economic reform in Russia. To conclude I argue that the difficulty of designing institutions that resolve disputes and enforce contracts impersonally has created a localized "quasi-market" that relies on vertical trading structures, personal ties, and private enforcers to minimize incentives to cheat.

2.0. The New Institutionalism and Contract Enforcement

In a recent review of new institutionalist literature, Randall Calvert (forthcoming) deemed the enforcement of property rights "a seldom addressed and poorly understood problem." Neoclassical accounts of exchange tend to assume that enforcement is a minor problem that can generally be excluded from formal models. The transaction costs literature in economics has recognized the importance of commitment and enforcement but has not systematically addressed these issues. Most accounts assume that enforcement is "either perfect or constantly imperfect" (North, 1990). Oliver Williamson has devoted considerable attention to this problem and argues that contracts are often structured to minimize opportunism (Williamson, 1975; 1985). As North notes, however, Williamson "generally assumes that enforcement is not perfect, but does not make it an explicit variable in his analysis" (North, 1990). Insufficient attention to the establishment of institutions to mitigate enforcement problems is unfortunate as the security of contracts is crucial for economic growth and, perhaps, democratic government.

North argues that enforcement mechanisms perform two functions. First, they establish a means to know when punishment is required. Second, because punishment is costly and often has the characteristics of a public good, they provide incentives to inflict punishment. Typically, punishment is costly and the enforcer has her own utility function that differs from those engaged in the exchange creating opportunities for bribery and extortion. This general discussion of enforcement provides a starting point for analyzing the institutions established to secure contract compliance on the commodity exchange.

2.1. Exchange in the Absence of a Third-Party Enforcer

Consider a single trade conducted in the absence of third-party enforcement. When contemplating the exchange, each trader has two strategies: he can be honest or cheat. If the game is played once, then each trader has an incentive to cheat. As both can foresee this logic, they will have little incentive to trade.

If, however, the traders know that they will trade with each other indefinitely, then each may have sufficiently strong incentives to be honest. Each trader calculates the payoff for each round, discounting expected future payoffs. If the present expected value of the stream of benefits from being honest are larger than the present expected value of benefits from cheating, then honesty is rational. As each trader assumes the other is rational, each can adhere to the contract with confidence that the other will follow suit (Taylor, 1976, 1987; Axelrod 1984).

The reputation for compliance can be transmitted to the community at large. If transactions are witnessed by the entire trading community, then the bilateral trading game described above can serve as a model for exchange between any two trading partners in the community. A reputation for being an honest trader can be a valuable commodity (Kreps, 1990). Yet the costs of keeping the members of the community informed about the past practices of trading partners can be significant. Adjudication can be costly because each party must gather evidence, verify it, present it in court, and perhaps hire specialists to conduct these tasks. Transparent exchange conducted among trading partners who are well informed about their past trading practices can reduce opportunism.

If the trading community is large or the trades are complex, then the costs of keeping informed about the trading practices of potential partners will be high. Traders may react by creating localized markets to increase the frequency of contact between traders or by resorting to private violence to change the structure of payoffs in this game.

2.2. A Precedent: The Medieval Law Merchant

Designing an institution that credibly ties an actor's past behavior to future benefits is difficult. First, actors who create an institution are generally aware of its future distributional consequences and may use the institution for personal gain. Second, designing institutions that rely on reputation and social sanctions to punish dishonest traders creates a collective action problem. Often, breaches of reputation are not punished by the state but by societal actors (Ellickson, 1991; Black, 1987). Gossip, ostracism, even vigilante expropriation may help remedy a breach in the absence of reliable state enforcement. Inflicting punishment is costly, however, and although all traders value the public good of enforcement, no individual trader may be willing to bear the costs of punishment.

One institution that increased contract compliance by relying on reputational effects and social sanctions in a structurally similar situation (weak public enforcement) was the medieval law merchant. Under the law merchant, a private judge registered contracts, settled disputes, and provided information about the trading practices of itinerant merchants during the Middle Ages (Milgrom, North, and Weingast, 1990). The law merchant was able to overcome the two problems cited above. A judge operating under the law merchant did not seek personal advantage because his profits depended on the number of cases he handled. If his decisions were perceived as dishonest or not credible, then he would handle fewer cases and earn lower profits. In addition, traders in the community overcame the collective action problem of inflicting social sanctions at low cost. Before engaging in an exchange, each trader paid a small fee to the judge for information about the past trading practices of a potential partner. If the partner had outstanding claims, the trade was not made. The judge provided this information to members of the trading community who would then boycott dishonest traders. The threat of boycott deterred dishonest traders provided their discount rate was sufficiently low. By "bundling" services valuable to individual traders with services valuable to the community, the judge warned the trading community about dishonest traders at low cost.

2.3. The Trading Environment in Russia

Economic agents in Russia face a very hazardous environment. The Russian government lacks the resources to be a reliable, neutral, third-party enforcer for many contracts. Legislation often lags behind practice, and honest economic agents are forced to operate in many grey areas. For example, commodity exchanges were operating for more than a year before the Russian Parliament passed the Federal Law on Commodity Exchanges in March 1992. With relatively few roads and a heavy reliance on railroads, the physical infrastructure is ill-suited to foster reliable exchange, and transporters are frequently subject to extortion and monopoly pricing. Transfers of money and goods often require weeks or months, which allows traders to look for better deals even after a contract has been signed. Law enforcement officials complain that they lack the resources to combat crime. The courts are overworked, often unpredictable, and have long waiting lists. State arbitration courts may take more than a year to hear cases and require a hefty deposit (often 10 percent of the contract value) from the plaintiff.

3.0. Commodity Exchanges in the Soviet Union and Russia

The first commodity exchanges in the Soviet Union were registered in the summer of 1990 often by odd alliances of private entrepeneuers, former bureaucrats from the state supply agency (*Gossnab*), and representatives of state enterprises. The exchanges gathered buyers and sellers under one roof and offered an alternative to a crumbling state supply network. Brokers bought and sold a variety of goods, including items traditionally traded on commodity exchanges, such as oil, grain, and sugar, and such atypical commodity exchange items as helicopters, computers, and cars. As most trade was conducted in nonstandard goods, often for barter, and without futures contracts, the Russian commodity exchanges were more akin to a bazaar than to their nominal counterparts in the West. Similar problems plagued commodity exchanges in the United States in the last century (Abolafia, 1985).

Before the price reform of January 1992, which curtailed the volume of trade, the commodity exchanges boomed. At the Russian Raw Materials and Commodity Exchange (RTSB) in October 1991, more than 2.3 billion rubles worth of goods changed hands (Yakovlev, 1991a). According to one estimate, 15 to 20 million tons of grain were traded on Russian commodity exchanges in 1992 (Zhurek, 1993). From September 1990 until January 1992, more than 400 exchanges opened in Russia. Why the boom?

Commodity exchanges in the former Soviet Union were established as profit-seeking organizations by their founders who provided the hall and the personnel to run the exchange and attracted brokers. In return brokers paid fees to the founders for service and remitted a small percentage (0.5 to 3 percent) of each deal made on the exchange. The founders also prospered by selling seats on the exchange, which often sold for several hundred thousand rubles at the old exchange rate of 30 rubles to the dollar. In the early days of the commodity exchange, the founders owned seats and competed with brokers for market share. By owning seats founders could divert goods to their traders before they reached the exchange floor—a clear example of insider trading. In addition, the commission that they paid to the exchange as brokers went back into their pockets as founders. In March 1991, the Council of Ministers banned this practice, but enforcement is difficult. Many exchanges simply created subsidiaries to engage in trade.

The exchanges also proved profitable for brokers and clients. Clients could arbitrage between state controlled and free prices. Enterprises, cooperatives, and retailers that offered goods for sale at high prices found buyers at the exchange who placed a high relative value on obtaining goods quickly, an important consideration in a shortage economy. (Cohen, 1991; Kokorev, 1992; Yakovlev, 1991a, 1991b; Zhurek, 1993).

The boom of 1990–1991 was followed by the bust of 1992–1993. From more than 400 exchanges operating in 1992, the number of active exchanges in Russia has fallen to less than twenty. Trade in April 1993 at the largest commodity exchange reached only 249 deals, totalling 17.6 billion rubles or roughly 13.5 million dollars (*Vek*, May 28, 1993: 1). Trade volume at commodity exchanges collapsed for two primary reasons.

First, price liberalization introduced in January 1992 severely limited the profitable practice of arbitraging between controlled and free prices. Second, the difficulty of enforcing contracts concluded on the exchange encouraged many brokers to find alternative means of trade, such as retail outlets or direct purchases from the factory. The institutional design of the commodity exchanges made contract enforcement problematic. The rate of contract violations varies across exchanges, but roughly 30 percent of all contracts signed on Russian commodity exchanges go unfulfilled (*Rossiskaya Gazeta*, March 10, 1993: 3).[3] The commodity exchange is being surpassed by retail outlets and direct sales between economic agents that offer the prospect of more secure trade (*Delovoi Mir*, September 8, 1992: 1). To better understand the difficulty of making credible commitments to contracts on the commodity exchange, I present the contracting mechanism in detail.

3.1. Contracting on the Exchange

Four actors are involved in each trade on the exchange: two brokers and their two clients. Brokers, those who have purchased the right to trade on the exchange, attract clients, who are trying to buy (or sell) a particular good. Brokers first scan their list of clients to see whether they can match a buyer and seller with another client of the brokerage firm without resorting to the exchange. If this match is made, then they receive commissions from both the buyer and seller. For many firms this fortunate outcome is rare. In most cases, the broker and the client sign a contract that specifies the terms of the exchange. Brokers often ask for 3 percent of the proposed deal as a retainer, a deposit of 15 to 100 percent of the deal in case of breach, and documentation that the client has either the money or the goods to conclude the deal. The broker takes this buy (or sell) order to the exchange. The commodity exchanges typically circulate a list of price quotes with payment conditions to the brokers each day. An auctioneer reads the quotes and asks for bids. Few goods provoke interest and competitive bidding is rare. When a good that satisfies the terms of the contract reaches the floor, brokers with buy orders place bids. If a bid is accepted, then the brokers for the buyer and seller sign a contract on the floor and register it with the exchange (or not register it as the case may be). Brokers negotiate the details of the contract, and if they fail to agree after registering their contract, then they pay a fine to the exchange, roughly equal to 3 percent of the proposed agreement.

Commodity exchanges in capitalist countries trade a limited number of goods that have few quality parameters. Oil, grains, and metals are traded in specified quantities according to standardized contracts. In contrast, idiosyncratic goods, such as computers and cars, dominate trading on Russian exchanges. Even commodities commonly traded on Western exchanges are not standardized (Woodruff, 1992). Oil and grains are offered in indivisible lots of varying quantities and quality. Trade in nonstandardized goods raises transaction costs and increases information asymmetry about the quality of goods. The wide assortment of goods offered on many commodity exchanges ensures that brokers will lack expertise in some goods and be fooled into buying substandard merchandise. Few commodity exchanges certify the quality of goods traded due to a lack of capital and expertise.

3.2. Contracts

Three types of contracts are written at the exchanges. Spot market contracts are fulfilled shortly after the deal is made on the exchange floor. After bidding, the buyer inspects the goods and pays the seller, often in cash but sometimes by transferring money into a bank account. This type of primitive trade is prevalent at many exchanges.

Forward contracts include intertemporal deals that require transportation of the good or transfer of funds from outside the region and the buyer waits to take possession until the good is delivered. Opportunities for breach are higher in forward contracts than in spot contracts. Buyers who commit money prior to receipt of the good are vulnerable, as are sellers who receive less than full payment prior to delivery.

Futures contracts, the soul of commodity exchanges in capitalist economies, are under intense study, but technical difficulties have severely limited their use. The Moscow Commodity Exchange has been conducting futures trades in U.S. dollars since October 1992 and is currently experiencing rapid growth. Trade has increased every month and reached \$3.8 million in July 1993 (*Kommersant*, August 7, 1993: 4). These trades are limited to hard currency and the standardized contracts are in denominations of only \$10, \$1,000, and \$10,000. Perhaps the exchange closest to introducing futures trading in commodities is the Moscow Ferrous Metals Exchange. In May 1993, brokers conducted two weeks of simulated futures trading in aluminum, and actual trading began September 1993 (*Kommersant*, May 22, 1993: 2). Nonetheless, the futures market for commodities is in its infancy in Russia.

3.3. Opportunities for Cheating

The institutional design and nature of trade on the exchange create many opportunities for deception. Clients or brokers can list their good on several different exchanges simultaneously, accept the highest bid, then renege on contracts concluded on other exchanges. Brokers can arbitrage between the price on the market and the client's acceptable price. If the client is unaware of the market price, then he can be easily duped. The most grievous form of deception occurs when clients accept prepayment for a good, fail to deliver, then disappear. The possibility that clients will abscond with prepayment or will provide a substandard good and then disappear are ever present.

Most violations occur between clients. Brokers interact regularly and value a good reputation. Over time they identify those who tend to represent trustworthy clients. If a contract is broken, they try to justify their actions to fellow brokers. In contrast clients interact rarely and have little interest in gaining a reputation for honesty on the exchange. Most important, traders foresee the difficulty of making credible commitments to contracts on the exchange and often forgo mutually beneficial deals.

4.0. Institutional Design and Contracts

As noted above the trading environment on the floor of the exchange appears to be a classic prisoner's dilemma. Without a third-party enforcer, the dominant strategy for clients conducting a single trade is to accept a good or payment, then to renege. The incentive not to comply can be mitigated if traders expect to meet repeatedly for an indefinite future and can be extended to the whole community if the costs of informing traders about past practices are low (Taylor, 1976, 1987; Axelrod, 1984; Kreps, 1990). If an institution reliably links a player's past behavior to future benefits, compliance should increase (Milgrom, North, and Weingast, 1990; Calvert, forthcoming; Clay, 1992).

In contrast to the medieval law merchant, the institutional design of the profit-seeking commodity exchanges has exacerbated, rather than mitigated, commitment and enforcement problems. First, the institutional design of the commodity exchanges encouraged brokers to make "off-exchange" deals (*vnebirzhevie sdelki*) that are not registered with exchange officials and have pernicious effects on contract compliance. By charging a commission on each deal and not offering any guarantees for the security of exchange, the founders of the exchange created a large market in off-exchange deals. These off-exchange contracts are legally binding between clients and are concluded by brokers who do not notify exchange officials that the deal was concluded on the commodity exchange. Clients avoid paying the exchange a commission by not registering their contracts with the exchange. Similarly, brokers often advertise a small quantity of their goods on the exchange to attract buyers and, once they have identified the buyer, negotiate a much larger contract that is not registered on the exchange. These off-exchange deals benefit the brokers who receive their commission and the client who does not pay a commission to the exchange.

The peculiar post-Soviet payment and tax system also encourages off-exchange deals. Two monies are used in Russia: cash rubles, *nalichnie rubli* and account rubles, *beznalichnie rubli*. The former includes cash held by individuals and are intended for everyday purchases. The central government has always limited the use of cash rubles and currently deals for larger than R500,000 (about $5,000) cannot be conducted in cash rubles (*Kommersant*, 27, July 12, 1993: 27). The latter are intended to be used by organizations and are processed through the Central Bank. It is more difficult to avoid taxes using account rubles because they leave a paper trail in the banking system. When possible, brokers use cash rubles to conclude off-exchange deals and discourage inquisitive tax collectors.

Off-exchange deals have one drawback. They do not give brokers or clients the right to use arbitration services provided by the commodity exchanges. Brokers calculate the benefits of off-exchange deals against the value of using private arbitration services in case of breach.

The number of unregistered deals is difficult to determine, but it has been estimated that for every deal registered on the exchange between twenty and forty deals are concluded off the exchange (*Ekonomicheskaya Gazeta*, 23, June 1992: 8). By raking a commission off each deal registered on the exchange, the founders increased incentives to make unregistered deals that are not widely publicized and made it difficult for a broker or firm to gain a reputation for honesty.

Off-exchange deals also make punishing dishonest traders problematic. As these unregistered contracts are generally private rather than public knowledge, the cost of adjudicating and enforcing disputes increases. Few brokers are willing to invest the time to learn the details of a case. Shortly after the opening of the exchanges, brokers tried to create a "black list" of unreliable clients, but the attempt failed because the cost of maintaining such a list was considered prohibitive by the brokers. All brokers benefit from information about the trading practices of clients and brokers, but given the large number of brokers on the exchange, it is not in any trader's particular interest to bear the costs of creating and maintaining the black list. Brokers are unlikely to know that a potential partner has a record of dishonest trading or that a breach has occurred in a particular case.

Brokers and clients on the commodity exchanges face additional difficulties in gaining a reputation for honesty. First, public opinion is generally skeptical of the commodity exchanges. Some brokers worked in the illegal sector of the planned economy, and many view the commodity exchanges as a haven for former "economic criminals." One complaint is that exchanges do not produce anything and are of little value to society. The notion that middlemen play a productive role in society is questioned by many Russians. Commodity exchanges have also been tarnished by the low quality of exchange goods and some people view exchanges as a dumping ground for defective or stolen products.

Similarly, gaining a reputation for honesty is complicated by the lack of information on past trading practices of potential partners. Few brokerage houses have been trading for more than two years, and given numerous changes in name and leadership, it is difficult to assess the reliability of a potential partner. One broker noted that it was common practice to liquidate brokerage firms periodically because over time even honest firms accrue dangerous enemies. Moreover, it is unclear to whom a reputation attaches. Does a reputation for honesty accrue to an individual or to a firm? If a firm's name or profile changes, does it retain its reputation?

Developing a reputation for honesty by repeated interaction is complicated by the high discount rate for many traders. The alarming rate of insolvency of firms in some sectors of the market reduces the probability that parties can expect to meet each other in a potential future trade (Litwack, 1991a, 1991b). Each side thus worries less about its reputation for being a reliable trader and opportunism becomes more attractive. Public skepticism toward brokers and the short shadow of the future make gaining a reputation for honesty difficult. The institutional design of the commodity exchanges exacerbated these problems by encouraging off-exchange deals.

The principal-agent problem has also restricted the volume of trade on commodity exchanges in Russia. In contrast to typical principal-agent problems, agents (brokers) on the commodity exchanges exhibit more concern for minimizing deception than the principals (clients). Most contract violations occur between clients rather than between brokers or between brokers and clients. Typically, contracts are broken by suppliers who receive prepayment for a good, but either fail to deliver the good or deliver it late. Brokers who interact regularly appreciate reputational concerns. To achieve a good reputation brokers are expected to check the financial status of their clients, but this can be time-consuming and expensive. Moreover, the client's true intentions remain private information. Clients interact through the exchange infrequently and have little concern for their reputation on the exchange.

Brokers on the commodity exchange also face an adverse selection problem (Akerlof, 1970). The exchanges have no means to prevent honest traders from meeting other honest traders at the exchange, then taking all their deals outside of the exchange. As trustworthy brokers and clients exit the exchange, the probability of finding an honest client or broker falls. As a result retailers who have developed a network of trustworthy suppliers have an efficiency advantage over dealers who work on the commodity exchange. Computers, cars, and other former staples of the commodity exchanges are now traded at lower prices and lower risk by retail stores. The benefits of repeated trade among brokers and clients are reduced by the exit of trustworthy brokers and clients.

4.1. Commodity Exchanges and Reputation

The salience of contract enforcement leads one to expect that commodity exchanges would have an interest in maintaining a reputation for reliability to attract brokers and clients. This reputation for reliability must be weighed against the formidable costs of creating institutions to punish wayward brokers and clients. The exchanges have tried several means to limit "off-exchange" deals and encourage brokers to use their services. Commodity exchanges provide their members with some selective benefits, such as access to information about the goods being traded, but once this information is released, it quickly becomes common knowledge among the brokers. Commodity exchanges offer arbitration services, but most do not assume responsibility for contracts concluded on the exchange. Arbitration services have found few takers, primarily due to weak enforcement procedures (*Bizness, Banki i Birzha*, 42, 19, 1992: 7).

The Moscow Commodity Exchange has tried to plug these drains on revenue by instituting a system of broker deposits. Each month the brokers pay a small fee to the exchange that is held against the commission paid by brokers to the exchange. The deposit is lost if the brokers make only off-exchange trades. The deposit system was instituted recently, and it is premature to judge its success. Brokers have long resisted such a system by theatening to move to other exchanges. One official at the

Moscow Commodity Exchange noted that the deposit fee was set at a low price in response to broker resistance. Commodity exchanges would like to establish clearing houses that hold payment until the good is approved by an independent expert, but they lack sufficient capital and expertise to do so.

5.0. Third-Party Enforcement

Third-party enforcement presents a slightly different theoretical problem than previously discussed. Sanctions in repeat-play games are applied by parties to the exchange, but in third-party enforcement, sanctions are applied by an entrepeneur, such as the state, who charges a fee for this service. As always enforcing contracts is costly, and sufficient incentives must be provided to encourage enforcers to do their job. Third-party enforcers have their own interests and may not simply behave as specified by the actors who hire them. Inflicting punishment is costly, and once an enforcer receives payment, there is little incentive to punish. An economic actor considering this payment can see this logic and will be reluctant to hire the enforcer out of fear of opportunism. The enforcer has an incentive to garner a reputation for honesty, and the client has an incentive to trust the enforcer, but the intertemporality of the exchange and the disparity in capacity for violence makes this difficult.

Third-party enforcement of contracts also raises the problem of monitoring the enforcer. If enforcing is very profitable, then third-party enforcers, such as the state or organized crime, have an incentive to extort revenue from the population (Bates, 1987, Tilly, 1985, 1991). If inflicting punishment is too costly, then it will be undersupplied, and beneficial trades will not be made (Ostrom, 1990). Brokers and clients use three types of third-party enforcement: arbitration services provided by the commodity exchanges, state arbitration courts, and private enforcers.

5.1. Commodity Exchange Arbitration Commissions

As an alternative to the overworked state arbitration courts, economic actors in Russia have established private dispute resolution services. The Association for Russian Bankers has established an arbitration court to settle quarrels among bankers, while entrepeneurs have created the Moscow Commercial Court to hear cases between any parties that agree to participate. Arbitration commissions have been active at commodity exchanges since their inception. They generally consist of a small number of arbitrators, many with experience in state arbitration courts, and brokers who settle disputes involving clients or brokers (Vinogradova, 1992; Vytransky, 1992). Arbitrators argue that their services have two advantages over state courts. They resolve disputes at lower cost, generally 3 to 5 percent of the sums involved rather than 10 percent as charged by state arbitration courts, and they decide cases more quickly than state arbitrators. Commodity exchange arbitrators usually render a decision within two months after a case is filed.

Despite these advantages, commodity exchange arbitration has several flaws. Enforcing compliance with decisions is difficult. Arbitrators can fine or dismiss brokers, but exchanges are reluctant to ban brokers because they will lose a source of revenue. The large number of brokerage firms in Russia ensures that a broker barred from one exchange can ply his trade elsewhere. As brokerage firms have diversified into retail and other activities outside of the commodity exchanges, the threat of banishment has become less powerful. A report by the Russian Raw Materials and Commodity Exchange (RTSB) noted laconically "blocking brokers from entering the hall has not always produced the desired results" (*RTSB godovoi otchet*, 1992).

The authority of the commodity exchange arbitration commissions has been undermined by the appeal process. Parties dissatisfied with private arbitration courts can appeal to state courts to retry their case. This provides a check on the behavior of arbitrators, but brokers and clients can use this right of appeal as a stalling tactic. As both sides foresee the costs of a lengthy legal bettle, commodity exchange arbitration committees resolve few disputes (*Delovoi Mir*, September 24, 1993: 3).

For most of their existence arbitration commissions have had limited powers. Until passage of the Temporary Statute on Arbitration Courts in December 1992, arbitrators could not issue subpoenas to force clients to appear in court. Many clients ignored arbitrators' requests to take part in the proceedings.

The effect of private arbitration services on contract compliance is positive but limited. The Moscow Commodity Exchange has one of the most developed arbitration commissions. Unlike most of its counterparts it has been financially independent of the exchange since its inception and earns revenue by charging a small commission of three percent. Yet in the sixteen months since its creation, it has handled only 123 cases. The arbitration committee at the RTSB handled more than 500 cases last year. These figures are striking given the high rate of contract violations (about 30 percent) on the exchanges.

A comparison of the medieval law merchant with commodity exchange arbitration commissions is instructive. In the former case traders applied sanctions by boycotting dishonest traders. In the latter case punishing brokers is difficult because of the prevalence of "off-exchange" deals. Second, traders under the law merchant system paid the judge for information about the past practices of potential partners before trading. At the commodity exchanges, gathering information about the trading practices of potential partners is difficult, as is identifying dishonest brokers and clients.

5.2. State Enforcement

One way to mitigate enforcement problems is to rely on the state for these services (Riker and Sened, 1991). North and Thomas argue that the state emerged to provide the public good of enforcement at lower cost than that provided privately (North and Thomas, 1973). Yet "bringing the state back in" to strengthen enforcement involves a tradeoff (Tilly, 1985, 1991). A state that is made strong enough to enforce contracts is also made strong enough to anull them (Weingast, 1993). Actors who fear the arbitrary use of state power may be unwilling to devote resources to strengthen the state's enforcement capacity.

As noted before tax avoidance is regularly practiced on the commodity exchange (*Bizness, Banki i Birzha*, 26, 1992: 5). Brokers engage in "off-exchange" deals using cash rubles rather than account rubles. To avoid taxes they also sign contracts to provide fictitious "consulting" services that actually cover part of the cost of the good they are selling. Private actors are reluctant to provide state actors with the material resources to provide the public good of reliable contract enforcement as they fear the "sucker payoff" of paying taxes while rivals consume the benefits of state enforcement without paying (Levi, 1988). An economic actor may find it more attractive to hire private enforcers who will work on his case specifically, rather then pay taxes toward the public good of state-backed enforcement.

The cost and uncertainty of state enforcement often makes it less attractive than alternatives. When considering the type of enforcement to employ, brokers and clients know that the docket in the state arbitration courts is full, and they may wait a year for a decision. Brokers also complain about the compensation rules followed by private and state arbitration courts. Judges are reluctant to index damages to the rate of inflation. The legal basis for indexing compensation is debated by jurists, but in practice judges generally shy away from indexing damages unless the formula for damages is written in the contract. As the 1992 inflation rate was approximately 2,000 percent and a court case can last a year, using the courts to redress damages is often unattractive. Second, compensation practices generally favor cash settlements rather than in-kind compensation (Kroll, 1987, 1989a, 1989b; Vytransky, 1992). In the shortage economy of Russia, brokers prefer compensation in-kind rather than cash and are therefore discouraged from using the court to redress injuries.

Due to the cost and uncertainty of the judicial process, brokers tend to use the courts only if the damages are large or the legal issues are simple. For example, in the summer of 1992 Alter-brok paid R32m (roughly $20 million) to a grain seller in Krasnoyarsk, only to be told that the shipment would not be forthcoming. State arbitration courts decided the case in roughly six months and the money was returned.

5.3. Private Enforcement

If the state undersupplies enforcement, then economic actors have strong incentives to hire private enforcers to ensure contract compliance. Private enforcers work on the case at hand and thereby eliminate the public goods problem of state enforcement. The use of private enforcers is common during periods of weak state rule. John Umbeck found that the during the California gold rush the six-shooter was the guarantor of property rights in the absence of state enforcement (Umbeck, 1981). Threats of force may violate the written law but can support contract compliance. In his study of violence in diverse social and temporal settings, Donald Black found that many "crimes" are really acts of self-enforcement by parties who have perceived a breach of formal or informal contract (Black, 1987).

The rise of legal and illegal enforcement agencies in Russia indicates that this option is increasing in importance. The Russian Parliament passed a Law on Private Security Agencies in the spring of 1992, and several hundred legal security agencies are active in Russia (*Izvestiya*, March 14, 1992: 1). The number of illegal enforcers is undoubtedly higher. State security agencies complain that private security agencies are luring their best officers with higher pay. The ease with which private enforcers can be employed may deter opportunism.

One of the largest legal security agencies in Russia is Aleks.[4] Formed in 1989 by the Isaakov brothers who worked in the Soviet Militia (police force), it has gathered a broad-based clientele by its promise to return any reasonable damages. Aleks provides body guards and security guards – complete with camouflage uniforms and truncheons – who will accompany goods to prevent diversion from their proper destination.[5] Aleks has an economic security division that acts as a credit and collection agency. Through ties with state and cooperative banks, Aleks claims to be able to rate a firm's creditworthiness, an important service in an information-poor economy. They deny threatening violence against those who breach contracts with their clients. They typically collect evidence that is presented to the alleged violators, and, in the words of the president of the firm, "they usually make the right choice."

As always, enforcement is costly and Aleks's fees are beyond the reach of many firms. Aleks's president declined to specify their rates, noting only that they are generally three times less than those charged by a Western security firm.[6] If force is necessary to gain compliance, then options other than expensive legal security agencies exist. It may be cheaper and as effective to hire someone to throw a rock through an offender's plate glass window (and force them to scour the country in search of plate glass) or to expropriate the good, than to rely on the state for enforcement.

In addition to high costs, private third-party enforcement raises additional problems. As noted above, private third-party enforcers have an incentive to gain a reputation for trustworthy behavior, but this is difficult to achieve. Aleks ameliorated this problem initially by engaging in activities that were easily monitored such as transporting goods on highways and railroads, protecting warehouses, and providing body guards. According to several sources it has been able to parlay this reputation for probity into other less verifiable areas such as credit checks and financial research.

A more intractable problem in private third-party enforcement is the potential for extortion. If private enforcers develop expertise and capacity for the use of force, then the incentive for extortion is great. As if to illustrate this point an Aleks manager was charged with extortion in the Urals in the summer of 1993. It is premature to judge the effect of this arrest on Aleks's business, but it will likely be negative.

Rendering payment to third-party enforcers creates a potential for extortion, but for the moment private security and enforcement services may well be cost-effective. The growing prominence of self-help measures is evident in Moscow. Private companies often devote significant portions of their operating costs to private security agents. The sale of locks and security alarms is booming, and the steel curtains that protect storefronts in large American cities have made their appearance in Moscow. We should distinguish between crime as retaliation for breach and crime as predatory behavior, but until a more effective public means of enforcing agreements is found, legal and illegal private security agencies will prosper.

6.0. Institutions and Credible Commitment

Russia's hazardous trading environment should not blind us to the many deals that are concluded. In response to the difficulties of trading on commodity exchanges, brokers and clients have established a number of institutions to reduce opportunism. Economic hostages, relational contracting, and vertical integration have enhanced contract compliance with varying degrees of success. Each institutional response has important theoretical and economic consequences.

6.1. Economic Hostages

Williamson argues that many economists overlook the pervasiveness of self-enforcing agreements (Williamson, 1985). He notes that hostages — asset-specific investments with little value in alternative uses — signal a commitment to fulfill contracts. The use of hostages to secure exchange is somewhat problematic because the holder of the hostage may contrive to expropriate it. An ideal hostage is valuable to the provider, but not to the holder, and thereby presents fewer expropriation problems. One type of hostage that has taken hold in Russia is deposits of money or goods held as collateral against breach of contract. As inflation has diminished the value of money deposits, brokers now ask for more secure deposits, such as apartments, cars, or goods. Clients were initially reluctant to provide deposits out of fear that brokers would not return them. Deposits often reach 100 percent of the proposed deal, and capital-starved clients are often unwilling or unable to post them. The sunk costs that brokers had to pay for their seats on the exchange reassured clients to some extent that deposits would be returned. If a broker withheld a hostage, than a client could find the broker at the exchange and deliver the punishment. Clients could also besmirch the broker's reputation among other clients and the exchange personnel. Brokers and clients have found success with hostages, but calculating a deposit that is large enough to deter opportunism by the seller, but small enough to discourage brokers from absconding with the funds, is difficult in an unstable environment.

One means of allaying the fear of unjustified confiscation is available to firms with close ties to banks. The buyer asks the bank to notify the seller that payment is enroute, when the bank is actually holding the money until it receives notice that the good has been received. This ploy gives the buyer time to query the seller about the delivery of her goods without the risk of losing her prepayment. Over time, however, this tactic can be countered by a sympathetic delivery company. The seller can send a notice that the good is enroute, but he will not make final delivery of the good until payment is made.

6.2. Vertical Integration

Contract compliance may be enhanced by creating or recreating vertical trading relationships (Williamson, 1975, 1985). According to Williamson, placing a transaction within the firm reduces opportunism and uncertainty by promoting convergent expectations between the two partners. Williamson suggests that hierarchical trading also attenuates the problem of information asymmetry. Placing exchange within the firm gives traders less incentive to conceal advantageous information. Finally he notes that disputes between entities within a firm may be resolved quickly by fiat, rather than by resorting to the courts.

Evidence on the extent of vertical integration in Russia is cloudy at the moment. A plethora of institutional forms exist, and relations between them are often obscure. Michael Burawoy and Kathryn Hendley spent several months in Moscow studying Rezina, a rubber factory trying to cope with the great uncertainty of economic reform (Burawoy and Hendley, 1992). One research goal was to analyze the networks of cooperatives at the factory, but they concluded "try as we might to disentangle the details of this network, we could not. Some cooperatives were empty shells or accounting devices, some were connected to ventures outside Rezina, others were merely fronts for dispensing overtime" (Burawoy and Hendley, 1992: 379).

A prominent tendency in the Russian economy is the creation (or often re-creation) of vertical trading lines as holding companies called financial industrial groups (*finansovo-promishlennie gruppi*) (FPGs). These FPGs generally include major industrial producers, their chain of manufacturers, and banks. Members of the FPG agree on pricing and production schemes to increase their share of the national and international market. For example, the FPG "Neftyekom" includes twenty-four enterprises that worked under the Ministry of Oil Chemical Production and comprised about 30 percent of producers of energy drilling equipment in the Commonwealth of Independent States (*Kommersant*, June, 2,

1993: 2). These FPGs attempt to give order to industrial production in the absence of third-party contract enforcement.

The creation and maintenance of hierarchical trading relationships creates a paradox for market reforms. As economic reform increases uncertainty, vertical integration becomes more attractive. With increasing degrees of vertical integration, however, the prospects for creating markets are reduced as large firms maintain their near-monopoly status.

6.3. Relational Contracting

Contractual compliance may also be enhanced by dense social relations (Dore, 1983; Williamson, 1985). Relational contracting relies on trust that has accrued over time and is driven by a desire to reduce search costs. Rather than searching for the "optimal" contract, traders engaging in relational contracting prefer the security of existing relationships. According to Williamson, relational contracting is used for recurrent and nonstandardized transactions. Relational contracting should be widespread in the current Russian economy (Solinger, 1991; Stark, 1990; Hellman, 1992).

Several factors complicate the development of relational contracting on the commodity exchanges. Turnover among brokers is high, and more important, their clients, the actual buyers and sellers of the goods, rarely interact through the exchange. Brokers tried to burnish their reputations by creating Brokers' Guilds with strict ethical codes, but these professional associations have little influence on trading floor.

The role of social norms to promote trade invites further research and findings will likely vary across economic sectors. Potential buyers and sellers often rely on personal ties to secure exchange (Stark, 1990; Johnson and Kroll, 1991; Hellman, 1992). Many groups that traded goods in the planned economy have retained a network of valuable personal ties. Trusted clients trade at low prices and are loathe to abandon these valuable relationships. A survey of enterprise managers found that they often use a three-tiered pricing system; one price for traditional customers, a second price (100 to 150 percent higher) for new customers, and a third (even higher) price on the exchange (*Rossiskaya Gazeta*, June 26, 27, 1992: 3).

Brokers and clients on specialized commodity exchanges, such as the Moscow Oil Exchange and the Moscow Ferrous Metal Exchange, have retained personal ties developed under the centrally planned economy.

The evidence is incomplete, but contracts made on these exchanges seem to have a higher compliance rate than those made on other exchanges. Arbitration courts at these exchanges handle fewer cases in percentage terms than universal exchanges. A broker at the Moscow Oil Exchange noted: "We are talking about large sums of money traded by people who know each other. No one deals with a stranger."

Similarly, surveys conducted by the Institute for Market Research reveal that brokerage firms that have long ties with clients have a higher survival rate than those that rely on one-time clients (*Bizness, Banki i Birzhi*, 22, 1992: 7). Personal ties developed under the centrally planned economy can account for the disproportionate influence that many former bureaucrats and Communist Party officials have in some economic sectors. Former officials of the ruling bodies of the *Komsommol*, (The Communist Youth Organization), and *Gossnab*, (the former State Supply Agency), are well represented among brokerage firms and exchange officials (Yakovlev, 1991a, 1991b).

The relationship between personal ties and exchange often involves a tradeoff. Economic actors must determine if it is more profitable to deal with trusted customers at lower prices or seek new clients at a potentially higher profit margin. A conclusion from the survey of enterprise managers cited above captures this calculation: "Executives look for sound reasons to break traditional ties so as not to draw condemnation within their circle and not to deprive themselves of similar benefits." Contrary to reports of economic conspiracies by former bureaucrats, this behavior may be an appropriate response to an environment of high uncertainty. Personal ties that provide information about past behavior may calm the fear of opportunism.

7.0. State of Russian Commodity Exchanges

The demise of the commodity exchanges in their current form is deep and permanent. Frustrated by the contracting problems of the commodity exchanges, brokers are resorting to alternative means of exchange. Retail outlets and direct sales between traders are replacing the commodity exchanges. Retail outlets provide transactions that are more transparent and offer a greater prospect for repeat trading than can be found on the commodity exchanges. Exchanges that do not create futures markets will probably disappear. To survive until futures trading is instituted, the commodity exchanges have resorted to lobbying the government for privileges and like all interest groups, brokers face a collective action problem. All brokers would like the collective benefits of lobbying, but individual brokers are unwilling to devote resources to this effort.

As the Russian Raw Materials and Commodity Exchange and the Moscow Commodity Exchange handle roughly 30 percent of all trade, they have strong incentive to bear the cost of collective action (Zhurek, 1993). Aided by this small group of wealthy founders, the commodity exchanges have begun to engage in partisan political ativity. Most lobbying is conducted by the professional associations that represent the commodity exchanges, such as the International Commodity and Exchange Union and the Russian Commodities Union. In May 1993, after a year of applying pressure on the government, they received a number of privileges. According to Governmental Decree 452 issued May 11, 1993, the commodity exchanges will receive a share (suggested 20 percent) of export quotas, and government help in finding and financing the use of warehouses, communication, and transport services. The government also pledged to buy an unspecified portion of traditional exchange goods, such as, oil, grain, and sugar on the exchanges (*Kommersant*, May 7, 1993: 3). To receive these privileges, commodity exchanges must become not-for-profit organizations and pledge to introduce futures markets.

8.0. Conclusion

A weak state and the uncertainty of the economic transformation have made contract enforcement in all sectors of the Russian economy problematic, but the institutional design of the commodity exchanges in Russia exacerbated these problems by making it difficult to identify dishonest traders and by inhibiting repeat trading. By charging a commission on each deal and by failing to provide exchange-backed guarantees, the exchanges gave incentives to brokers to make deals off the exchange, which complicated contract enforcement.

More important, the failure to create institutions that provide the collective good of contract enforcement has encouraged brokers and clients to rely on private means to secure exchange. Economic hostages, vertical integration, and relational contracting are currently being used with varying degrees of success to reduce opportunism. The most alarming trend is the rise of legal and illegal private security agents to enforce contracts. Hiring a private security agent may be individually rational, but the consequences for the economy as a whole can be very detrimental. The race between private and state enforcement will determine the shape of political units of Russia. Those organizations, the central government, regional governments, private security agents, organized crime, or any combination of the above, that are best able to resolve the problems of adjudication and enforcement will likely emerge as the most powerful actors in Russia.

Notes

1. The author gratefully acknowledges the support of the National Council on Soviet and East European Affairs, the Harriman Institute, and the Wallis Institute of Political Economy, and would like to thank Jack Snyder, Dave Weimer, William Riker, Joel Hellman, Elena Vinogradova, Alexander Yakovlev, Rostislav Kokorev, Pavel Mochalov and the members of the Comparative Property Rights Project at the Wallis Institute, University of Rochester, for helpful comments.

2. Evidence provided is based on field research conducted in Moscow in June 1992 and May 1993. I conducted forty hours of interviews with brokers, analysts, and political actors involved with the exchanges in Moscow. Field research was conducted primarily at the two largest exchanges, the Moscow Commodity Exchange and the Russian Raw Materials and Commodity Exchange. Less time was spent at the Moscow Oil Exchange, the Moscow Ferrous Metal Exchange, and the Moscow Trade House. I have also surveyed the relevant Russian language sources. *Kommersant; Bizness, Banki i Birzha*; and *Birzheviie Vedemosti*, were especially helpful, as was *Birzhi v SSSR: Pervii god raboty* (Yakovlev, 1991a). I also benefitted from survey research conducted by the Institute for the Study of Organized Markets, a Moscow research institute.

3. *Bizness, Banki i Birzha*, 34, 1992. When asked to cite the percentage of contracts that go unfulfilled, brokers responded as follows

Unfulfilled contracts	*Percentage of brokers responding*
<10%	33%
11–25%	18%
26–50%	28%
51–75%	11%
>75%	10%

4. Much of the information on Aleks was obtained during interviews with the president and vice president on June 18, 1992. When possible the information was corroborated with secondary sources.

5. One observer noted that "Aleks is a reverse protection racket" (*Eto peket, no v obratnyuyu storonu*).

6. For analytical purposes, this essay does not examine the potential for a union between the state and private security agencies. The president of Aleks claimed that his firm provided security services for the government.

References

Abolafia, Mitchel Y. (1985). "Self-Regulation as Market Maintenance: An Organizational Perspective." In Roger Noll (ed.), *Regulatory Policy and the Social Sciences* (pp. 312–347). Berkeley: University of California Press.

Akerlof, George. (1970). "The Market for Lemons: Quality, Uncertainty and the Market Mechanism." *Quarterly Journal of Economics* 84(3): 488–500.

Axelrod, Robert. (1984). *The Evolution of Cooperation*. New York: Basic Books.

Bates, Robert. (1987). *Essays on the Political Economy of Rural Africa*. Berkeley: University of California Press.

Black, Donald. (1987). "Crime as Social Control." *American Sociological Review* 48(1): 34–45.

Burawoy, Michael and Hendley, Kathryn. (1992). "Between Perestroika and Privatisation: Divided Strategies and Political Crisis in a Soviet Enterprise." *Soviet Studies* 44(3): 371–402.

Calvert, Randall L. (Forthcoming). "The Rational Choice Theory of Social Institutions: Cooperation, Coordination, and Communication." In Jeffrey Banks and Eric Hanushek (eds.), *Political Economy of Institutions and Decisions*. New York: Cambridge University Press.

Clay, Karen. (1992). "Trade, Institutions and Law: The Experience of Mexican California." Stanford University, November, 1–35.

Cohen, Ariel. (1991). "The Developing Soviet Market: Commodity Exchanges." *Report on the USSR* 17 (May): 11–16.

Dore, Ronald. (1983). *Flexible Rigidities: Industrial Policy and Structural Adjustment in the Japanese Economy, 1970–80*. Stanford, CA: Stanford University Press.

Eggertsson, Thrainn. (1990). *Economic Behavior and Institutions*. New York: Cambridge University Press.

Ellickson, Robert. (1991). *Order Without Law*. Cambridge, MA: Harvard University Press.

Greif, Avner. (1992). "Cultural Beliefs and the Organization of Society: A Theoretical Reflection on Collectivist and Individualist Societies." Stanford University, November: 1–41.

Hellman, Joel. (1992). "The Revenge of the Past: Building Market Institutions in Soviet-Type Economies." American Political Science Association, Washington, DC: 1–28.

Johnson, Simon and Heidi Kroll. (1991). "Managerial Strategies for Spontaneous Privatization." *Soviet Economy* 7(4): 281–316.

Kokorev, Rostislav. (1992). "Brokerstvo kak institut organizatsii rynka v perekhodnoi ekonomike." Dissertation, Moscow State.

Kreps, David. (1990). "Corporate Culture and Economic Theory." In James E. Alt and Kenneth A. Shepsle (eds.), *Perspectives on Positive Political Economy* (pp. 90–143). New York: Cambridge University Press.

Kroll, Heidi. (1987). "Breach of Contract in the Soviet Economy." *Journal of Legal Studies* 16(1): 119–148.

———. (1989a). "Property Rights and the Soviet Enterprise: Evidence From the Law of Contract." *Journal of Comparative Economics* 13(1): 115–133.

———. (1989b). "Reform and Damages for Breach of Contract in the Soviet Economy." *Soviet Economy* 3(2): 276–297.

Levi, Margaret. (1988). *Of Rule and Revenue*. Berkeley: University of California Press.

Litwack, John. (1991a). "Legality and Market Reform in Soviet-Type Economies." *Journal of Economic Perspectives* 5(4): 77–89.

———. (1991b). "Discretionary Behavior and Soviet Economic Reform." *Soviet Studies* 43(2): 255–279.

Milgrom, Paul R., Douglass C. North, and Barry Weingast. (1990). "The Law Merchant, Private Judges, and Champaigne Fairs." *Economics and Politics* 2(1): 1–23.

North, Douglass, C. (1990). *Institutions, Institutional Change and Economic Performance*. New York: Cambridge University Press.

——— and Robert Paul Thomas. (1973). *The Rise of the Western World: A New Economic History*. New York: Cambridge University Press.

Ostrom, Elinor. (1990). *Governing the Commons: The Evolution of Institutions for Collective Action*. New York: Cambridge University Press.

Riker, William and Itai Sened. (1991). "A Political Theory of the Origins of Property Rights: Airport Slots." *American Journal of Political Science* 35(4): 951–969.

Solinger, Dorothy. (1991). "Urban Reform and Relational Contracting in Post-Mao China: An Interpretation of the Transition from Plan to Market." In Richard Baum (ed.), *Reform and Reaction in Post-Mao China* (pp. 104–123). New York: Routledge Press.

Stark, David. (1990). "Privatization in Hungary: From Plan to Market or From Plan to Clan?" *East European Politics and Society* 4(3): 351–392.

Taylor, Michael. (1976). *Anarchy and Cooperation*. New York: Wiley.

———. (1987). *The Possibility of Cooperation*. New York: Cambridge University Press.

Tilly, Charles. (1985). "War-making and State-making as Organized Crime." In Peter Evans, Dietrich Reuschmeyer, and Theda Skocpol (eds.), *Bringing the State Back In* (pp. 169–191). New York: Cambridge University Press.

———. (1991). *Coercion, Capital and European States*. Ithaca, NY: Cornell University Press.

Umbeck, John. (1981). "Might Makes Rights: A Theory of the Formation and Initial Distribution of Property Rights." *Economic Inquiry* 19(1): 38–59.

Vinogradova, Elena. (1992). *"Arbitrazhnie Kommissii: Obyazatelstvo ili Pravo?" Khozyastvo i Pravo* 2(3): 106–114.

Vytransky, V.V. (1992). *Zashchita Imushestvennikh Prav Predprinimatelii*. Moskva: Pravo i Ekonomika.

Weingast, Barry. (1993). "Constitutions as Commitment Devices." *Journal of Institutional and Theoretical Economics* 149(1): 286–311.

Williamson, Oliver. (1975). *Markets and Hierarchies: Analysis and Antitrust*

Implications. New York: Free Press.

———. (1985). *The Economic Institutions of Capitalism*. New York: Free Press.

Woodruff, David. (1992). "The Commodity Fiction and Competition in the Post-Soviet Economy: Theoretical Reflections on Russia's Commodity Exchanges." University of California at Berkeley.

Yakovlev, A.A. (ed.). (1991a). "*Birzhi v SSSR: pervii god raboty*." Moscow: Institut issledovaniia organizovannikh rynkov.

———. (1991b). "*Kak kupit' i prodat' tovar na birzhe*." Moscow: Institut issledovaniia organizovannykh rynkov.

Zhurek, Stefan. (1993). "Commodity Exchanges in Russia: Success or Failure?" *RFE/RL Research Report* 5 (February): 41–43.

4 THE RATIONAL CHOICE THEORY OF INSTITUTIONS: IMPLICATIONS FOR DESIGN

Randall L. Calvert

1.0. Introduction

Almost all accounts of policymaking organizations stress two important features. First, the process of policymaking, and the life of any organization, consists of a sequence of similar or related situations in which members of the organization must take actions. Second, the actions they take tend to fall into patterns: they behave in similar ways in similar situations, which is how we recognize a policy, an organization, or an institution in the first place.

A third feature of organizations figures importantly in many accounts of how policy is made and carried out: individuals within the policymaking organization or agency have individual interests or preferences, which may differ from the ostensible purposes of the organization or of the policy set out by an agency's principal. Thus any patterns of behavior that the members follow must consist of rational actions given the actors' environments, which include the actions of other individuals in the organization and in other organizations; the actions of bureaucratic superiors; the requirements of outside professional, political, or clientele groups; and other already established patterns of outside action and expectations.

The actions of all these agents together determine the outcome of organizational decisionmaking and the level of satisfaction of each participant given this process and outcome.

To understand how policies are determined and carried out by an organization, one needs a theoretical approach that emphasizes these features of institutional life. A natural candidate is the theory of repeated games. This approach would portray a typical situation of policymaking or policy implementation as a stage game played among relevant actors, and repeated from time to time perhaps with variations in the participants, their opportunities, and their preferences. In a game-theoretic equilibrium, the participants' behavior over a series of these situations must form a consistent pattern given their preferences and their mutual expectations about the game and about one another's actions. The result of such an analysis is a set of statements about how the behavior of players in the game, and the outcome of the game, are determined by the parameters of the game and the expectations of the players.

The designer of a policymaking institution has some ability to design the "rules" of this game that agents will play as they make policy decisions. However, this freedom to determine the rules is never complete. If a designer wishes to set the payoffs for agents by having a supervisor apply rewards and punishments in response to the agents' actions, then the designer must worry about the fact that the supervisor is also a player in the game and also has preferences that may not correspond exactly with the designer's goals. The supervisor too must be given incentives that make it rational to apply these punishments and rewards in the ways envisioned by the designer.

At some margin, however, the agency will be affected by already existing agencies with already determined ways of doing business: courts, for example, in which lawyers and judges apply the law according to general principles that will not be affected by the design of the new policymaking agency; or legislators who will react in predictable ways to the effect of policy choices on their potential voters and contributors; or wider professions in which the future standing of agency officials may be affected by how well they adhere to professional norms in carrying out their policymaking duties. This is the institutional designer's starting point; it defines a game within which the new policymakers will act.

Within this fixed political and policy environment, the institutional designer can do two things. First, she can determine some of the parameters that will affect the payoffs of the agents, by setting lengths of terms of office, managerial structures, civil service ranks and professional requirements for officials, requirements for reporting to outside actors, and the like. Such formal structural features need not absolutely constrain real policymakers, but they may make certain actions harder and others easier to accomplish or to conceal from monitoring. Still, the fundamental lesson of viewing policymaking as a repeated game is that many patterns of action within that game can be maintained as stable equilibria.

The institutional designer can use a game-theoretic approach to gain insights into what makes agents cooperate, compete, work together smoothly without confusion, act in ways productive for organizational goals even when supervisory monitoring is impossible, and so on. The starting point of such an analysis is that agents won't automatically do these things; rather it is necessary to provide both incentives and expectations so that the desired behavior will be rational for them to maintain. Relatively simple game theoretic models can provide general insights about problems of cooperation, coordination, and information sharing. I examine some of these below. In addition, more specialized models may offer prescriptions about specific incentive schemes useful to induce healthy competition, habitual cooperation, or other desired patterns of behavior in a specific policymaking problem. I hope to make the techniques for doing this clear in the course of the chapter.

2.0. The Theory of Repeated Games with Variation and Its Applicability to the Problem of Institutional Design

Before turning to some of these specific tasks, however, it is necessary to clarify how the theory of repeated games can be regularly applied to the somewhat complicated general conditions of institutional design for policymaking. To capture many of the phenomena of interest in the design of policymaking institutions, it is important that our model provide explicitly for the presence of variations from one policymaking situation to the next, and of incomplete information among the players concerning their true preferences as well as about events in the policymaking environment. As usually presented, the theory of repeated games relies on the simple repetition of a stage game, as well as complete information about the game's structure.

After reviewing the basic elements of the standard theory of repeated games, this section presents the general argument for how a policymaking organization can be successfully modeled using that theory. From this it is clear that the well-known "folk theorem" concerning the existence of multiple equilibrium in repeated games applies. Structuring the problem in this way makes clear the two main avenues for institutional design:

influencing the parameters of the game and influencing the choice of equilibria by the participants.

2.1. The Theory of Repeated Games

The standard theory of repeated games deals with situations of the following sort: a game G is to be played by a set of players. This "stage game" G might involve opportunities for discovery of information, the monitoring of other players, or communication among the players, as well as the taking of actions that will determine outcomes. In a repeated game, once G is played, the players observe the outcome, receive the payoffs, and then play G again. In the typical application, we imagine that G is repeated indefinitely, with the players discounting future payoffs by some factor d ($0 < d < 1$) to take account of their uncertainties about continued participation in the game, as well as the opportunity costs of delayed payoffs. In a policymaking setting, the extent of discounting may depend on economic factors, the participant's plans for retirement or career change, the frequency with which the participant makes a certain kind of decision or encounters a certain other participant, and so on.

A player's *strategy* is a plan for playing each repetition of G, perhaps conditional on the outcomes of all previous plays of G. Such strategies may be extremely simple (for example, "no matter what has happened before, always defect") or extremely complicated, making use of some finely tuned summary of previous outcomes and the actions that led to them.

An *equilibrium* in the repeated game is a profile of strategies for all the players such that each player, expecting the others to play according to the equilibrium, cannot improve his or her payoff by departing from it. Typically an equilibrium might involve strategies that react to other players' previous moves in ways purposefully designed to deter the other players from certain actions and encourage them to take certain other actions. In some settings, interesting equilibrium strategies involve reacting to other players' actions in ways that allow the players to transmit information to one another about their beliefs or intentions.

For any equilibrium (or indeed for any strategy profile at all) we can calculate in advance the expected payoff that would result for each player ("expected" because the actual payoffs may depend on the outcomes of random "moves by nature" incorporated in G, or on the realizations of mixed strategies employed by the players). Suppose that V_n is player n's expected payoff for some equilibrium in the repeated game; then n's *per-*

period average payoff for that equilibrium is defined as $(1 - d)V_n$, that is, the number that, if summed over infinite repetitions and discounted, would add up to V_n.

An important result in the theory of repeated games is the so-called folk theorem, which guarantees that in general a repeated game will have a great number and variety of equilibria (see, for example, Fudenberg and Maskin, 1986). It can be stated using a little more notation. Let v_n^* be the lowest expected payoff that player n could be forced to in G, even if the other players ignored their own payoffs and just concentrated on harming n; this is called n's "minimax" payoff. Choose any list of payoffs v, one value for every player, that satisfies two criteria: first, for each player n, $v_n > v_n^*$; and second, this list of payoffs is achievable from some outcome of G, or at least as the expected values from some randomization over the outcomes of G. Then the folk theorem says that, provided the discounting of future payoffs is not too heavy, there is a subgame-perfect equilibrium[1] of the repeated game that has v as the list of expected per-period average payoffs for the players.

The folk theorem tells us that in nearly any repeated game of interest, these is a great variety of equilibrium patterns of play yielding different payoff values. Experience with repeated games also tells us that, even for a given level of average per-period payoffs, there are likely to be many equilibria that would yield that same vector of payoffs. The folk theorem presents a problem for the analyst, in that we have no dependable criterion for choosing among the equilibria of the game in order to make a prediction. Nevertheless, it provides an opportunity for explaining several phenomena previously regarded as outside the purview of rational choice analysis, such as leadership phenomena and "corporate culture" (Calvert, 1992; Kreps, 1990; Miller, 1992).

2.2. Variation and Incomplete Information Within a Stage Game

The theory of repeated games extends to include the interesting aspects of variation and incomplete information necessary for modeling policy-making processes, provided we represent the stage game in the right way. The now-standard method (see Harsanyi, 1967–1968) of treating single-play games of incomplete information is to represent the various information states as the results of an initial move by "nature" that determines the true values of information held by all players; all players know the probabilistic rules by which this determination is made, but each player sees the result only in terms of his or her own private information. Such games are solved by deriving a strategy for each possible information state or "type" for each player, representing the expectations of all players in equilibrium about how each player will behave conditional on being each possible type. For present purposes we can simply include such a type-determining "move by nature" at the beginning of each stage game, so that the repeated game is still simply a repetition of identical stage games, even though the types may now vary from one iteration to the next.

A similar technique will allow us to absorb stage-game variation into the standard theory of repeated games. Suppose that the policymaking situation to be faced by an organization can always be represented by one of a large set of games, whose differences reflect differences in the policy problem, client preferences, market forces, and so on. Let the "stage game" consist of an initial move by nature, in which one of the games in this large set is selected to be played in the current iteration. Then a strategy for the stage game consists, formally, of a plan for playing any of the subgames that could arise, even though nature's choice of a subgame will be known before any of those plans is put into effect. With this approach, the overall game then consists technically of an identical stage game repeated in each iteration, as required for the standard theory.

Thus these extended models can be rewritten into the standard form of repeated games, and such basic results as the folk theorem continue to apply. The appendix to this chapter presents more formally a general version of the repeated game model that allows for variations among the stage games and that provides the machinery for analyzing situations of incomplete information. It also presents a more formal statement of a folk theorem for that generalized setting.

2.3. Equilibrium Selection by Players: Solving the Coordination Problem

The existence of multiple equilibria presents a problem not only for the analyst trying to make a prediction, but also for the players in a repeated game. If some players use strategies consistent with one equilibrium while others use strategies consistent only with a different one, the result may be a lower payoff for all players. For instance, if the game in question is a repeated prisoner's dilemma and the equilibria involve different patterns of prescribed cooperation and of punishment for noncooperation, then players intending different equilibria may end up punishing one another for behavior that was intended to be cooperative, punishing those punishments, and so on, at the cost of lost cooperation gains. In such cases the repeated game presents the players with a problem of coordinating on some single equilibrium: they have to arrive at agreement in order to avoid bad payoffs for everyone.

I return to the detailed analysis of coordination problems in Section 4, but some general remarks are helpful now in understanding the importance of the multiple equilibria for institutional design. Game theorists writing about coordination problems have explored many processes by which participants may overcome the difficulty and achieve coordination without undue loss. These include the use of strategies known to be "prominent" for exogenous reasons (Schelling, 1960); the use of "tracing" procedures for eliminating undersirable strategies and arriving at a unique expectation through independent ex ante reasoning (Harsanyi and Selten, 1988); communication among the players about their intentions (Farrell, 1987); the identification of asymmetries among the participants that can be used to assign them to various action-choosing roles (Sugden, 1986); and repeated play of identical coordination problems (Crawford and Haller, 1990). Some of these methods presuppose the solution of prior coordination problems, as in the use of tracing procedures or asymmetries among players. Others appeal to factors extraneous to the game but common to the players' histories, as in the identification of prominent "focal points."

Although the theory of coordination games, or more broadly of equilibrium selection in games, is still quite an open subject, it nevertheless offers several tools with which to close the analysis of repeated games by explaining how the players arrive at one out of a multitude of possible equilibria. If one assumes that players who find themselves out of equilibrium will continue to search for better courses of action, then it seems appropriate to maintain the standard game-theoretic assumption that behavior in a stable organization will correspond to some equilibrium. The analyst of repeated games can say something useful about the process by which the players arrive at that equilibrium and, more important, about what will happen to the equilibrium if conditions of the game change in ways not anticipated by the players or (equivalently) if new circumstances with which the players have never before dealt, arise in the course of play. This type of information can be useful to the designer contemplating the robustness of various possible institutional arrangements.

In general, the theory assigns quite an important role to the interaction among the players in determining which equilibrium they will end up playing. Their initial expectations about equilibrium may be important as well, however, and the institutional designer has this one advantage over the game theoretic analyst: the designer can influence those initial expectations to attempt to make some types of equilibria more likely than others.

2.4. Levers for Institutional Design

If policymaking in an organization can be represented as a series of games, then the theory of repeated games is a valuable tool for understanding how policy outcomes depend on the interests, expectations, histories, and opportunities of the participants. In particular, different interests or different expections lead, in general, to different actions by participants and thus to different policy outcomes, and the analysis of repeated games elucidates precisely this relationship.

The institutional designer is typically interested in ensuring that certain kinds of outcomes will occur once the organization's policymaking is under way. The first tool available for influencing these outcomes is the interests and preferences of the participants. In the typical setting, there will be some participants (clientele groups, for example) whose preferences form part of the backdrop of policymaking and are beyond the reach of the designer. Likewise, some aspects of policymaker preferences, such as the inclination to protect one's own job, are likely to be givens for the designer. The designer is likely to have some leeway, however, over the preferences of the policymakers. Most obviously, the career patterns and compensation and incentive schemes for members of the organization influence their derived preferences over actions and outcomes. If workers can be fired when clients are unhappy, then they behave differently than if they could not be fired at all. If they are paid for piece work, then they behave in different ways than if they are paid a wage. It matters for the quality of policy decisions whether workers are held strictly responsible for standard operating procedures or are instead evaluated for how sensitively they determine and articulate appropriate actions for special policy problems and circumstances. Designing the conditions of employment and compensation helps determine player payoffs in the policymaking game within the organization.

In addition, professional incentives may help determine policymakers' preferences. Bureaucrats in a federal agency may be lawyers, economists, scientists, engineers, or generic federal employees. They may be political appointees or career civil servants. These characteristics help determine their "payoffs" from taking various actions in the course of policy formation. Due to professional pressures outside the organization, such professionals often seek to maintain their credibility among their peers by taking actions that will be respected by the professional community at large (Bardach and Kagan, 1982). For example, it is much easier for a lawyer in the Federal Trade Commission to recommend the regulation of business practices than it would be for an economist in the same position to do so. Many lawyers and economists in the FTC eventually leave to find other employment in their profession and need to maintain their reputations in their fields. Also, each can benefit later from different types of experience; hence FTC lawyers look for chances to get court experience, while FTC economists might seek to perform original economic research publishable in a professional journal (Katzmann, 1980). Whether the Bureau of Competition is staffed with lawyers or economists, then, has an important effect on the outcomes of its research and recommendations and ultimately on agency regulations. Equilibrium patterns of interaction among those professionals, other regulators, clienteles, and politicians will depend on the preference patterns of the professionals. To choose a certain kind of person for a position is to choose a certain collection of payoff values for the players in the policymaking game.

The information that players have is an important feature of any game, and this too is a subject important to the policy designer. An organization or official can be given more or fewer resources for determining objective facts about a case, and this will obviously affect policymaking. More interesting from a game theoretic point of view, the information that participants have about one another's actions, preferences, and beliefs is likely to affect the way they react to one another's actions. The designer can provide for extensive communication and the kinds of incidental contact that promote familiarity or can discourage such information transfer and force participants into situations of uncertainty about one another. Either approach might be desirable depending on whether the designer wishes to constrain or promote certain kinds of coalition building, teamwork, collusion, or conspiracy within the organization.

Another important factor in the outcomes of policymaking games is the extent to which participants discount future payoffs. Discounting is partly a function of factors that may be outside the designer's control — age, economic discount rates, or uncertainty in the economic environment. Other factors that go into discounting are more manipulable, though. If one policymaking participant has to coordinate her actions with another, the development of that cooperative relationship will depend partly on how often they interact or how likely they are to interact again in the near future. The institutional designer can influence the existence or difficulty of long-rum, regular interactions among different participants and thus influence the patterns of behavior they will adopt.

By choosing participants who share experience in another organization, or who have worked together in some other context, the institutional designer can partly choose the participants' history of interaction and thus influence the selection of equilibrium in the new organization. If a high-rise construction company hires its metalworkers largely from a nearby Indian reservation, then the cooperation and work norms of their employees is likely to reflect previous habit among those same people. If the CIA staffs an operation with members of the Mormon church, it is likely buying into a certain pattern of trust and responsibility among those agents. Likewise, if a policymaking organization hires people with postgraduate training in the humanities or veterans of a different policymaking agency, then the new organization is likely to inherit certain patterns of interaction among its members.

The institutional designer has other opportunities to influence equilibrium choice in an organization by influencing the initial expectations of participants. The details of organizational structure help to do this: if a particular manager is designated as my supervisor, then my initial expectation will be that all participants will expect me to follow the direction of that manager and not of some other manager elsewhere in the organization. More generally, initial instructions to participants can influence the long-term patterns of interaction that result. If workers in one office are told that it would be a good idea to cooperate with workers in another office, then they are likely at least initially to try that; if such cooperation is made rational by the incentives inherent in worker preferences, policy effects, and organizational incentives, then such behavior may well persist. On the other hand, if such cooperation had not been initially suggested, then the same office may fall into a pattern of ignoring or undercutting what the other is doing, with internal rewards and sanctions being adjusted to support such behavior.

By taking advantage of the opportunity to influence preferences, discounting patterns, information, expectations, and experience of the participants, the institutional designer fills in the details of the game that they will play in the course of making policy. These details determine what equilibrium patterns of behavior are possible, what equilibrium is likely to emerge, and thus what the nature of policy choices and organizational responsiveness will be. Although it is unlikely that any institutional designer will ever be able to analyze a game theoretic model of policy-making that provides more than a stylization of the real problem, important lessons about relevant aspects of a design problem can be learned from such an effort. The overarching idea here is to take interacting incentives and strategic behavior (or its equivalent, rational mutual adjustment of behavior) seriously into account when trying to design an institution to yield certain behavioral or policy results.

Two general approaches suggest themselves, both having important uses. One is to create a stylized version of a specific policy problem, such as the regulation of prices in a natural monopoly by an agency that will be subject to certain political pressures. There is considerable precedent for such modeling in the literature, as I recount in Section 6 below, and although such efforts have not explicitly aimed at institutional design, they present the kinds of results needed by institutional desingers. The second approach is to identify common types of interactions thought to be universally important in policymaking institutions, and create and interrogate models that exhibit those types of interactions in a general form. The latter is the main business of this chapter and the subject of Sections 3, 4, and 5 below.

3.0. Cooperation in Institutions: The Repeated Prisoner's Dilemma

One of the types of interaction in organizations most commonly of interest to analysts of policymaking is cooperation. For our purposes here, cooperation is any behavioral pattern in which individuals in a policymaking situation take actions that are, in themselves, costly to their interests but that, because they are accompanied by other such actions by other actors, provide a net overall benefit to the participants in the interaction. A cooperation "problem" is a situation in which the actors could achieve such gains if they would all engage in the appropriate behavior but in which there is a temptation for each to let the other players contribute unilaterally and thus reap even larger individual benefits. An institutional designer may either wish to promote cooperation (such as when she wishes organizational actors to take the time and trouble to exchange information that will produce better policy choices) or discourage cooperation (such as when she wishes to prevent the collusion of regulated firms to mislead a regulatory agency and reap larger profits). In either case, the designer needs to know what factors tend to promote or retard the development of cooperative behavior among institutional actors.

To illustrate this type of analysis, consider the most straightforward example of a cooperation problem, the simple two-player prisoner's dilemma (PD) game. This game might represent some simple element of policy implementation in which a functionary in one agency may or may not cooperate with someone in another agency to help one another in making some implementation decision. To help is costly, but mutual help is mutually beneficial. Note that these costs and benefits are strictly in terms of the two agents' own personal interests; the agents may or may not share their organizations' respective goals. Finally, in any given iteration of this repeated situation, each of the two agents must choose her actions without first learning the other's choice, and only then is the outcome of the situation revealed: mutual help, mutual withholding of assistance, or one-sided helping.

The repeated PD model is well known from the literature (see, for example, Axelrod 1984) and has the elements shown in Table 4.1. The stage game, played at each repetition, has the normal form shown in the table, where the first number in each pair indicates the utility of the outcome to player 1 and the second that to player 2. Here $a > 1$ represents the payoff from having the other player help unilaterally, and $b > 0$ that from being the one who helps unilaterally. In this example we adopt the standard assumption that $a - b < 2$, so there is one efficient way to "cooperate" in the repeated game (namely, for both palyers to "help"), and we can ignore the alternative possibility that the players take turns unilaterally "helping." As always in the prisoner's dilemma game, then, each player has a dominant strategy of not helping, and the lower right cell is the only possible equilibrium outcome.

If the game is repeated indefinitely, with future payoffs being discounted by a factor of d per period ($0 < d < 1$), cooperation becomes possible in equilibrium provided that d is large enough relative to a and b. How large d has to be depends on the strategy by which the players intend to punish defection. For example, if the players use the well known tit-for-tat (TFT) strategy,[2] then, as Taylor (1976: 31–39) shows, the parameters of the game (a, b, and d) must meet the following requirement: d must be at least as large as the maximum of $(a-1)/a$ and $(a-1)/(b+1)$. With this provision, tit-for-tat is an equilibrium strategy, so cooperation can thereby be maintained among rational players.[3] If a stronger punishment

Table 4.1.

	Player 2 helps	Player 2 does not help
Player 1 helps	(1, 1)	($-b$, a)
Player 1 does not help	(a, $-b$)	(0, 0)

scheme is used, such as in the strategy of permanent retaliation (in which a player helps as long as the other player has always helped, but once the other player fails to help a single time, the first player never helps in any future iteration), then cooperation is possible under a weaker condition – namely, that the payoff from continued mutual help is at least as great as that from one period of unilateral advantage-taking, followed by a discounted eternity of mutual nonhelp: $1/(1-d) \geq a$, that is, $d \geq (a-1)/a$; this is weaker than the tit-for-tat condition provided that $a-b>1$.

These results are the source of some specific predictions about how the behavior of the players will respond to unexpected exogenous changes in the parameters. Suppose that indeed $a-b>1$, and that initially both players are using the tit-for-tat strategy, for which d meets the condition for that strategy to be in equilibrium. Suppose that d is then decreased. As long as the conditions for equilibrium are still met, it would be rational for both players to continue to use the TFT strategy; any unexpected departure from the prescribed pattern of cooperation should be met with a one-period punishment in kind. When d dips below $(a-1)/(b+1)$, however, TFT is no longer viable as an equilibrium, and a change must occur. The players could, for example, switch to never helping; alternatively, they could continue cooperating in the mutual expectation that any departure would now be met with permanent retaliation from the other player, ending all cooperation. Clearly, the prediction about what happens in case of a departure from the prescribed cooperation would change. If d is lowered past the threshold $(a-1)/a$, then cooperation is no longer possible in equilibrium under any strategy, and the players would cease helping one another.[4] Similar predictions result from changes in the payoff values a and b: decreasing a eventually makes cooperation unachievable; increasing b does the same under the TFT strategy but has no effect under the permanent retaliation strategy.

Do these predictions have real-world referents? Making the translation to the real world is not a trivial matter, but there are several reasonable real-world versions of these parameter changes. If the policymaking situation occurs less often, then the discount factor is, in effect, reduced; the same thing happens if one of the agents becomes more likely to depart the interaction through retirement or promotion. Changes in b correspond to changes in the costliness of helping: b decreases if communication or information-retrieval technology change so as to make help less time-consuming to provide and increases if the agents acquire new supervisors who frown more on helping the other agency on the side. Finally, the parameter a represents the stakes in mutual help; if it becomes more difficult to accomplish the agents' (personal) goals without, say, pooling their information about the case at hand, then cooperation is more important and a has increased.

4.0. Coordination in Institutions: The Battle-of-the-Sexes Game

Another type of interaction extremely important in any organizational or policymaking setting is coordination. For our purposes coordination is any behavioral pattern in which individuals in a policymaking situation take actions that fit together to achieve outcomes that all participants regard as superior to what would have happened had they chosen an inappropriate combination of actions. In a coordination "problem," participants agree that outcomes of a certain kind would be preferable to those of another kind, but among the preferred kind of outcomes they have opposing preferences, and they must make effectively simultaneous decisions that will together determine those outcomes. Coordination problems may be solved through various applications of communication, precedent, and leadership. Again, an institutional designer may wish either to promote coordination, in order to get coherent policymaking actions, or to retard it, as for example in preventing workers from devising informal norms to limit the amount of work they perform without being discovered by monitors.

Besides being important in its own right as a factor in institutional performance, the analysis of coordination provides an important illustration of a type of predictive statement that did not occur in the analysis of cooperation in the prisoner's dilemma. This is because game-theoretic models of coordination often involve so-called mixed strategies, in which identical actors in identical situations may sometimes take one action and sometimes another, seemingly at random from the point of view of the analyst or of other players. Different parameter values in the game representing a coordination problem require different frequencies of the alternate behaviors in equilibrium. These variations imply variations in the frequency with which successful coordination is achieved, and an understanding of them is thus important to the institutional designer.

Suppose that a regularly recurring policymaking situation involves individuals from two agencies, with two differences from the previous model. First, the same two decision makers do not interact repeatedly; rather, a different pair of actors, one from each agency, is involved in each iteration, and they do not have perfect information about previous interactions among other decision makers. Second, the policy problem itself is not a prisoner's dilemma, but rather one involving a problem of coordination. For concreteness, let me refer to agency *A* and agency *B*, and suppose that they can both choose between a policy favored by agency *A* (call it policy α) and one favored by agency *B* (policy β). If both agencies choose the same policy, then the outcome is "good" for both, and if they choose differently, uncoordinatedly, then the outcome is "bad" for both. However, within the "good," or coordinated, outcomes, each agency most prefers the one in which its own favored policy is chosen. Game theory knows this type of interaction as the "battle-of-the-sexes" game (Luce and Raiffa, 1957), and it takes the form shown in Table 4.2, where the first number in each pair indicates the payoff to the decision maker in agency *A* and the second that to the decision maker in agency *B*, and where $x > 1$. This game has equilibria in pure strategies, in which one agency gets its preferred outcome with certainty; however, if there is really a "problem" of coordination in some real-world setting, focusing on these pure-strategy equilibria assumes away that problem without explaining how it is solved. A more revealing way to understand coordination is to examine the mixed-strategy equilibrium, in which each player chooses her most favored policy with probability $x/(1+x)$. For different values of the payoff parameter x, which represents the stakes that decision makers in each agency perceive for making sure that the favored rather than the unfavored policy is chosen,[5] the equilibrium probability of insisting on one's own favorite policy will vary. Hence a higher value of x (more strongly favored policy, or less relative importance placed on avoiding coordination failure) means a higher value of $x/(1+x)$, and thus more insistence by agencies upon their more favored policy, and more frequent coordination failures (which occur with probability $2x/(1+x)^2$). Likewise if one agency faces higher stakes than the other, the frequency of coordination on the two diagonal cells will differ, favoring the agency with the *lower* stakes: If *A*'s payoff from both choosing α is x, and *B*'s from both choosing β is y, with $x > y > 1$, then in equilibrium *A* chooses α

Table 4.2.

	Agency B chooses policy α	Agency B chooses policy β
Agency *A* chooses policy α	$(x, 1)$	$(0, 0)$
Agency *A* chooses policy β	$(0, 0)$	$(1, x)$

with probability $y/(1 + y)$ and B chooses β with probability $x/(1 + x)$, so that policy α is chosen by both with probability $y/[(1 + x)(1 + y)]$ and both choose β with probability $x/[(1 + x)(1 + y)]$.

In the prisoner's dilemma example, predictions were in the nature of threshold phenomena: if a condition on the parameters ceases to be met, then cooperative relations will disintegrate. In the battle-of-the-sexes example, the prediction is a standard rate-of-change or comparative statics statement: changes in the parameter yield corresponding changes in behavior as a continuous function of the parameter. More frequent coordination requires lower values of x (and of y). In order to promote coordination, the institutional designer would wish to have the agencies' internal incentives in as little conflict as possible, so that they do not disagree strongly on which of two policies is better. Such an ideal is sometimes beyond the designer's capacity to produce, though, and it is necessary instead to consider the process by which disagreeing agencies might learn to coordinate using such devices as repeated play, communication, and other complications not appearing in the simple battle-of-the-sexes model.

5.0. More Substantial Models: Variation and Communication

The examples of the prisoner's dilemma and battle-of-the-sexes games are simple ones indeed, but they illustrate how such game-theoretic models of policymaking institutions can offer predictions about behavioral responses to the conditions of policymaking and to changes in those conditions. It remains to indicate how more substantial phenomena might be similarly treated. To this end I first review some of the features likely to arise in examining games with more than two players. I then summarize how to go about modeling asymmetries, variation, and incomplete information in the context of the simple games constructed above, including an example of a repeated game in which the stage game varies from one iteration to the next. More specialized models can be built and interrogated in similar ways.

5.1. Games with Multiple Players

The two-player models given previously hold important general lessons concerning cooperation and coordination in games because it is straighforward to extend such models, and fairly straightforward to extend those equilibria, to games having more participants. Two complications arise in considering such extensions, though, and can lead both to further understanding of general phenomena of cooperation and coordination and to an important conceptual tool for understanding institutions generally.

Many real-world situations of cooperation and coordination involve many players, but they interact only in pairs. In that case, the reasoning in the two-player case carries over straightforwardly, although discounting now depends not only on one's rate of time preference but also on the frequency of interaction of any given pair of players (Calvert, 1995).

Other applications, of course, really do involve multiple players interacting at the same time. In a public goods or generalized prisoner's dilemma problem with many players,[6] it is still true that cooperation in equilibrium requires some structure of expected retaliation, and its possibility depends on the size of the discount parameter and the relative values of payoffs. However, there are now many forms that such retaliation could take, and the parameter requirements for cooperation to be chosen depends on the form chosen. The most obvious generalization from the two-player cooperative equilibrium would require all players to punish any deviant by refusing in turn to cooperate. This approach has several new complications, however: if retaliation is in the form of noncooperation, as before, then it harms the nondeviants as well as the original deviant. In that case, an efficient punishment scheme may require just the right number of players to "retaliate" while the remainder continue to provide public goods for the rest. In that case, the question of who gets to assume the role of punisher presents a significant problem of coordination. If, on the other hand, retaliation were to be carried out by each player separately through noncooperation with a deviant in other, pairwise relations – as in the case of shunning as a punishment for moral violations – then there is always the temptation to cheat by not punishing the deviant and thereby enjoy the gains from cooperation in the two-player setting. This type of solution to the cooperation problem generates yet another cooperation problem (Laver, 1983: 55–59; Calvert, 1991).

A common type of retaliation scheme for enforcing cooperation in the many-player setting involves some form of centralized monitoring and punishment. Where retaliation by noncooperation, and pairwise retaliation by "shunning," require the same behavior of all players, these more structured approaches assign different roles to different players. An example is the studies by Milgrom, North, and Weingast (1990) and Greif, Milgrom, and Weingast (1994) of the problem of economic trade between actors who do not interact repeatedly. In those studies, an actor is designated to serve as a central clearinghouse for information about previous cooperative behavior by a player; in the equilibria of interest, all other players are required to consult this information source, pass information to it themselves, and punish another player when the clearinghouse reports that punishment is in order.[7] This type of equilibrium represents an analytical breakthough of critical importance to the study of institutional design: an aspect of organizational structure (the role of clearinghouse, the requirements for passing information and applying punishment) is portrayed not as a fixed "rule of the game," but rather as an aspect of an equilibrium in some more primitive underlying game describing the players' basic opportunities for interaction (Calvert, 1995). This approach allows the analyst to study the conditions under which such emergent "rules" can persist, given rational behavior by the players. For institutional features that cannot be effectively enforced from outside an organization, this is precisely the kind of condition that must be created in order for the institution to work as intended: the rules of behavior must be self-enforcing within the institution. This includes the behavior of any organizational leader who is supposed to enforce such rules: the willingness of the leader to enforce a particular set of rules is subject to the same kind of incentive problems as is the willingness of subordinates to behave as the institutional designer intends (Miller, 1992).

Obviously, in principle, more elaborate structures could be treated in similar fashion. A common pattern of enforcement in any organization is for certain specialized players to have the special duty of monitoring adherence to certain rules and of punishing deviations. Those specialists are in turn compensated by higher organizational leaders for their efforts. A central problem in any effort at institutional design is to make sure that such enforcers will act to monitor and enforce as the designer intends, but will not misuse their attendant authority to extract benefits for themselves at the expense of intended organizational goals.

5.2. Asymmetries, Information, and Variation

Even if a recurrent policymaking problem of interest did take one of the simple forms examined above, it would be surprising to find such perfect regularity, symmetry, and information. One might suspect that more realistic imperfections would be highly relevant to predictions about behavior and to questions of institutional design. It is possible to examine such imperfections fruitfully in the same theoretical context. First, and most obviously, policymaking situations differ from one occurrence to the next, and so differences between the players' payoffs (even after normalization) are likely to occur and to result in games that are more complicated to analyze than the simple ones above. These complications, however, are readily addressed. The condition for both players using tit-for-tat to be an equilibrium, for example, now becomes two conditions, one for each player; the players in the battle of the sexes may now use different mixed strategies in equilibrium and thus generate two sets of comparative statics predictions, one for each player.[8] Second, for similar reasons we may expect that payoffs may vary over time in ways known only imperfectly to the players in advance. Representing this uncertainty by subjective probabilities, we can construct equilibrium strategies that depend on the particular circumstances of play in a given "iteration" as well as on the players' expectations about future payoff values. Variations in the opportunities (actions or strategy sets) available to the players can be equivalently represented by payoff variations: an action that is impossible for a player to take in a given case has, in effect, an extremely low payoff, so that the player avoids it under all circumstances. Asymmetries and variations such as these are subject to exactly the same sort of game-theoretic analysis, and to the same type of examination of predictive results, as in the simple examples presented above; versions of the same comparative-statics predictions continue to hold true.[9] In addition, interesting new wrinkles may now emerge.

5.3. Example of a Repeated Prisoner's Dilemma Game with Variation Across Iterations

Consider a version of the repeated prisoner's dilemma game in which payoffs are a simple additive function of benefits provided by each act of cooperation or helping (a benefit of 1 to each player if one player cooperates, and 2 if both cooperate), minus a cost of cooperation for a player who cooperates. Suppose, however, that this cost varies from iteration to iteration, taking on values c_1^t and c_2^t in iteration t that are revealed only at the beginning of that iteration. For now, I continue to assume that these values are known to both players. Then one interesting equilibrium is a version of TFT in which each player i is required to cooperate when c_i^t is less than some criterion value, which is a function of d and of the distribution from which the c_i^t are drawn, but not required to cooperate otherwise. Failure to cooperate when expected precipitates retaliation on the next turn in which the wronged player would have otherwise been expected to cooperate. The payoff matrix for the stage game in iteration t is shown in Table 4.3. In keeping with the spirit of this example, I assume that each c_i^t is a realization of a random variable c_i whose cumulative distribution

Table 4.3

	Player 2 helps	Player 2 does not help
Player 1 helps	$(2 - c_1{}^t, 2 - c_2{}^t)$	$(1 - c_1{}^t, 1)$
Player 1 does not help	$(1, 1 - c_2{}^t)$	$(0, 0)$

function is F_i, and which takes on only values greater than 1. Thus for some players in some iterations, the cost of cooperating is so high that the player would prefer mutual defection to mutual cooperation. However, the question is whether that player might still cooperate in order to ensure future mutual cooperation when costs are lower.

This repeated game has a large number of equilibria; in order to display some phenomena of interest, I assume for illutrative purposes that $F_1 = F_2$ and concentrate once again upon symmetric equilibria of the following type: to begin with, each player i cooperates when c_i^t is less than or equal to some threshold value C, and defects otherwise; but if a player ever defects when cooperation was expected, both players defect forever after.

First, an important point for institutional engineering in a situation such as this is that the highest overall payoffs are achieved when C is set equal to 2. To see this, let c' represent the expected value of c_i^t conditional on c_i^t being less than or equal to C.[10] Then the expected payoff to either player from following this strategy, before any cost value is known, is $(2 - c')\,F(C)/(1 - d)$.[11] Setting the derivative of this expression's numerator with respect to C equal to zero (recall that c' is a function of C also) gives $C = 2$, and because the second derivative at $C = 2$ can readily be seen to be negative, 2 is the ex ante expected payoff-maximizing value of C for this kind of equilibrium. In other words, if one is free to determine which equilibrium the players will adopt and wishes to maximize overall payoff to the players, the best symmetrical equilibrium to choose will be either one in which neither player ever cooperates, or one in which each cooperates only if her current cost is less than the "total benefit" (1 to each player) of cooperating.

Second, other equilibria of this type are possible, depending on the extent of discounting and the form of the distribution function for costs. Setting C high requires one to bear the cost of cooperating more often, but also means that the other player will cooperate more often, providing a free benefit. In general it may be possible to set C at many different values consistent with rational ongoing cooperation by the players. Consider as an illustration the case in which F is the uniform distribution on the interval [1, 3], so that $F(C) = (C-1)/2$ and $c' = (C+1)/2$. The binding constraint that any such threshold strategy must satisfy to be an equilibrium is that it must be rational to cooperate when a low enough cost value has been drawn. Suppose, then, that the players have just drawn their cost values in iteration t. Seen from this point, the value of continued cooperation in iterations $t+1$, $t+2$, is

$$V = d(2 - c')F(C)/(1 - d) = d(-C^2 + 4C - 3)/[2(1 - d)], \quad (1)$$

while the short-term gain of not cooperating in iteration t is $c_i^t - 1$, which must be less than V for all $c_i^t \leq C$ for the strategy to be in equilibrium. As this condition is most difficult to satisfy when cooperation cost is at its maximum, C, the general condition for equilibrium is thus, after rearranging terms,

$$dC^2 + 2(1 - 3d)C + 5d - 2 \geq 0. \quad (2)$$

In general this inequality is satisfied on an interval of C-values (not necessarily all feasible because the interval may lie partly outside of [1, 3]), one of whose endpoints is $C = 1$. If d is sufficiently large, $C = 1$ will be the lower bound of the interval, so there will be permissible values of the cost threshold for cooperation; as d grows, the highest allowable C will decrease until the point is reached at which cooperation can be sustained only at $C = 1$ (at which value the individual's own benefit from cooperation outweighs the cost). As long as $d \geq 1/2$, cooperation can be sustained for some values of C greater than 1. If $d \geq 2/3$ then the efficient value $C = 2$ can be sustained as an equilibrium, and as d approaches 1, cooperation can be sustained even for values of C approaching the maximum of 3 (although such a high level of required cooperation would be dysfunctional in that it would yield all players a lower total payoff than when $C = 2$).

The qualitative lessons for the institutional designer is that lighter discounting allows the choice of equilibria sustaining more frequent cooperation. Yet the cost of cooperation may sometimes be so high that the resulting benefits are not worth obtaining, even though they are obtainable by rational agents in equilibrium. In that case, if the designer has the choice of cooperation patterns and wishes to maximize benefits to agents, cooperation must be required only when its costs are not *too* high.

By similar means, more ideas about institutional design can be derived from other embellishments to the simple models presented here, such as improving coordination through communication about intentions (Farrell,

1987); the presence of information known to some players that affects the desired actions for other players (Banks and Calvert, 1992; Calvert, 1993); and interactions among larger groups of players (Milgrom, North, and Weingast, 1990; Crawford and Haller, 1990). Surprising results with important general implications sometimes emerge from such modeling: for instance, the introduction of incomplete information may improve payoffs in a coordination problem (Banks and Calvert, 1992); and the introduction of the slightest doubt about the selfish rationality of a player can enable cooperation in a limited-horizon cooperation problem in which complete information makes strictly rational cooperation impossible (Kreps, Milgrom, Roberts, and Wilson, 1982).

6.0. More Substantial Models: Tailoring the Game to the Real Policy Problem

Of course, designers of policymaking institutions are interested in more than just the cooperation and coordination problems that occur in the process. Specific policy problems involve specific questions of information, planning, incentives, and accommodation to technological, social, and political constraints that determine the success of a policy. Any such problem, however, can be portrayed as a situation in which various agents having different goals choose actions that jointly determine the policy outcome by some given (perhaps probabilistic) set of rules. Thus a game-theoretic analysis of the policymaking institution can still provide insights about how its members and their clientele will behave, and how rules and expectations might be designed to provide the best possible outcomes, either from the point of view of some or all of the participants, or by some external standard. Even though the assignment of specific payoff values and discount factors is unlikely to be feasible in building such models, one can always interrogate the models to learn how changes in preferences, expectations, frequencies of interaction, and the other conditions of the situation will affect the actions of participants and thus the quality of outcomes.

The literatures on the theory of organization and on the theory of regulation hold numerous examples of the kind of approach I am describing. The textbook by Milgrom and Roberts (1992) presents examples of organization-theory modeling in which aspects of the relations between different organizational units and levels are analyzed from the standpoint of noncooperative game theory. Versions of the problems of cooperation, coordination, and strategic use of information play the leading roles in these models. The same theoretical tools that I suggest applying to those general problems also serve to investigate problems specific to a given institutional setting. The literature on principal-agent relations, for example, uses these tools to examine incentives in and optimality of specific contract types such as "tournament" competiton among subordinates for incentive rewards; and standard employment agreements in which, based on performance, a worker is either retained at a given salary or fired.

A survey article by Baron (1992) recounts several lines of work that apply methods of noncooperative game theory to regulatory policymaking situations, revealing how the strategic behavior of firms and regulators, and ultimately the welfare properties of production in regulated industries, depend on the preferences and information of regulators and the regulated. Often in the existing literature, the regulator and the firm are portrayed as unitary actors. Banks (1989), Banks and Weingast (1992), Laffont and Tirole (1988), and Salant and Woroch (1992) examine various aspects of the dynamic relationship between the regulator and the firm, or equivalently between a bureaucratic superior and subordinate, analyzing problems of proposal and response, information revelation, commitment to a regulatory policy, and efficiency among multiple equilibria. Other recent work directly examines the complications of having many participants in the regulatory process. Baron (1985a, 1985b) constructs models in which the firm is regulated by multiple agencies, each having different jurisdictions and interest (for example, a public utility whose price is regulated by a utility regulator and whose production processes are regulated by an environmental agency). Conversely, Baron and Besanko (1992, 1993) investigate the regulatory problem of an agency whose regulated "firm" consists of several units, each of which contributes to the overall regulated service (such as a local telephone company and a long-distance service provider), that set their policies partly indepently of one another.

The recent literature on the noncooperative game theory of organizations and regulation mostly addresses the nature of equilibria that can arise in those processes, the strategies that are available to the players in various equilibria, and the welfare (efficiency) properties of those equilibria. These results carry direct lessons for the institutional designer: most obviously, if various equilibria are possible in a given regulatory problem, then presumably the designer would want to lead participants to focus on one that has good welfare properties for consumers. Indirectly, the same models carry predictions concerning how strategies and the availability of various equilibria may change with changes in the political, economic, and technological parameters of the games. This same modeling approach could, in principle, be applied to any problem of institutional design: the basic policy problem faced by an organization is characterizable by certain patterns of opportunities, outcomes, and payoffs, and these determine a game among the participants. The designer, again, has some capacity to influence these basic parameters, as well as to influence the choice among available equilibria in the resulting game. Specific problems of cooperation or coordination, or specialized political, economic, or informational problems, can all be examined in the context of game theory models prior to the design of institutions.

7.0. Conclusion

This analysis has proposed several principles about the role of game-theoretic models in institutional design. The primary one is simply that the game-theory modeling of institutions is a potentially important tool of analysis for design. The designer needs to understand interacting incentives of policymakers and other participants in the process, and the structure and rules of any policymaking institution are, in part, internally enforced. Such an institution will deal repeatedly with similar decisionmaking situations. The theory of repeated games, in an appropriately modified form, is the key to applying game theory to these problems.

One immediate result of this approach is that an institution may be seen, not simply as a set of rules of the game assumed by the analyst, but as a set of behavioral regularities emerging in equilibrium that, in combination, force rational participants to continue to conform. Using the tools described here, the institutional designer can understand the problems of establishing and maintaining a given structure of rules. More pertinently, the designer can use the controllable features of the institution, such as what kinds of people will be employed in a policymaking organization, how easy it will be for them to interact, and how they will be hired, fired, and compensated, to affect their private interests in the process and thus to affect the parameters of the game. These parameters, in turn, determine what patterns of behavior can persist in equilibrium.

The analysis of general forms of cooperation and coordination problems, as undertaken in Sections 3, 4, and 5, yields general advice about institutional design. Game-theoretic modeling produces "comparative statics" statements about the predominance of cooperation and coordination in equilibrium, and these statements can guide the institutional designer by connecting controllable parameter values with future behavior. In particular, discounting discourages cooperation, as does a high payoff to noncooperative behavior relative to the gains from cooperation. Communication and frequent repetition of similar situations aid in the establishment of coordination, whereas ambiguity about the comparability of different coordination problems will make coordination difficult. Also, the sharper the disagreement about the relative merits of different "coordinated" outcomes, the more difficult it will be to establish coordination in the absence of some previously existing focus or precedent.

An understanding about how the parameters of a game determine the set of feasible equilibria, however, is not sufficient for institutional design. In general, game-theoretic models of policymaking institutions have multiple equilibria. One means by which the institutional designer can influence the future course of policy outcomes is to help create a "focus" on some particular equilibrium or class of equilibria, by initial instructions, basic structure, statement of intent, initial standard operating procedures, and other such means. In any event, the designer must generally worry about which of the many equilibrium patterns of behavior possible within a given organizational structure will emerge among the participants.

The cooperation and coordination problems attempt to address only simple versions of very general problems faced by institutional designers. Even though more "realistic" models can rapidly become intractable if the analyst is not careful, the game-theory approach to institutions can accommodate many of the complexities likely to arise in specific institutional design problems. These include more complicated features in cooperation and coordination games, such as asymmetry, information, multiple players, and variation across iterations; the same lessons continue to apply, but new prescriptions emerge when we interrogate such complexities. Likewise, institutional designers can use the same methods to examine the special political, economic, technical, or informational features of a given policymaking problem, as demonstrated by the game-theory literatures on organizations and regulation.

Appendix: Formal Model of Repeated Games with Variation

A.1. The Setting for Repeated Games with Variation

Let Γ represent a set of possible "stage games" G, and N an overall set of participants. Let P be a probability measure over the games in Γ; at each iteration t, nature chooses the game $G = G^t$ to be played next, according to the probability distribution given by P. P is common knowledge among the players in N. Payoffs (as specified below) accrue to the players with the completion of each stage game; possible payoffs in future iterations are discounted by some factor d. A repeated game, then, is completely described by the triple $<\Gamma, P, d>$.

A.2. Stage Games with Incomplete Information

Each $G \in \Gamma$ is a game in normal form[12] (in general, a game of incomplete information), described by a set of players $N^G \subseteq N$, a set of actions $A_n{}^G$ available to each player n, and a payoff function for each player. In general the players may have different information about the payoffs of other players in the game; this uncertainty is represented by assigning to each player n a set of possible *types* $I(n)$; each type i in $I(n)$ represents a particular state or value of the information actually known to player n. For example, if the payoff function of a player is private information, then $I(n)$ indexes the set of possible true payoff functions for player n.[13] Let $i(n)$ represent n's true type. Each player n knowns $i(n)$, but players other than n know only some probability distribution over $I(n)$. I summarize this incomplete information as follows: Abusing notation slightly for convenience, let $I(N^G)$ be the Cartesian product of all the $I(n)$ for N in N^G; then let Q^G be a probability measure on $I(N^G)$ that represents the knowledge of players about each others' types when G is played. Thus in general the payoff to player n takes the form of a function $u_n^G\ (a;\ i)$ describing the utility value to each player n when the players in N^G take actions

$$a = (a_m)_{m \in N^G}$$

and the true type of player n is i. We can also think of a, the profile of actions taken in G, as an *outcome* of G. Let A^G denote the set of all possible outcomes of game G, the Cartesian product of the action sets $A_n{}^G$ over all n in N^G.

A.3. Strategy in the Repeated Game

Suppose that $t-1$ iterations of the repeated game $<\Gamma, P, d>$ have been completed, and that each stage game G^s had outcome a^s. The *history* of play as of iteration t is then $H^t = (a^1, a^2, \ldots, a^{t-1})$; H^1 is defined as an arbitrary constant. If game G^t is to be played next, a player might wish to make her actions in that stage game depend on the outcomes of previous games, for example in order to take some sort of learning into account or to exercise a possibility of retaliating against some previous action of another player. I designate by $s_n\ (a_n;\ i,\ G^t,\ H^t)$ the probability of choosing pure strategy a^n in player n's (mixed-strategy) plan for playing G^t given all previous outcomes H^t, if player n is of type i. Although player n knows her type and thus will not have to use a strategy for any type other than $i(n)$, as we will see, other players must maintain expectations about what player n may do in order to compute their own optimal strategies; however, only $s_n\ (\cdot;\ i(n),\ G^t,\ H^t)$ is actually implemented by a player, and the outcome of G^t depends on the realizations of these mixed strategies only. Then let σ_n be the entire collection of plans by player n for all types, all stage games, and all histories; this is player n's *strategy* for the repeated game. Finally, let $\sigma = (\sigma_n)_{n \in N}$ be the *strategy profile* describing a strategy for each type of each player in every possible stage game with every possible history.

A.4. Equilibrium in the Repeated Game

In order to define equilibrium, I need to define a player's payoff function for the repeated game, and in order to do that I need some notation for the probability of a given history of play. This definition will be easiest to construct recursively. For $t = 2, 3 \ldots,$ the probability that at iteration t the sequence of outcomes thus far will have been H^t given that the history at time $t-1$ was H^{t-1} is

$$R^t(H^t \mid H^{t-1}) = \int_\Gamma \int_{I(N^G)} \sum_{a \in A^G} \prod_{n \in N_G} s_n(a_n; i(n), G, H^{t-1}) \, dQ^G(i(N^G)) dP(G).$$

The overall probability, as seen from the beginning of the game, that H^t will be the history at time t can then be given recursively as

$$R^t(H^t) = \sum_{H^{t-1}} R^t(H^t \mid H^{t-1}) R^{t-1}(H^{t-1}),$$

where the sum is taken over all possible histories H^{t-1}; and of course $R^1(H^1) = 1$ by definition.

Player n's payoff function in the repeated game $<\Gamma, P, d>$ is then given by

$$u_n(\sigma) = \sum_{t=1}^{\infty} d^{t-1} \sum_{H^t} R^t(H^t) \int_\Gamma \int_{I(N^G)} \sum_{a \in A^G} s(a; i(N^G), G, H^t) u_n^G(a, i(n)) \, dQ^G(i(N^G)) dP(G).$$

A strategy profile σ is an *equilibrium* in the repeated game $<\Gamma, P, d>$ if and only if, for each player n,

$$u_n(\sigma) \geq u_n(\sigma_{-n}, \sigma'_n),$$

where (σ_{-n}, σ'_n) represents the strategy profile in which all players besides n use strategy σ but player n uses the alternative strategy σ'_n. This definition represents the standard Bayesian Nash equilibrium; similar definitions can be given as needed for refinements such as perfect equilibrium.

A.5. The Folk Theorem

Ignoring the incomplete information case for the moment, the extension of the folk theorem to the present setting is fairly straightforward. Suppose $I^G(n)$ is a singleton for each G and n, and let $v_n{}^G$ represent the minimax payoff for player n in game $G \in \Gamma$; that is,

$$v_n^G = \min_{a_{-n}} \max_{a_n} u_n^G(a,i).$$

Then define the minimax value across Γ for player n as

$$v_n^* = E_\Gamma\, v_n^G = \int_\Gamma v_n^G\, dP(G).$$

As usual I define the expected per-period average payoff from a repeated-game strategy σ to be $(1 - d)\ u_n(\sigma)$; notice that this payoff represents an expectation taken over possible realizations of sequences of stage games G. Let V' be the set of all such payoff values: $V' \equiv \{ \mathbf{v} \in \mathbb{R}^{|N|} |$ for some σ that is a strategy for $<\Gamma, P, d>$, $v_n = (1 - d)u_n(\sigma)$ for all $n \in N\}$. Let V be the convexification of V'. Then (still for the case of complete information) the folk theorem can be stated as follows:

> Let $\mathbf{v}$ be a vector of payoffs in V, such that for each $n \in N$, $v_n > v^*{}_n$. If the discount parameter d is sufficiently large, then there exists a subgame perfect equilibrium strategy profile σ for $<\Gamma, P, d$ such that $(1 - du_n\ (\sigma) = v_n$ for each $n \in N$.

To prove this, one need simply restate the model in the fashion used in Section 2 of the chapter and apply any conventional proof of the folk theorem, such as that in Fudenberg and Maskin (1986).

Proving a general folk theorem of this sort under incomplete information seems to be infeasible. $I^G(n)$ could include types for whom any designed "punishment" turns out to be a reward, and if opponents do not know a deviant's type they will be unable to ensure the right punishment. Nevertheless, it is only reasonable to expect that, in general, repeated games with incomplete information will have a great variety of equilibria. This is the only feature of the result on which the remarks in the text, concerning influence opportunities for the institutional designer, depend.

Notes

1. That is, an equilibrium in which no player's strategy would ever require her, should another player deviate from the equilibrium, to carry out any punishment or other reaction that would not be a best response under the circumstances (see Selten, 1978).

2. Begin by helping in the first iteration; in each subsequent iteration, do exactly what the other player did on the previous iteration. Thus every defection is punished with a defection, until the opponent returns to cooperation. A slight modification of this strategy renders it "subgame perfect" – that is, rational to carry out the threat of punishment: if a player does depart from the required pattern of cooperation, that player "apologizes" by unilaterally helping on the subsequent turm (see Sugden, 1986).

3. For the subgame-perfect version of tit-for-tat, the additional criterion $d \geq b/(1+b)$ must also hold so that off-the-equilibrium-path "apologies" are rational. Notice, however, that this condition is redundant when $a - b > 1$.

4. Obviously if the players had some beliefs as to what was causing d to be reduced, and therefore could make predictions about what value d were likely to take on in the future, these thresholds would be altered. Given any specific set of beliefs about d, however, some similar sort of prediction of how d affects behavior would still follow.

5. In units defined by the simple value of coordinating – that is, the utility difference between coordinating on one's less favored equilibrium and failing entirely to coordinate. Thus in the formalization given, the relative value of the preferred equilibrium, x, can in effect be decreased by increasing the simple value of coordinating.

6. In either case I refer strictly to games in which, at least within some relevant range of size of contribution to a public good, not contributing (contributing less) is a dominant strategy. Other forms of public goods games common to the literature involve so-called threshold provision problems, in which a certain level of contribution is required to realize the production of a unit of the public good – that is, the public good is "lumpy". Games of the latter type are really problems of coordination, not cooperation. Sea van de Kragt, Orbell, and Dawes (1983) for a presentation of the latter type of game as a "public good" problem and Calvert and Wilson (1984) for a commentary on the difference.

7. Actually the Milgrom et al. and Greif et al. models employ an uninterested outside actor as the clearinghouse, and the former portrays retaliation as a separate process of "fines" outside the prisoner's dilemma interaction itself. Calvert (1995), however, demonstrates how to construct similar equilibria by compensating a player to act as the clearinghouse, including the provision of incentives to keep that player honest and how to make retaliation work through the cooperation decision itself rather than through outside fines.

8. There is still a strong argument in the asymmetric battle-of-the-sexes for concentrating on the mixed-strategy, rather than one of the two pure-strategy, equilibria: predicting a pure-strategy equilibrium begs the central question of how coordination is to be achieved, while the mixed-strategy representation as least embodies the central problem in the coordination game, which is that uncertainty about the other actor's intention may lead to a coordination failure.

9. For example, if one player's discount factor drops below the threshold for cooperation by that player to by possible in equilibrium, cooperative behavior by both players ceases; when payoffs vary probabilistically, such threshold conditions can be restated in terms of expected payoffs, and cooperative behavior made always contingent on the current payoff values.

10. That is, $c' \equiv \int_1^C x \, dF(x)/F(C)$.

11. This is calculated as follows: in any iteration, both players will cooperate with probability $F(C)^2$, receiving payoffs of $2 - c_i'$ each; a player will cooperate unilaterally with probability $F(C)[1 - F(C)]$, receiving payoff $1 - c_i'$; the second player will cooperate unilaterally with the same probability, and in that case the first player will receive a payoff of 1; and finally with probability $[1 - F(C)]^2$ neither player will cooperate and each will receive zero. Adding up these probability-weighted payoffs and using the conditional expected cost of cooperating, then discounting over all future repetitions, gives the desired result.

12. More generally, one might want to portray each stage game in extensive form and take advantage of the more detailed techniques for analyzing such games. This would add considerable complication and little explication for current purposes, however, so I stick to the more conventional repeated normal-form game model.

13. For convenience I just let $I(n)$ include indexes for all the types that player n could take on in *any* of the games G in Γ. Some of the types may of course be irrelevant to any particular game G, and these will receive probability weights of zero when G is played.

References

Axelrod, Robert. (1984). *The Evolution of Cooperation*. New York: Basic Books.

Banks, Jeffrey S. (1989). "Agency Budgets, Cost Information, and Auditing." *American Journal of Political Science* 33(3): 670–699.

Banks, Jeffrey S. and Randall L. Calvert, (1992). "A Battle-of-the-Sexes Game with Incomplete Information." *Games and Economic Behavior* 4(3): 347–372.

Banks, Jeffrey S. and Barry R. Weingast. (1992). "The Political Control of Bureaucracies under Asymmetric Information." *American Journal of Political Science* 36(2): 509–524.

Bardach, Eugene and Robert A. Kagan. (1982). *Going by the Book: The Problem of Regulatory Unreasonableness*. Philadelphia: Temple University Press.

Baron, David P. (1985a). "Noncooperative Regulation of a Nonlocalized Externality." *Rand Journal of Economics* 19(3): 553–568.

———. (1985b). "Regulation of Prices and Pollution under Incomplete Information." *Journal of Public Economics* 28(2): 211–231.

———. (1995). "The Economics and Politics of Regulation." In Jeffrey S. Banks and Eric A. Hanushek (eds.), *Modern Political Economy: Old Topics, New Directions*. New York: Cambridge University Press.

Baron, David P. and David Besanko. (1992). "Regulation, Information, and Organizational Structure." *Journal of Economics and Regulatory Strategy* 1(2): 237–275.

———. (1993). "Hidden Gaming in an Information Hierarchy." Photocopy, Stanford University.

Calvert, Randall L. (1991). "Elements of a Theory of Society Among Rational Actors." Photocopy, University of Rochester.

———. (1992). "Leadership and Its Basis in Problems of Social Coordination." *International Political Science Review* 13(1): 7–24.

———. (1993). "Communication in Institutions: Efficiency in a Repeated Prisoner's Dilemma with Hidden Information." In W. Barnett, M. Hinich, and N. Schofield (eds.), *Political Economy: Institutions, competition, and Representation* New York: Cambridge University Press.

———. (1995). "Rational Actors, Equilibrium, and Social Institutions." In Jack Knight and Itai Sened (eds.), *Explaining Social Institutions*. Ann Arbor: University of Michigan Press.

Calvert, Randall L. and Rick K. Wilson. (1984). "Comment" (on A. van de Kragt, J. Orbell, and R. Dawes, "The Minimal Contributing Set as a Solution to the Public Goods Problem"). *American Political Science Review* 78(1): 496–497.

Crawford, Vincent P. and Hans Haller. (1990). "Learning How to Cooperate: Optimal Play in Repeated Coordination Games." *Econometrica* 58(3): 571–595.

Farrell, Joseph. (1987). "Cheap Talk, Coordination, and Entry." *RAND Journal of Economics* 18(1): 34–39.

Fudenberg, Drew and Eric Maskin. (1986). "The Folk Theorem in Repeated Games with Discounting or with Incomplete Information." *Econometrica* 54(3): 533–554.

Greif, Avner, Paul Milgrom, and Barry Weingast. (1994). "Coordination, Commitment, and Enforcement: The Case of the Merchant Guild." *Journal of Political Economy* 102(4): 745–776.

Harsanyi, John C. (1967–68). "Games with Incomplete Information Played by Bayesian Players." *Management Science* 14(3,5,7): 159–182, 320–334, 486–502.

Harsanyi, John C. and Reinhard Selten. (1988). *A General Theory of Equilibrium Selection in Games*. Cambridge, MA: MIT Press.

Katzmann, Robert A. (1980). *Regulatory Bureaucracy: The Federal Trade Commission and Antitrust Policy*. Cambridge, MA: MIT Press.

Kreps, David M. (1990). "Corporate Culture and Economic Theory." In James E. Alt and Kenneth A. Shepsle, (eds.), *Perspectives on Political Economy* (pp. 90–143). New York: Cambridge University Press.

———, Paul Milgrom, John Roberts, and Robert Wilson. (1982). "Rational Cooperation in the Finitely Repeated Prisoners' Dilemma." *Journal of Economic Theory* 27(2): 245–252.

Laffont, Jean-Jacques and Jean Tirole. (1988). "The Dynamics of Incentive

Contracts." *Econometrica* 56(5): 1153–1175.
Laver, Michael E. (1983). *Invitation to Politics*. Oxford: Robertson.
Luce, R. Duncan and Howard Raiffa. (1957). *Games and Decisions: Introduction and Critical Survey*. New York: Wiley.
Milgrom, Paul R., Douglass C. North, and Barry R. Weingast. (1990). "The Role of Institutions in the Revival of Trade: The Law Merchant, Private Directors, and the Champagne Fairs." *Economics and Politics* 2(1): 1–23.
Milgrom, Paul and John Roberts. (1992). *Economics, Organization, and Management*. Englewood Cliffs, NJ: Prentice-Hall.
Miller, Gary J. (1992). *Managerial Dilemmas: The Political Economy of Hierarchy*. New York: Cambridge University Press.
Salant, David J. and Glenn A. Woroch. (1992). "Trigger Price Regulation." *RAND Journal of Economics* 23(1): 29–51.
Schelling, Thomas C. (1960). *The Strategy of Conflict*. Cambridge, MA: Harvard University Press.
Selten, Reinhard. (1978). "The Chain Store Paradox." *Theory and Decision* 9(2): 127–159.
Sugden, Robert. (1986). *The Economics of Rights, Co-operation, and Welfare*. Oxford: Basil Blackwell.
Taylor, Michael. (1976). *Anarchy and Cooperation*. London: Wiley.
van de Kragt, Alphons J.C., John M. Orbell, and Robyn M. Dawes. (1983). "The Minimal Contributing Set as a Solution to Public Goods Problems." *American Political Science Review* 77(1): 112–122.

5 CONVENTIONS AND NORMS IN INSTITUTIONAL DESIGN

Patrick Croskery

1.0. Introduction

A world without conventions and norms is almost unimaginable. We use conventions and norms to make countless predictions (generally confirmed) about the future behavior of others: our co-workers will appear at work each day, other drivers will remain on the right side of the road, the restaurant will accept payment in dollars, people giving us directions will do so honestly, long-term friends will help us with minor needs, and so on. Without this ability to predict the behavior of others, we would be unable to fulfill almost all of our plans: saving money for the future, making improvements to our homes, getting an education to qualify for a job, and so on.

Recognizing the importance of conventions and norms, rational choice theorists have developed basic accounts of these social structures. To work effectively with conventions and norms, however, the institutional designer must go beyond the basic accounts provided in the rational choice literature. Standard rational choice theory assumes that individual actors have unlimited cognitive resources, but real-world institutions must reflect the fact that these resources are scarce. For the purposes of institutional design, then, some account must be given of how conventions and norms are instantiated in individual actors. In addition, standard rational choice approaches ignore the influence of culture and community on the choices people make, but these appear to play a significant role in actual decision making.

In this chapter I sketch a framework for a more comprehensive understanding of conventions and norms and discuss the implications of this framework for the purposes of institutional design. The framework is illustrated in Table 5.1.

Conventions, which have been analyzed in the rational choice literature as the outcome of iterated coordination games, are instantiated in individuals in the form of *habits* and grouped together into larger structures I call *cultures*. In a parallel fashion, norms, which are generally viewed as resulting from games with a Nash equilibrium that is inefficient (the most famous example being the prisoner's dilemma), are instantiated in the form of *virtues* and grouped together into larger structures I call *communities*. While my use of these terms does not precisely correspond to their standard usage in English, the connotations of these terms is appropriate: the first set of concepts is understood in nonmoral terms, while the second set involves moral considerations.

My discussion is presented in two stages; I provide the entire account of conventions before turning to the account of norms. This approach has several advantages. First, the account of norms makes use of the account of conventions because the selection of norms poses a second-order coordination problem. Any difficulties and opportunities that arise in considering conventions will therefore have equivalents when we consider norms. Second, the account of norms, virtues, and community roughly parallels the account of conventions, habits, and culture; having the basic structure of the account of conventions in hand will make the account of norms easier to understand.

Table 5.1. Comparison of Conventions and Norms

	Convention	*Norm*
Iterated strategic structure	Coordination	Prisoner's dilemma
Form in individual	Habit	Virtue
Social structure	Culture	Community

2.0. Conventions, Habits, and Culture

2.1. Conventions

The analysis of conventions in terms of iterated coordination games is a familiar one (Lewis, 1969; Ullmann-Margalit, 1977; Sugden, 1986). A brief sketch of this way of understanding conventions, along with some of its implications, provides a useful starting point for understanding the relationship between conventions, culture, and habits.

While traveling in Paris, a husband and wife accidently become separated. They do not have a hotel room (they were visiting for the day) and did not discuss in advance where to meet under these conditions. Where should they go? The two are facing a one-play coordination game without communication. Each wants to end up where the other is: there is no conflict of interest. But there is more than one location from which they must choose. Under these conditions, one location may be especially salient or prominent (Schelling, 1960) for psychological reasons. Perhaps they both know they must leave Paris by train, so they meet at the train station. Or perhaps they try to think of a prominent landmark, such as the Eiffel Tower, and meet there. Or perhaps one goes to the train station and the other to the Eiffel Tower, and they fail to meet.

Were they able to communicate (say by each calling their hotel back in London and leaving or receiving a message), coordinating would be simple. Alternatively, if this had happened to them before, and they had happened to meet at the Eiffel Tower, the Eiffel Tower would have a significant salience this time, and coordinating would again be simple.

While the one-play cases are intriguing, iterated coordination situations are a much greater part of our lives. Conventions can be understood by looking at contexts in which the coordination circumstances arise repeatedly. A convention is a rule that makes one solution the default. The usefulness of convention is twofold. First, where communication is possible but has some cost associated with it, the convention eliminates or reduces that cost. Second, where communication is not possible, the convention provides a salient solution. Thus, if you find a lost mitten in a department store, you cannot contact the owner, but both you and the owner know that the department store's lost and found (or customer service) is the appropriate place to turn in and pick up the mitten.

How do conventions emerge? They can result from explicit planning and communication. A company may lay out a set of policies; a goverment can announce a set of standards. In addition, they may spontaneously emerge. Salience is a self-feeding process; as a particular solution is used, it becomes more salient, which makes it more likely to be used, and so on. A solution that is salient for a large number of people is a convention.

2.2. Habit

Our understanding of conventions and culture must reflect the fact that people do not have unlimited cognitive resources to devote to learning and using conventions (Simon, 1992). Reflecting the limits of cognitive resources in decision making generally is currently an active if unsettled topic in economics and cognitive science. A wide range of approaches are being developed (McCain, 1992; Thaler, 1991, Simon, 1992). For the particular case of conventions, the most important approaches are those that explore the way that individuals store their knowledge of the world (including expectations about the behavior of others) in the form of standardized and simplified *scripts* (Schank and Abelson, 1977) or *frames* (Minsky, 1975) or *schemas* (Mandler, 1984). By storing expectations in frames, individuals reduce the storage space required, as well as the processing time required to make an appropriate decision.

Thus, when an individual goes out to a restaurant, he makes use of the frame for "eating at a restaurant," which includes the behavior he can expect from the waiter at various stages of the meal and also informs him of the behavior the waiter will be expecting in return. Both participants can perform their roles habitually—that is, with minimal conscious processing.

2.3. Culture

Frames, to reduce cognitive costs, must be simple, apply to a significant range of interactions, and be shared by those who are interacting. Cognitive costs are further reduced if the frames themselves are arranged hierarchically, with lower–level frames being subsumed under higher-level frames (Madler, 1985). Thus, the frame for shopping in a grocery store and the frame for shopping in a department store are subsumed under a frame for shopping.

I use the term *culture* to refer to a widely shared complex structure of interdependent frames (that is, combinations of conventions). It is worth noting that this does not exactly match the standard use of the term *culture*, which often implicitly includes norms. Later in this chapter I use the term *community* to refer to structures that include norms as well.

Under this definition, then, cultures can be found of greatly varying complexities. A particular corporation may have a set of distinctive conventions, which then forms its culture. An entire society may have a range of conventions that form its culture. To understand the corporation in the context of that society, it may be necessary to know both sets: the corporation's conventions will have developed in the context of the conventions shared in the society. In this sense, then, any institution has a culture, which is related in more or less complex ways to the surrounding society and other institutions.

2.4. Implications of the Account of Conventions for Institutional Design

An institution has as part of its structure a particular constellation of conventions. On the rational choice account of conventions, the institutional designer can expect a set of conventions to be self-maintaining once in place, assuming that the strategic conditions do not change. In addition, even in the absence of central planning she can expect conventions to spontaneously emerge under appropriate conditions.

Where then is the work of the institutional designer? The task of the institutional designer is to guide the process of emergence to generate an efficient set of conventions. She needs, then, to pay attention to sources of inefficiency in the process of convention formation. Four sources stand out. First, conventions may be slow to establish thenselves. Second, a nonoptimal convention may establish itself. Third, a convention may not respond to change as effectively as some alternative. Fourth, where conventions develop in two separated groups two different conventions may be established, hindering coordination when those groups are no longer separated. I briefly illustrate these four sources of inefficiency along with an appropriate response by the institutional designer.

If a situation is sufficiently complex, or communication is difficult, or if the participants involved frequently change, a convention can be very slow to emerge. Thus, engineers have a need for a wide range of technically sophisticated standards. While such standards might be expected to emerge spontaneously over time, this process can be greatly facilitated by the work of standards groups, whether private or governmental. The standards group can provide a given standard with salience, accelerating its acceptance. In general, the task of the institutional designer is to generate salience for the conventions her institution requires. Industry groups, laws, policies laid down by firms or agencies, and public debate can all serve this purpose.

Spontaneously emerging standards are extremely responsive to salience in the initial conditions. A partucular rule might be salient for reasons that are completely independent of efficiency. The QWERTY typewriter system is a familiar example. If she has input at the beginning of the process, the institutional designer can select among the possible rules on the basis of efficiency considerations, and provide the favored rule with the salience necessary to make it a convention (perhaps the Dvorak keyboard).

What the cognitive perspective brings out is that the costs of remembering and acting on the convention also need to be taken into account in a complete consideration of efficiency. All things considered, a simple convention might be preferable to a highly complex convention with higher potential payoffs. If cognitive resources were unlimited, then there would be no reason not to include a special clause for all possible exceptional cases, but in this world the exceptions that can be included are strictly limited. How complex a convention ought to be depends on the circumstances for its use. For example, the more important an issue, the more cognitive resources may be devoted to it.

The efficiency of a convention is not restricted to the complexity of the convention itself, however. Because conventions are joined together into larger frames and even larger cultures, the possibility arises of economizing on costs by making use of existing frames when developing new conventions. Thus, when a new store opens up, it will make use of price tags, payment lines, sales, advertisements in the local paper, and so on. This reduces the cost to the customers of understanding the workings of the store. Likewise, state tax forms closely resemble federal tax forms, making the process of filing out the forms somewhat less burdensome.

Where conventions can be expected to change steadily in response to a changing environment, the surrounding frames are particularly important. Preexisting frames will give the participants expectations about the direction and range of changes. Thus, a firm hiring someone could look for the highly specific set of skills it currently needs. Or it could anticipate growth and change and hire someone with a standard collection of skills, such as an accountant, anticipating that the skills the accountant learned in school that are not currently needed are likely to be the ones that will be required later on.

Because conventions develop somewhat arbitrarily based on initially salient factors, there can be wide variation where conventions have developed in isolation from one another. This variation is found between nations but also between corporations, governmental agencies, clubs, and neighborhoods. When groups that have different conventions need to interact with one another, this variation poses a problem. Were there no preexisting conventions, we would expect a set to emerge. However, each group has a stable, self-maintaining set of conventions, as well as a substantial investment in their habitual knowledge of those conventions.

The solution the institutional designer should pursue under these conditions depends on the nature of the interaction. If the two cultures are going to need to blend (as in a corporate takeover), there is no choice but to force either one or both groups to incur some changeover costs. On the other hand, if the cultures are going to be interacting for some restricted set of purposes, it is possible to develop a limited set of conventions instead: conventions that have a reasonable fit with both cultures, at least for some restricted purposes. Pidgin languages are instances of conventions that permit groups to communicate without either giving up their significant investment in their own languages or incurring the cost of learning an entirely new language. More modest pidgin conventions might be helpful if, say, two divisions of a company use different conventions for the reporting of sales figures. Reports to central headquarters might use a set of conventions that combined elements of the two divisions' reporting schemes.

3.0. Norms, Virtues, and Community

3.1. Norms

The rational choice account of norms begins with a game that has an inefficient Nash equilibrium. The example most commonly used is the prisoner's dilemma (PD). Robert Sugden (1986: 106) provides a particularly clear illustration of this strategic structure. You inherit a postage stamp and decide to sell it. You place an ad, and someone calls and agrees to your price. You suggest that he send you the money at which point you will send the stamp, while he suggests that you send the stamp at which point he will send the money. Ultimately you each agree to send your part of trade right away. However, as you are putting the stamp into the mail, you realize that if you do not put it in the mail, it will not affect whether or not he sends you the money, so you might as well not send him the stamp. He realizes that whether or not he sends the money will not affect whether or not you send the stamp, so he might as well not send the money. Even though each of you prefers the outcome where the trade is successfully made, if you both act rationally the trade does not go through.

Mutual defection is the uniquely dominant strategy in one-play PDs. In fact, mutual defection is the dominant strategy for any finite series of PDs, due to the chain-store paradox (Selton, 1978). As both players will defect in the last round, neither can use the threat of defecting in that round to force cooperation in the second to last round. But this means that neither can use the threat of defecting in the second to last round to force cooperation in the third to last round, and so on.

If two players are involved in an infinite series of PDs, however, then while defection remains a perfect equilibrium outcome, a number of cooperative strategies are equilibrium outcomes as well. Thus, for example, the strategy of tit-for-tat (cooperate, and then do what your opponent did the last round) is an equilibrium strategy (Axelrod, 1984). According to the folk theorem, in fact, there are a large (potentially infinite) number of such cooperative strategies that are equilibria of this game.

The existence of many equilibria poses a second-order coordination problem, in which one strategy (preferably not mutual defection) gets selected. A norm, on this account, is the outcome of this second-order coordination problem—a set of self-sustaining mutual expectations. As a result, norms can vary substantially in their efficiency, a fact that has significant implications for institutional design.

The requirement that the interaction be infinite can be weakened in two ways. First, all that is required is that the probability that the interaction ends at any given round is sufficiently small. Second, if there is an effective reputation system, the interations need not be between the same two players (Milgrom, North, and Weingast, 1990).

Up to this point there is general agreement on the workings of cooperation. One quite unsettled issue remains: the role of moral motivations. If people follow and police norms at least in part for moral motives, then a different range of norms is possible and different instituional designs are appropriate than if they do not. In addition, different norms and institutions are possible depending on what sort of moral motivation they possess.

The possibilities that have been raised include policing done for entirely self-interested reasons (Calvert, 1992; Milgrom, North, and Weingast, 1990), nonconsequentialist, nonmoral motives (Elster, 1989), nonconsequentialist, moral mitives (Etzioni, 1988), and consequentialist, moral motives (Hardin, 1988). Thus, for example, if policing is done for consequentialist, moral motives, the institutional designer will need to persuade the participants of the consequentialist merits of his institution (or his proposed modification to an existing institution).

3.2. *Virtues*

To properly understand the range of conventions one finds in the world, we had to recognize the significance of the limits of cognitive resources. Given that norms represent the solution to a second-order coordination problem, we must consider the same constraints when looking at the instantiation of norms in individuals.

The frames in which we store our knowledge of the world must include not only expectations based on pure coordination considerations but also those based on norms. For a norm to exist, it must be the case that there be a set of self-sustaining mutual expectations, and these expectations will be stored in our network of frames.

Conventions, however, can become completely habitual (that is, acted on without much conscious processing) without much risk, other than the occasional framing error. We do not need to worry about looking for defections by others, nor do we have anything to gain by defecting ourselves. We also do not face the costs of keeping track of the history of any individual's interactions, nor the costs of communicating the results of our interactions with her to others. All of these are important considerations in the case of norms. However, the typical norm, like the typical convention, is habitual in the sense that people do not explicitly choose to follow it or not in each particular circumstance.

Another important fact about norms is that they can be internalized. Although the process of internalization is not well understood, it at least involves some sanctions that we impose on ourselves when we violate a norm. There are a number of theories of the nature of these sanctions, including the view that they are emotional constructs (Frank, 1988) or more general motivational constructs (Gibbard, 1990) or the result of a basic "desire to keep the good will of others" (Sugden, 1986: 152) or the outcome of "a process of preference formation" (Manion, 1993: 39).

An account of the process of internalization must be combined with an account of the role of moral motivations in the policing of norms. One might, therefore, have an account of norms that holds that they are emotional constructs reflecting consequentialist moral considerations. Alternatively, one might hold that norms are a result of a desire to keep the good will of others and reflect nonconsequentialist, nonmoral considerations.

A norm, then, is instantiated in individuals in the form of a virtue: an habitual expectation about ourselves and others that includes sanctions we impose on ourselves or others for violation. Which virtues people actually adopt will vary depending on which account of internalization is correct.

3.3. Community

Just as our understanding of virtues built on our understanding of habits, so too community is best understood in the light of the account of culture. The frames in which we store conventions combine into larger, shared networks of conventions, or cultures. Likewise, the frames in which we store norms combine into larger, shared networks of norms, or communities. On this account, the term *community* applies to a broad range of cases, from highly integrated traditional communities to more diffuse communities, such as the medical or legal communities.

Like virtues, and unlike culture, the concept of community involves resources for sanctioning. In the case of community, sanctions are given by membership itself, as well as by status. One of the most serious sanctions available for the violation of a norm is exclusion from the relevant community. If membership in a community is valuable, then a violation that will involve a loss of membership has very high opportunity costs.

A loss of status in a community can also be a sanction. In its simplest form, a loss of status is simply a change in one's reputation, with a corresponding change in the range of beneficial interactions in which one can engage. For a first-time criminal offender, the loss of status involved in becoming an ex-con might be a greater cost than the prison term. This sanction does not apply to repeat offenders, of course, but repeat offender is itself a status.

4.0. Implications of the Account of Norms for Institutional Design

Seen as an alternative or supplement to directly enforced rules, norms are useful to the institutional designer in at least three ways. First, norms can supplement enforcement where compliance with the rules is difficult to detect. Herbert Kaufman (1960) considers the role of norms in the work of forest rangers, who, by the nature of their jobs, often must work without any direct supervision. Second, norms can be helpful where only group output can be effectively measured. Gary Miller (1992), in his reinterpretation of the observations of F. J. Roethlisberger and W. J. Dickson

(1939), explores the development of norms in the setting of a bank wiring room, where groups of workers wired banks of terminals in telephone switching systems. Third, norms can be required where the resources available for enforcement are not sufficient by themselves to implement a policy; even if the resources exist to enforce a policy directly, the costs of that enforcement may be reduced if supporting norms can be generated. Melanie Manion (1993) analyzes the effort by Chinese leaders to implement a policy of retirement by way of norms.

To make systematic use of norms, an institutional designer must arrange the institutional structures so as to create the conditions necessary for the emergence and maintenance of norms. Four general conditions are required: interactions must be indefinitely iterated, the second-order coordination problem suggested by the folk theorem must be solved, the norms must be internalized, and the norms must fit appropriately with the existing community norms. A number of strategies are available to the institutional designer to generate these conditions.

4.1. Indefinite Iteration

The first general condition for norms to emerge and be maintained is that the interactions in question be indefinitely iterated. Indefinite iteration is required for the existence of a cooperative equilibrium. The institutional designer can either directly make long-term relationships a part of the structure of her institutions or she can make use of reputation systems.

The Forest Service provides an instance of the strategy of building long-term relationships into the structure of the institution. Kaufman (1960) describes the process of hiring and training used by the Forest Service in a successful effort to generate norms. By carefully selecting individuals who were highly motivated to be involved with the service (p. 164), requiring a substantial training period (p. 169), and promoting from within (p. 180), the Forest Service ensured that the rangers had a long-term commitment. Interestingly, the Forest Service also used the fact that norms require long-term relationships to prevent the formation of disruptive norms. By having a policy of regular rotation, the Forest Service limited the influence of local norms, whether of the community or of a particular station (p. 217).

The background norms of a given community can affect the likelihood of repetitions. Mark Casson (1991: 221) argues that the strength of norms of loyalty vary from one group to another, and that loyalty enhances the stability that makes norms possible. While the existence of such a background norm is not directly in the control of the institutional designer, it is a resource that can be exploited where it is available.

An alternative to long-term relationships is a reputation system, illustrated by David Kreps's (1990) discussion of the interaction of workers and firms. He suggests that firms can have reputations with prospective workers that permit the development of norms, even though each worker cannot count on his own future interactions to generate the cooperative outcome (p. 92). Rather, the worker counts on his ability to affect the reputation of the firm with other prospective workers to protect his interests. As a result, firms and workers can enter into contracts with one another that do not fully specify all the conditions of employment. Such contracts are desirable because of the pervasiveness of unforeseen contingencies.

Because reputation systems have substantial reporting costs, the institutional designer can increase their effectiveness by reducing those costs. Paul Milgrom, Douglass North, and Barry Weingast (1990) suggest that a system of private judges can serve such a purpose. Where "it is too costly to keep everyone informed about what transpires in all trading relationships...the system of private judges is designed...to transmit *just enough* information to the right people in the right circumstances to enable the reputation mechanism to function" (p. 3). The judges, in effect, reduce the information costs of using a reputation system to create the indefinite iterations necessary for cooperative norms to emerge and be maintained.

Membership in certain organizations can be thought of as part of a reputation system. Milgrom, North, and Weingast discuss the Champagne fairs, where a condition of entry was that a merchant be "in good standing" (1990: 20). In general, an institutional designer can create a club in which membership is conditional on meeting certain norms and use exclusion to enforce those norms. For this approach to work, it is essential that membership be valuable. Interestingly, membership can be valuable just because it stands as an assurance to others that one is meeting certain norms.

4.2. Resolving the Second-Order Coordination Problem

The second general condition required for norms to emerge and be maintained is the resolution of the second-order coordination problem suggested by the folk theorem. The institutional designer faces the same difficulties and opportunities here as she did in generating conventions, with some additional complications. Her task is to make one particular (efficient) cooperative strategy salient.

One strategy for creating the expectation that a norm will be followed involves creating an association between the new norm and existing norms. Manion (1993: 50) suggests that "norms are more likely to emerge when there are generally shared frames of reference, easily accessible in the psychological inventory, and for which few conflicting frames readily present themselves." The Chinese leaders, in their effort to generate a norm of retirement, explicitly linked this new norm to three pre-existing frames of reference: "leave of absence for convalescence," "special retirement as quite simply a new work assignment," and retirement as fulfilling duties "as communist party members" (p. 51). As Manion points out, this approach only works to the degree that an effective association can plausibly be made.

Casson (1991: 184) suggests that an effective leader might generate the expectation that a given norm will be followed by making a self-validating prediction that the norm will be followed. If the leader has established credibility in other regards, then she might be successful in this effort. Interestingly, even though her prediction is to some extent ungrounded, its very success increases her credibility and thus increases her ability to use this technique.

A leader can help this process along by rigging the evidence that compliance is occurring, an approach Manion describe as "exemplary conformers." Pointing out a few highly visible individuals following the norm provides evidence that the standard is already in place (p. 57). Had the Chinese leaders themselves retired, for example, the norm might have been more rapidly adopted; however, they wished to have a norm of retirement that applied to everyone but themselves, which limited the effectiveness of their use of exemplary conformers (p. 240).

4.3. Internalization

The third general condition required for norms to emerge and be maintained is that the norms be internalized. As I suggested earlier, there are a number of accounts of the role of moral considerations in the process of internalization, ranging from accounts based purely on self-interest to those based on nonconsequentialist moral considerations. Which strategies for generating internalization succeed depends on which account of internalization is, in fact, correct.

If norms are internalized in response to consequentialist, moral considerations, then the most obvious strategy for generating internalization is to provide arguments directly that a given norm will provide benefits (Manion, 1993: 51). Eugene Bardach and Robert Kagan (1982: 133) suggest that this is a significant role for an effective regulator. They consider the example of water pollution inspectors who explain the uses of the water downstream, and the Wages and Hours Law Enforcement Office "selling" the "theory of industrial fairness underlying the law."

There are limits to the effectiveness of direct argumentation, however, which may reflect other forces in the process of internalization. Edward Shils and Morris Janowitz (1984: 313) found that propaganda efforts by the Allied Forces involving "ideological attacks on German leaders" and "the justness of our war aims" were ineffective in increasing the rate at which soldiers surrendered. However, the fact that these moral arguments were encountered in propaganda may have limited their effectiveness.

The hiring and training process used by the Forest Service that Kaufman (1960) discusses not only generates long-term relationships, it also helps to generate moral motives for compliance. Kaufman suggests that the Forest Service's policy of frequently transferring rangers had the effect of leading the rangers to rely on the Service for continuity and structure in their world and as a consequence to "'internalize' the perceptions, values, and premises of action that prevail in the bureau" (p. 176). This "identification" with the Forest Service was intensified by the use of symbols (p. 183), the ranger's role as representative of the Forest Service to the local community (p. 193), and the fact that headquarters frequently consulted with the rangers about policy (p. 185). This strategy is compatible with a range of accounts of internalization.

Constructing a set of rules can contribute to the internalization of norms, if those rules are seen as coming from a body with some moral authority. Manion (1993: 55) considers the role of exemplary rules as an alternative to direct argumentation. She suggests that an exemplary rule gives people information about the overall benefits of a policy by inductive rather than deductive means. Thus, in trying to generate a norm for retirement, the Chinese leaders "issued about two hundred regulations, measures, notices, and decisions on cadre retirement" (p. 56).

Under some conditions, however, rigidly enforced rules can be counter-productive. Miller (1992: 211), looking at the case of manufacturing workers, suggests that "participation in high-level plant decision making" influences the development of strong norms. Norms are particularly likely to be developed where workers have a high degree of involvement in their work, and he recommends policies such as "control over performance standards," profit-sharing plans, and "more challenging tasks with wider scope" as ways of increasing that involvement (p. 211). In contrast, he suggests that "hierarchy reduces worker motivation, and the imposition of clearly defined rules induces employees to do no more than the minimum specified by those rules" (p. 209).

4.4. Integration with Existing Community Norms

The fourth general factor the institutional designer must consider is the way that the norms she wishes to create and maintain fit in with the existing community norms. She must take into account considerations of efficiency, context, and conflict.

The overall efficiency of a norm includes its use of cognitive and social resources. A norm might appear to be efficient in the abstract but be prohibitively expensive for people to remember and act on. For norms that involve communication (such as those that are enforced in part by reputation effects), Kreps (1990: 126) argues that "the simpler the message being sent and the more internally consistent it is, the easier it will be to communicate." A simple and internally consistent norm also makes effective use of cognitive resources. If that norm also fits in with the larger pattern of norms that form the community, then it will make effective use of those social resources.

When introducing a norm into an existing tradition, the institutional designer has to consider the way that contextual expectations will influence the interpretation of that norm. Michael Walzer (1983) suggests that the kind of expectations we have varies with different "spheres" of life, including political office, the marketplace, education, family, and religion, among others. If an institutional designer is introducing a norm into an area in which family relationships are important, then he will need to take into account different factors than if he is introducing a norm into a market environment. The norms surrounding adoption and surrogate mothers reflect this source of tension.

Just as two independently developing cultures can have quite different conventions, posing difficulties when circumstances change and they need to interact, so too independently developing communities can encounter difficulties in interacting due to differences in their norms. The appropriate response of the institutional designer depends on the extent of the interaction. If the two communities must merge, then there will be a very difficult transition period while the norms adjust. On the other hand, if the communities only need to cooperate for a limited range of purposes, then the institutional designer has the option of attempting to encourage a set of pidgin norms – a set of norms that draw support from both cultures (perhaps in quite different ways) that permit the cooperation. This is one way of understanding John Rawls's (1987) notion of an "overlapping consensus" supporting norms of toleration.

5.0. Conclusion

The framework I have just sketched integrates simple accounts of conventions, norms, cultures, communities, habits, and virtues, in a manner generally consistent with the rational choice approach to human behavior and institutional design. Assuming that this framework is useful in its basic outlines, future research would focus on considering how richer and more complex accounts would fit into it. Such extensions might be expected to occur in three general areas. First, further work might be done on the dynamics of coordination and cooperation, including reputation systems, communications systems, and the like. Second, work might be done extending the model to account for situations that do not reduce to coordination and cooperation—where conflict is more deeply embedded (Knight, 1992; Ullmann-Margalit, 1977). Third, work might be done more tightly linking the results from cognitive science and sociology into the rational choice framework.

What this framework should make clear, however, is that research in cognitive science, moral philosophy, sociology, and anthropology is relevant to a comprehensive account of conventions and norms, even one that is within the rational choice tradition. While the theoretical accounts involved in these other disciplines may not always be compatible with the rational choice understanding of human behavior, many of their observations and results can be carried over into the framework sketched in this chapter.

References

Axelrod, Robert. (1984). *The Evolution of Cooperation*. New York: Basic Books.

Bardach, Eugene and Kagan, Robert. (1982). *Going by the Book: The Problem of Regulatory Unreasonableness*. Philadelphia: Temple University Press.

Calvert, Randall L. (1992). "The Rational Choice Theory of Social Institutions: Cooperation, Coordination, and Communications." In Jeffrey Banks and Eric Hanushek (eds.), *Political Economy of Institutions and Decisions*. New York: Cambridge University Press.

Casson, Mark. (1991). *The Economics of Business Culture*. Oxford: Oxford University Press.

Elster, Jon. (1989). *The Cement of Society*. New York: Cambridge University Press.

Etzioni, Amitai. (1988). *The Moral Dimension: Toward a New Economics*. New York: Free Press.

Frank, Robert. (1988). *Passions Within Reason: The Strategic Role of the Emotions*. New York: Norton.

Gibbard, Allan. (1990). *Wise Choices, Apt Feelings: A Theory of Normative Judgment*. Cambridge, MA: Harvard University Press.

Hardin, Russell. (1988). *Morality Within the Limits of Reason*. Chicago: University of Chicago Press.

Kaufman, Herbert. (1960). *The Forest Ranger: A Study in Administrative Behavior*. Baltimore: Johns Hopkins Press.

Knight, Jack. (1992). *Institutions and Social Conflict*. New York: Cambridge University Press.

Kreps, David M. (1990). "Corporate Culture and Economic Theory." In James Alt and Kenneth Shepsle (eds.). *Perspectives on Positive Political Economy* (pp. 90–143). New York: Cambridge University Press.

Lewis, David. (1969). *Convention: A Philosophical Study*. Cambridge, MA: Harvard University Press.

Madler, George. (1985). *Cognitive Psychology: An Essay in Cognitive Science*. Hillsdale, NJ: Lawrence Erlbaum.

Mandler, Jean Matter. (1984) *Stories, Scripts, and Scenes: Aspects of Schema Theory*. Hillsdale, NJ: Lawrence Erlbaum.

Manion, Melanie. (1993). *Retirement of Revolutionaries in China: Public Policies, Social Norms, Private Interest*. Princeton, NJ: Princeton University Press.

McCain, Roger A. (1992). *A Framework for Cognitive Economics*. Westport, CT: Praeger.

Milgrom, Paul R., Douglass C. North, and Barry R. Weingast. (1990). "The Role of Institutions in the Revival of Trade: The Law Merchant, Private Judges, and the Champagne Fairs." *Economics and Politics* 2(1): 1–23.

Miller, Gary J. (1992). *Managerial Dilemmas*. New York: Cambridge University Press.

Minsky, Marvin. (1975). "A Framework for Representing Knowledge." In Patrick Henry Winston (ed.), *The Psychology of Computer Vision* (pp. 211–280). New York: McGraw Hill.

Rawls, John. (1987). "The Idea of an Overlapping Consensus." *Oxford Journal of Legal Studies* 7(1): 1–25.

Roethlisberger, Fritz J. and William J. Dickson. (1939). *Management and The Worker*. Cambridge, MA: Harvard University Press.

Schank, Roger and Robert Abelson. (1977). *Scripts, Plans, Goals and Understanding*. Hillsdale, NJ: Lawrence Erlbaum.

Schelling, Thomas. (1960). *The Strategy of Conflict*. Cambridge, MA: Harvard University Press.

Selton, Reinhard. (1978). "The Chain-Store Paradox." *Theory and Decision* 9(2): 127–159.

Shils, Edward A. and Janowitz, Morris. (1948). "Cohesion and Disintegration in the Wehrmacht in World War II." *Public Opinion Quarterly* 12(2): 280–315.

Simon, Herbert, Massimo Egidi, Robin Marris, and Riccardo Viale. (1992). *Economics, Bounded Rationality and the Cognitive Revolution*. Brookfield: Edward Elgar.

Sugden, Robert. (1986). *The Economics of Rights, Co-operation and Welfare*. Oxford: Basil Blackwell.

Thaler, Richard H. (1991). *Quasi Rational Economics* New York: Russell Sage Foundation.

Ullmann-Margalit, Edna. (1977). *The Emergence of Norms*. Oxford: Oxford University Press.

Walzer, Michael. (1983). *Spheres of Justice: A Defense of Pluralism and Equality*. New York: Basic Books.

6 INSTITUTIONS FOR THE SETTLEMENT OF TRADE DISPUTES: THE CASE OF THE CANADA–UNITED STATES FREE TRADE AGREEMENT

Kenneth B. Woodside

1.0. Introduction

Trade disputes among competing countries have become increasingly common and contentious in recent years. They also receive a great deal of attention in the media. Indeed, they have taken on the character of minor battles between contending industries and countries with the trade actions called, variously, "provocations" or "threats" by one country against another. These trade skirmishes have acquired new significance over the last decade as the volume and relative importance of international trade and investment has grown. My purpose in this chapter is to examine and assess the workings of the trade dispute settlement institutions established under the trade liberalization agreement negotiated between Canada and the United States in 1987. These dispute settlement institutions have now been in operation for several years since the implementation of the Canada–United States Free Trade Agreement (FTA) in January 1989 and will be retained, although with significant modifications, under the North American Free Trade Agreement (NAFTA). My primary objective is to assess how well these institutions have served the two member countries under the FTA and how one might anticipate they will work under the NAFTA.

The main reason for the increased importance of trade disputes among countries has been the enormous liberalization of international trade and of the conditions governing foreign investment that has occurred over the last decade. This expansion has many sources. Among the most important are the reduction in levels of tariff protection, the widespread moves to deregulate markets, including financial markets around the world, and the development of new or renewed trading areas (Brean, Bird and Krauss, 1991). Among these new trading regimes one would include the move toward a single market in the European Community, the negotiation of the FTA and the NAFTA in North America, and negotiations toward some form of Asian or Pacific trading area. The resulting increase in international trade and investment, which has substantially outstripped the growth of domestic economic activity worldwide, has increased economic interdependence and increased both the potential for trade disagreements and their likely importance when they occur (Woodside, 1993). This increased economic interdependence has, therefore, resulted in growing vulnerability and related sensitivity by governments to the actions of other countries with whom they trade. These new trade regimes are intended to encourage the further growth of this interdependence, and thus they make the possibility of more disputes ever more likely.

Trade disputes can take many forms. The most common form is one in which one country alleges that one or more foreign companies are dumping goods in their market at unacceptedly low prices and thus threaten the economic viability of domestic producers. The governmental agencies that allege such dumping proceed to impose duties that reflect the extent to which these imports are said to be underpriced. Other types of disputes include claims that another government is unfairly subsidizing its exports, that there has been an excessive surge in imports in a particular industry or sector, regardless of the reason, and that this surge needs to be slowed to allow domestic adjustment, that national treatment has been denied to a foreign investor, and that technical or environmental standards of one sort or another are being used to impede imports. In all of these cases the real intentions of the exporting and importing countries are questioned, and demands from domestic interests for some form of retaliation are forthcoming.[1] An element of ambiguity is often present as to how fairly the laws of the country initiating the trade action have been applied. This is the setting in which international trade dispute institutions are called into action.

A focus on the role of political institutions in resolving disputes has become much more common over the last decade (March and Olsen, 1989; Evans, Rueschemeyer, and Skocpol, 1985). In part, this is a reaction to the widespread changes that have occurred in the forms of governance during this period. With the emergence of new institutional structures, attention has naturally focused on their relative effectiveness. In particular, what incentives for cooperation are created by the new institutions, and are the new structures appropriate to the circumstances in which they must operate? Are the institutions capable of providing a mutually acceptable solution to the dispute? Are the decisions of the international dispute settlement institutions treated with sufficient respect? These are some of the questions that I address in this study.

This chapter is divided into three sections. The first deals with the role of dispute settlement institutions in the politics of trade and provides a framework for our examination of the institutions set up under the FTA and the NAFTA. The second section offers an assessment of the evolution of these institutions under the FTA. The third section describes the proposed changes under the NAFTA and how these changes may affect the working of the dispute settlement institutions. The research on which I base this essay is in its very early stages, and, consequently, its conclusions should be treated with some caution. The major sources that have been employed are a small number of interviews with participants in the process as well as the panel decisions under the FTA and the trade agreements themselves.

2.0. Dispute Settlement Institutions and the Politics of Trade

The FTA and the NAFTA along with the European Community have been described as examples of *minilateralism* among trading regimes (Yarbrough and Yarbrough, 1992). Unlike multilateral agreements such as the General Agreement on Tariffs and Trade (GATT), a minilateral agreement can involve as few as two countries. As with a multilateral arrangement, however, they are also based on the establishment of supranational institutions to provide a form of third-party enforcement of the provisions of the agreement (Yarbrough and Yarbrough, 1992: 6). In order for these institutions to be effective, the member states must be willing to concede to them some role in resolving the trade disputes that are likely to arise. This involves, in effect, some effective delegation of sovereignty by the member governments to the institutions they established in order to resolve problems created under the trade regime. The need for some de facto delegation of power is an ongoing problem in such agreements because the sovereign powers of states are usually guarded jealously. Any apparent attempt to constrain sovereignty is likely to be controversial.

The origins of interest in Canada in some form of trade agreement with the United States date from the early 1980s when a growing loss of faith in existing approaches to domestic economic policy merged with a renewed interest in market-based solutions (Doern and Tomlin, 1991; Woodside, 1993). The Canadian economy was not only very dependent on its exports to the United States, but this dependence had continued to grow throughout the post–World War II period. This increased dependence continued despite some feeble attempts at diversifying Canadian exports through official advocacy of a so-called third option during the 1970s as well as the growth of Canadian nationalism and concern over foreign control of the economy. Part of the reason for this strong dependence on the U.S. economy was the preponderant role of major U.S.-based multinational corporations in the Canadian economy. This served increasingly to integrate the two economies. These corporations had a strong interest in putting constraints on the Canadian government's capacity to legislate economic nationalist measures against foreign (i.e., U.S.) investment. For its part, the U.S. government also sought to guarantee American access to Canadian energy resources.

On Canada's part there were growing concerns that Canadian access to the United States market was threatened. As American businesses faced increased pressure from foreign competitors, they turned with growing frequency to so-called trade remedy laws or contingent protection as the solution (Gold and Layton-Brown, 1988; Bovard, 1991). A new trade regime seemed to be an attractive way of evading the potential threat posed by these trade actions. The extent of Canadian dependence on the U.S. market — 75 percent of Canadian exports going to the United States when exports constituted about 25 percent of Canada's gross national product (GNP) — made any reasonable possibility of exemption from U.S. trade law very attractive. More important for our purposes, it also made the choice and effectiveness of trade dispute settlement institutions central to perceptions about whether a trade agreement with the United States would be successful.

Canada was apparently willing to support the establishment of a dispute settlement institutional structure (DSIS) that would have substantial authority over the resolution of Canada-U.S. trade disputes. This willingness to compromise Canadian sovereignty to protect access to the U.S. market existed despite the growth in Canadian nationalism over the last few decades. However, it was not shared by the U.S. negotiators of the agreement. Rather than an organization that would have had extensive authority over trade actions taken by the two countries, the FTA resulted in a DSIS that had the responsibility to review the actions of the two member countries to determine whether the governments had given sufficient attention to due process and had used acceptable data and methods in arriving at their decisions.

It is worthwhile examining and assessing the performance and evolution of the DSIS from two perspectives. First, how effectively have these institutions worked internally so far? I pay particular attention to such factors as the development of standard operating procedures, the growth of an organizational culture that contributes to the effectiveness of the institution, and whether the nationality of the panelists has been an important factor in determining panel decisions. The second perspective considers the relationship of this institution to other related institutions. Have the DSISs had any effect on the behavior of domestic institutions involved in trade disputes, and do these institutions in the two countries respect the decisions taken by the DSIS panels? This would include institutions such as the United States International Trade Commission (ITC) and the Canadian International Trade Tribunal (CITT). Thus my focus is not only on how the organization has evolved internally but also what kind of effect it has had on its external environment. Has it successfully encouraged institutions to adjust their approaches and operating procedures, or has it largely been ignored? As the effectiveness of international institutions is largely dependent on whether the interested countries want them to succeed, the relationship between the DSIS and the other institutions in their environment is important.

3.0. Dispute Settlement Institutional Structures under the FTA

The dispute settlement structures established under the FTA are basically threefold in character. Under Chapter 18, a system of panels can be established to adjudicate general disputes between the two parties to the agreement. For example, a case in 1989 involved a disagreement over whether Canada could legitimately require that salmon and herring caught in its coastal waters be landed in Canada prior to their export. The main concern of Chapter 18 panel inquiries is how the FTA should be interpreted and applied. The FTA emphasizes negotiated settlements, but if this fails, recourse can be taken to either binding arbitration under Article 1806 or nonbinding arbitration under Article 1807.[2]

The second structure for dispute settlement is mandated in Chapter 19.

In this chapter each of the parties to the agreement reserves the right to apply its laws to combat dumping and export subsidies. However, if such trade action is taken, then the other party can request a panel review of the decision under Article 1904 of the FTA. The review by this panel replaces judicial review by the courts, and the panel can either affirm the legitimacy of the trade action or it can remand the decision back to the appropriate administrative agency for purpose of a reconsideration of its decision. The Chapter 19 decisions are binding (Article 1904.9), and any remand is supposed to be complied with by the designated agency.[3] As of the end of 1992 there had been over thirty cases dealt with under the Chapter 19 provisions. This chapter also provides for the possibility of a challenge to a binding panel decision if there has been some serious error by a panel or some malfeasance is alleged. There have been two occasions when this "extraordinary challenge procedure" has been invoked. The panels that are established under Chapter 19 were intended to be temporary in character, with the two countries intending to negotiate a common subsidies code that would clarify which subsidies would be permissiable under the FTA and which ones would no longer be employed. This subsidies code would have eliminated at least some of the trade disputes between the two countries. Negotiation of the subsidies code was delayed through the early 1990s because of ongoing GATT negotiations on some of the same issues. The third dispute settlement structure involves financial services. These disputes are resolved outside the panel system through negotiations between the United States Treasury and Canada's Department of Finance. (For a description of the institutions see Table 6.1.)

The panels, themselves, are binational in character. Each country maintains a roster of twenty-five individuals who are eligible to hear a case. Any particular panel is composed of two panelists from each country and a fifth member selected jointly by both parties or, in the absence of agreement, by lot. The panel produces a written report explaining how it came to its decision and detailing any changes required of the original agency decision. Panels established under Chapter 19 for which the decision is binding and the focus is on procedural fairness must include a majority of lawyers among their members. There is no such requirement for a majority of lawyers for Chapter 18 panels, reflecting their broader jurisdiction that allows them to examine other nonlegal issues that may be relevant to the case. If an Extraordinary Challenge Committee is required, it was to be composed of three judges with one selected by each of the governments from a common roster and the third chosen from the roster by the two justices already selected.

The FTA also established two more permanent institutions. The first is the Canada–United States Trade Commission established under Article 1802. Headed up by the United states Trade Representative (USTR) and Canada's Minister for International Trade, this Commission is responsible for ensuring the effective operation of the FTA through consultation and negotiation. The second institution is a Binational Secretariat established under Article 1909. It has offices in both Ottawa and Washington and the Secretariat's function is to organize and manage the dispute settlement institutions under both Chapters 18 and 19, arrange for the distribution of panel decisions, and maintain the rosters of potential panellists.

3.1. The Internal Operation of the DSIS

In this section I consider three salient aspects of the operation of the dispute settlement institutions. The first aspect is that of the operation of the panels themselves. Each of the governments has established a common set of rules to govern the responsibilities of the Secretariat with respect to the panels, how the panels will operate, how and when the panels will accept and use various kinds of information, and a host of other factors that affect how a particular panel will operate (Canada, 1992). In this respect there has been a substantial formal and legal elaboration of the institutional structure of the DSIS.

Another component of the operation of the panels is that of the speed of decision making. One of the main goals of those who designed the panel system was to create a system that could produce decisions more quickly. Disputes adjudicated within the GATT take years to reach resolution. Judicial review through the U.S. Court of International Trade often takes two years or more. The FTA panels are intended normally to come to a final decision within 315 days as outlined in Article 904(14) and all panels except for two have been resolved within this time frame (Horlick and DeBusk, 1992). In this respect the DSIS system has been successful.

One major concern about the operation of the panel system was that the panels might divide along national lines. This fear has not, as yet, materialized. A good number of the decisions have been unanimous, and almost all of the others have involved but one dissenting vote. It appears that the two secretariats and the panelists themselves have made a considerable effort to make the system work and make the resultant decisions credible. A norm that stresses consensus has seemingly taken root within the DSIS of the FTA and contributed to a relatively smoothly run operation.

Table 6.1. FTA-NAFTA Dispute Settlement Institutions

	Jurisdictions	*Structure*	*Strengths*	*Weaknesses*	*Results*
Chatper 18 (FTA)	General disputes between countries	Five panelists, two from each country and one jointly selected	Reviews agency decisions, encourages negotiation	More subject to nationalist pressure than Chapter 19	Mixed, regarded as uneven and unsatisfactory
Chapter 19	Dumping and export subsidy cases	Five panelists, two from each country and a third from one of the two	High level of consensus and cooperation among panelists	Uneven response from domestic agencies in each country, expecially U.S.A.	Widely seen to be very successful
Extraordinary Challenge Committee	Any panel cases where malfeasance or serious error is alleged	Three judges, one chosen by each country and the third by the first two judges	Gives finality to process, not used often	Could potentially be used too frequently	Used twice as of January 1997
Canada-U.S. Free trade Commission	The effective operation of the entire FTA	Headed by U.S. Trade Representative and Canada's Minister of International Trade, work done by public servants	Provides opportunity to negotiate and consult	Raises issue to political level for settlement	Relatively inconspicuous role

Binational Secretariat	Organization and management of panels for Chapters 18 and 19. Becomes permanent under NAFTA	Secretariat housed in both Ottawa and Washington	Porvides continuity, support	None apparent	Effective management
Chapter 20 (NAFTA)	Replaces Chapter 18 review under FTA	Panelist for each country selected by other party	Hopefully provides far more objective panel decisions	Remain advisory in character	Unknown
Free Trade Commission (NAFTA)	Replaces Canada-U.S. Free Trade Commission, oversight power over entire NAFTA; jurisdiction over investment and financial services disputes added	Larger staff, more use of advisory committees	Unknown	Unknown	Unknown

Thus, in assessing the evolution of the operation of the panel system, the conclusion would have to be a favorable one.

At this stage I can only speculate on why this norm of cooperation or consensus has taken hold so firmly, especially since it was initially intended that the panel system would be a temporary one. One possible explanation is that panelists on both sides anticipated that a subsidy code would not materialize because the U.S. Congress would never agree to a code that would limit its freedom to subsidize. The fact that Canada depends more on expenditure subsidies and the U.S. on other policy instruments such as tax exemptions to subsidize activities posed cultural impediments in the negotiation of a subsidy code.[4] A second explanation would stress the desire of individual panelists to see the trade dispute institutions succeed, not only because they created new jobs and income but also because the legitimacy of the FTA depended to a great extent on the capacity of the panel system to resolve disputes effectively. As such they could see a marriage of pecuniary self-interest and a desire to contribute to more responsible government. A third possible explantion is that the behavior of domestic institutions involved in trade disputes is undisciplined in their choice of methodologies and blatantly protectionist (Bovard, 1991). The panelists in doing their jobs could hardly avoid finding common ground against such practices.

The second important aspect of the evolution of the DSIS relates to the internal effectiveness of the structure. In this area the evidence is more mixed. While most of the decisions have been complied with eventually, in a number of cases the effectiveness of the panel system has been threatened. In an early case of alleged dumping, referred to as the *Red Raspberries from Canada* case, the panel had to remand the case back to the Department of Commerce twice before it received an adequate explanation of why the Department had calculated the extent of dumping in the way that it had (Binational Secretariat, 1989b). Commerce did not have an adequate explanation for its choice of methodology and eventually applied the approach insisted on by the panel. With the new methodology in use, the supposed dumping disappeared.

In another case, referred to as *Fresh, Chilled or Frozen Pork from Canada*, the International Trade Commission (ITC) ruled that subsidized pork imports from Canada threatened the U.S. pork industry with material injury. A panel was established to review the allegation, and it ruled that the ITC decision was based on statistics that, at best, appeared to be questionable and that the choice of statistics overly influenced the ITC's decision (Binational Secretariat, 1991a). Consequently, the decision was remanded back to the ITC. The ITC subsequently reissued the same decision, attempting to rework the data, and a second FTA panel remanded the second ITC decision back to the agency again. This time the ITC complied with the panels required approach, and the threat of material injury disappeared. However, the United States requested that an Extraordinary Challenge Committee (ECC) be established to review the second remand order of the FTA panel (Binational Secretariat, 1991b). The ECC ruled that there was no justification for calling for an ECC and the second remand order was sustained.[5] As both the raspberries and fresh pork cases indicate, the main internal problem this posed for the effectiveness of the system is that the panel process could become indeterminate, making resolution of disputes difficult. The ECC stage, which originally was intended to be employed very infrequently, may eventually become a more common feature of dispute settlement as a means of ending the process. In early 1993 another panel decision involving *Live Swine from Canada* has become the target of an ECC, once again stretching out the decision-making process in another case. An overall assessment of the internal effectiveness of the evolving FTA DSIS must be more guarded. Despite the existence of terms such as "binding decisions" in Chapter 19 of the FTA, there is really no such thing as a binding legal decision in international relations. The DSIS requires commitment to its effective functioning in order to achieve the goals sought by the participants.

The third aspect in the internal evolution of the DSIS worthy of note is the kind of law that it has generated. In particular, there has been some discussion of the problems associated with the absence of a real role for precedent in the body of FTA panel decisions. The FTA's DSIS is intended to review the decisions taken by domestic tribunals and agencies to determine that the decisions taken reflect a proper attention to due process and appropriate standards of review. Some analysts and participants argue for the need for a common case law for all cases under the FTA. As things stand, panels can ignore the decisions of previous panels on different cases, and each remand in a particular case has the potential to raise new issues and even introduce new information. As panels can only confirm or remand, there is also the possibility of an ongoing review process that will eventually eliminate any benefits of accelerated timing under the FTA. In the cases involving live swine from Canada, petitioners have sought and received separate hearings from the U.S. government agencies, the ITC and Commerce, over the exports from Canada for each successive year in order to determine whether Canada was guilty of providing export subsidies for live hogs. The fact that previous panel decisions had consistently rejected the allegations did not prevent the next year's imports from being investigated on the same grounds. Each new year brings a new case against live hogs imported from Canada. With the introduction of precedent, this continuing process might be stopped. However, there is little reason to expect this to occur.

As an arena of international decision making, domestic political considerations will always be crucial driving forces behind the panel process, and one must be appropriately modest in one's expectations. In terms of the internal operation of the DSIS, the norm of consensus and cooperation that has characterized decision-making has been the most impressive achievement in institutional growth. It has been the source of much of the success of the panel system.

3.2. The External Operation of the DSIS

We have focused, so far, on the internal operation and evolution of the DSIS. Yet a fuller assessment of the effectiveness of the design of its institutions requires that one examine the relationship of the DSIS with the related structures with which it must interact. Under the FTA the key institutions with which the DSIS must deal are the Canadian International Trade Tribunal (CITT) and Revenue Canada and, in the United States, the Department of Commerce and the International Trade Commission (ITC). These institutions are the bodies involved in determining whether a trade remedy law needs to be invoked. In each country one of the institutions determines whether an infraction has taken place, and the second determines whether this infraction, having taken place, is causing material injury to the domestic producers in the same industry.

The decisions of these agencies are the ones that are reviewed by the panels set up under the FTA's DSIS. The FTA panels have the responsibility of passing judgment on the quality of the decisions of these domestic agencies. One key question is how seriously do these administrative bodies treat a remand from one of the FTA's DSIS panels. Does the agency have an incentive to respect a remand from these panels? As the implementation of decisions of an international governance structure requires a form of voluntary compliance with its decisions, the domestic agencies must see their interests as sharing something in common with those of the DSIS. Second, what effect have the DSIS panels had on the operating procedures of these agencies? It is a constant concern in the politics of international trade that the domestic political institutions are not really concerned with whether justice is being served by their decisions. Their real concern is to protect the interests of domestic producers. However, an effective liberalized trade regime requires that a measure of cooperation evolve among the relevant participating institutions. Our interest in this section is to assess the nature of these relationships as part of our exercise in examining the success of the DSIS as established under the FTA.

3.2.1. External Institutions in Canada Revenue Canada has the responsibility for determining whether a trade infraction such as dumping has occurred. It acts on receipt of a complaint, and once the complaint has been properly documented the Deputy Minister of Revenue Canada, the leading civil servant in the department, has thirty days in which to decide whether or not it will further investigate the matter. After another ninety days Revenue Canada is required to issue a preliminary determination as to whether dumping has occurred or an export subsidy exists. If this determination claims that such a situation appears to exist, the full review process including the CITT moves into action. Given that Revenue Canada, like equivalent institutions in other countries, often uses indirect measures such as a "constructed cost" approach to determine whether dumping exists, the openness of the procedures utilized is important (Stone, 1984; Magnus, 1989).

As a result of its role in the collection of tax revenue, Revenue Canada has tended to be relatively secretive in its activities. This secretiveness in assessing trade cases has been under attack for some time, going back certainly to the 1984 Special Import Measures Act, which substantially predates the FTA and its DSIS. This pressure continues to grow, however. One example is the demand for fuller explanations of decisions taken. For instance, in a case where three U.S. breweries were alleged to be dumping their beer in the British Columbia market, the panel that was set up remanded back to Revenue Canada the part of its final determination that dealt with the calculation of dumping margins. It required that if the agency were unwilling to change its methodology, it should provide a better explanation for its decision (Binational Secretariat, 1991a: 7–9). Increased transparency or openness in the making and justifying of decisions taken by Revenue Canada continues to be sought and the FTA's DSIS has helped to generate pressure for such change.

It is the responsibility of the CITT to determine whether the dumping that is alleged to have occurred has caused material injury to the production in Canada of like goods. Unlike Revenue Canada, the CITT operates in a manner quite close to a court with a wide-ranging adversarial examination of the allegations and full opportunities for participation by all parties to the case. Thus decisions taken by the CITT are subject to substantial and open debate. However, once the CITT has taken a decision, the decision is final for the most part. The CITT has a privitive clause giving finality to its decisions that largely protects them from judicial review (Hogg, 1977: 137–138). This finality only holds where the CITT has not exceeded its jurisdiction, has not made a mistake in its application of the law, and has not acted in an obviously unreasonable manner (Magnus, 1989: 176). While this measure provides protection and autonomy for the CITT and its decision-making process, there has been increasing pressure from U.S. trade officials for its elimination. The existence of panel review under the FTA makes its absence under the GATT more unacceptable. Another effect of the FTA has been to require that the CITT play closer attention to its choice of procedures for review in order to ensure a perception of fairness. The fact that under the FTA its decisions are subject to review by the panels and have been subject to remand has contributed to this development, probably also improving the fairness of reviews by the CITT of cases involving other GATT members.

3.2.2. External Institutions in the United States The most important external institutions in the United States that deal with the DSIS are the Department of Commerce and the International Trade Commission. It is the role of the Department of Commerce, on receipt of a petition from a U.S. firm or trade organization, to investigate whether the alleged dumping of goods or existence of an export subsidy is supported by the evidence. The role of the International Trade Commission is to determine whether there has been material injury to the domestic industry caused by the dumping or export subsidy. These two institutions carry out their investigations concomitantly with each stage in the investigation of one, such as the preliminary finding, triggering a new stage in the investigation by the other (Horlick, 1989). Both of these agencies are supposed to be independent of the Congress, but in practice they must resist ongoing pleas from congressmen as well as elected state politicians.

The DSIS panels have frequently found that the Department of Commerce has exaggerated the amount of dumping that occurs. Part of the reason for this may derive from the origins of its mandate. In 1979 Commerce was given responsibility for the determination of dumping as a result of dissatisfaction with the performance of the Treasury. Commerce is quite aggressive in its pursuit of dumping, taking a more adversarial role than its counterpart in Canada. Further, U.S. dumping legislation prevents Commerce from considering the interests of other parties, such as consumers, in its assessment of dumping or export subsidies. As the process involves considerable discretion arising in part from the fact that many business practices in the home market can be alleged to involve dumping, the capacity of the DSIS panels to relate effectively with these agencies is important. To date the result has been mixed. In the cases involving live swine from Canada, Commerce continues to investigate the existence of export subsidies in Canada with a new case each year. While this reflects the absence of deference to precedent in the decisions of the DSIS panels, it also reflects the fact that the panel process still has a long way to go in establishing its legitimacy in the eyes of the Department of Commerce.

The International Trade Commission has also had an uneven relationship with the DSIS panels. The panels have frequently found that the ITC was claiming injury where the panels could find none. The major exception to this situation was the case involving replacement parts for paving equipment from Canada where injury was substantiated. There has also been a tendency to treat the panel decisions with less than complete respect. In the case involving fresh, chilled, or frozen pork from Canada, the panel remanded the ITC's decision twice before it received an appropriate response from the agency. At the same time the ITC's majority opinion on the second remand order continued to criticize the DSIS panel decision while, at the same time, complying with it. In this case an Extraordinary Challenge Committee was requested by the United States Trade Representative, and it supported the decisions made by the panel. To the extent that agencies like the ITC fail to give sufficient respect to the panel remands, it may be necessary to invoke the ECC mechanism more frequently than was originally intended.

What incentives can lead domestic trade institutions to comply with the decisions of DSIS panels? One is the potential for embarrassment. In the United States, the courts were significantly more deferential to domestic agency decisions prior to the FTA than the panels have been since its implementation (Boddez and Trebilcock, 1993). The more aggressive stance of the panels may encourage more attention to panel decisions by the domestic agencies. The fact that panel decisions also involve nationals as panelists gives their decisions more legitimacy. However, in the final analysis, agency cooperation remains an uncertain result, subject to domestic political pressures and fluctuating perceptions about how well the trading relationship is working.

3.3. Common External Problems

One other problem involving relationships between the panels and external agencies is the phenomenon that is sometimes called "forum shopping."

This refers to the capacity of governments to choose between either the GATT panels or the FTA panels in deciding where to take cases. The FTA allows the two countries to use either the GATT or the FTA panels, but once one has been selected, the case cannot be taken to the other DSIS panel. For instance, in the case of *Live Swine from Canada*, the Canadian government both challenged at the GATT the legislation on which Commerce had based its export subsidy decision, alleging that the legislation was inconsistent with the GATT obligations of the United States, and initiated a panel review of the injury determination by the ITC under the FTA. Each country can choose which of the alternative dispute forums that it will use; we expect each to do so on the grounds of which is likely to generate the most favorable result.

The danger that this poses for the DSIS panels is that it may undermine the legitimacy of the panel decisions. If it is believed that a GATT panel might have produced a different result from an FTA panel, the FTA remand may receive much less respect from the agency that it seeks to discipline. The remand becomes just one of a range of potential responses that the agency might have received, and the two countries may be more likely to invoke the ECC procedure more frequently. As the panel process gets more complicated, as it will under the NAFTA, this problem may become more important.

4.0. The Panel Process Under the NAFTA

The North American Free Trade Agreement (NAFTA) involves a number of important changes to the FTA DSIS. These changes go beyond the fact that the NAFTA includes a third member, Mexico, and provides for the accession to the treaty of other states in the future. In the first place, the panel review system set up under the FTA is no longer a temporary one. The idea of negotiations to establish a common subsidy code among the member states has been abandoned. Instead, each country will continue to apply its own trade remedy laws and these domestic agency decisions will continue to be reviewable by the DSIS set up under the NAFTA. As a reflection of the more permanent status of the panels, there are a number of related changes that could further enhance the internal cohesiveness of the DSIS. The Free Trade Commission, which replaces the Canada–United States Trade Commission, has been given complete responsibility for oversight of the operation of the entire agreement. The Binational Secretariat will now become permanent and assist the Commission in overseeing the NAFTA (Article 2002). The Commission also will now have the power to call on outside advisory groups, boards, and committees as it sees fit, thereby increasing its capacity to challenge the decisions of domestic institutions that regulate trade policy and to try to deal with trade irritants as they emerge (Articles 2007.5 and 2015).

Second, apart from these changes in the institutional capacity of the DSIS under the NAFTA, the agreement also makes some significant changes in how the panelists will be selected. Rather than each country having its own roster, the NAFTA provides that the member countries will establish common rosters from which the panelists will be chosen. Under Chapter 19, there will be a common roster of seventy-five members, twenty-five per country, and under Chapter 20 (replacing Chapter 18 of the FTA) there will be a separate common roster of thirty. It will be possible, however, to go outside the rosters if it is necessary (Articles 2009 and 2011). Not only will this roster be a consensus roster, but, in Chapter 20 cases, each of the disputing parties will get to choose the panel members for the other country from among the common roster members from that other country. While the FTA provided that each country chose two of the five panelists from its own national roster, the NAFTA requires in Chapter 20 cases that each country choose the panelists that will be nationals of the other country. This change in procedure seems to be designed to strengthen, in Chapter 20 panel decision making under the NAFTA, the norm of cooperation and nonnational decision making that has characterized panel decision making under Chapter 19 of the FTA. Another procedural feature that may contribute to consensual decision making is the requirement that panelists not be individually identified with majority or minority decisions. The NAFTA also introduces the possibility of third-party participation in the panel decisions. This participation can take the form of participation as panelists or just being in attendance at the panel hearings. A major test for the new panel structure will be its capacity to integrate the greater cultural diversity represented by Mexico into the previously more homogeneous cultural setting under the FTA. A critical part of the success of the FTA panels was their capacity to come to decisions that were unanimous or close to unanimous and thus avoid national divisions. This consensus is bound to be more difficult to sustain.

A third feature of the DSIS under the NAFTA is the great expansion in its mandate. At the same time that the panel system was made permanent, the number of areas of potential disagreement that are subject to its purview was substantially increased. Whereas under the FTA financial services disputes were left to the Treasury and the Ministry of Finance, under the NAFTA they come under the jurisdiction of the general panels set up under Chapter 18 of the FTA and now found in Chapter 20 of the NAFTA. However, they will have a separate roster from those panels that handle other matters under that chapter (Article 1414). The decisions of customs officers will also be subject to review (Article 510.2). Most importantly, however, the NAFTA establishes a separate dispute settlement structure to deal with conflicts between the government of one of the parties to the NAFTA and investors of another party to the agreement. This investor-state provision involves the establishment of another common roster of potential panelists and has significant implications for Mexico where these rights have been less well protected in the past. Over the long haul, this provision may turn out to be the most controversial and important provision in the NAFTA. In itself it involves the application of all the rights and protections for property characteristic of a first world legal system to a third world country. It also underscores the reality that the NAFTA is as much if not more about the protection of investor rights as it is about trade itself (Articles 1115 to 1138).

Whether or not this DSIS, as established under the NAFTA, will turn out to be the supranational institutions that may be necessary to achieve an effective liberalized trading regime, we are not yet in a place to judge. Internally, it is clear that much thought has been given to how to integrate a new and culturally distinctive society into the process. External relations between the DSIS and domestic agencies are likely to develop more slowly under the NAFTA. While the FTA's DSIS panels showed considerable deference to domestic agency decisions and this certainly contributed to its consensus approach to decision making, it will be harder to sustain this approach under the NAFTA. There is bound to be considerable suspicion in the United States and Canada over the decision-making practices of Mexican agencies as well as the competitive practices of Mexico-based firms. At the same time the proliferation of separate panel systems with their separate rosters may increase the possibility of "forum shopping" under the NAFTA itself as well as between the NAFTA and the GATT.

5.0. Conclusion

The DSIS that has been operative under the FTA and will be carried over under the NAFTA, although with significant changes, shows some important signs of growth as an effective supranational institution charged with overseeing the emerging North American trade regime. Probably the greatest success story of its internal evolution has been the avoidance of national divisions. The emergence of a norm of cooperation and consensus has given much greater legitimacy to panel remands. The panels also appear to have had some positive effect on the behaviors of domestic agencies, although the gains in this area, as might be expected, have been more modest. Finally, it can be expected that the DSIS will be seriously challenged under the NAFTA. The factors that have contributed to panel success under the FTA will be harder to sustain under the NAFTA, at least in the short term.

Notes

1. These problems are complicated by the fact that each country may have different ways of calculating whether dumping is occurring or an export subsidy is being provided. For instance, United States law governing dumping requires that the normal or undumped price must include provision for a profit of 8 percent on the part of the company making the sale. In Canada, while there is also a provision that a margin of profit exist in an undumped price, the law does not specify what that profit margin should be. Therefore, the Canadian law gives Revenue Canada some discretion as to what profit it will require whereas the U.S. law is quite specific.

2. As of the end of 1992, there had been only three cases adjudicated under Chapter 18.

3. The use of the term *binding* indicates that if the offending country fails to take the appropriate action as requested by the panel, the other party may take action to impose trade penalties of equivalent effect on any exports of the offending party. Where the economic and political resources of the two countries sharply differ as in the case of Canada and the United States, the binding criterion is of much greater value to the stronger country, which likely will be more willing to exercise its rights.

4. According to one Canadian participant in the negotiation of the FTA, his U.S. counterparts never liked or appreciated the idea of duty remission where duty is remitted if certain conditions are met. This was an approach they regarded as too interventionist.

5. It appears that the asking for an ECC hearing on the *Fresh, Chilled or Frozen Pork* decision was part of the price extracted by Congress for agreeing to grant fast-track authority to the executive for the negotiation of the NAFTA (Horlick and DeBusk, 1992). The fast-track authority is one of the means authorized for the passage of trade legislation under the U.S. Trade Act of 1974. The fast-track mechanism provides limited time periods for the passage or defeat of trade legislation, and, most importantly, the legislation cannot be amended in the process.

References

Brean, D.J.S., R.M. Bird, and M. Krauss. (1991). *Taxation of International Portfolio Investment*. Halifax: Centre for Trade Policy and Law and the Institute for Research on Public Policy.

Binational Secretariat. (1989a). *Fresh, Chilled or Frozen Pork from Canada.* USA-(19)89-1904-11.

———. (1989b). *Red Raspberries from Canada.* USA-(19)89-1904-01.

———. (1991a). *Certain Beer Originating in or Exported from the United States.* CDA-(19)91-1904-01.

———. (1991b). *Fresh, Chilled or Frozen Pork from Canada.* ECC-(19)91-1904-01USA.

Boddez, Thomas M. and Michael J. Trebilcock. (1993). *Unfinished Business: Reforming Trade Remedy Laws in North America.* Toronto: Howe Institute.

Bovard, James. (1991). *The Fair Trade Fraud: How Congress Pillages the Consumer and Decimates American Competitiveness.* New York: St. Martin's Press.

Canada Department of External Affairs. (1992). *Rules of Procedure for Article 1904 Binational Panel Reviews.* Ottawa: Queen's Printer.

Doern, G. Bruce and Brian W. Tomlin. (1991). *Faith and Fear: The Free Trade Story.* Toronto: Stoddart.

Evans, Peter B., Dietrich Rueschemeyer, and Theda Skocpol (eds.). (1985). *Bringing the State Back In.* Cambridge: Cambridge University Press.

Gold, Marc and David Leyton-Brown. (1988). *Trade-Offs on Free Trade: The Canada-U.S. Free Trade Agreement.* Toronto: Carswell.

Hogg, Peter W. (1977). *Constitutional Law of Canada.* Toronto: Carswell.

Horlick, Gary N. (1989). "The United States Antidumping System." In John H. Jackson and Edwin A. Vermulst (eds.), *Antidumping Law and Practice* (pp. 99–166). Ann Arbor: University of Michigan Press.

Horlick, Gary N. and F. Amanda DeBusk. (1992). "The Functioning of FTA Dispute Resolution Panels." In Leonard Waverman (ed.), *Negotiating and Implementing a North American Free Trade Agreement* (pp. 1–27). Vancouver: Fraser Institute/Centre for International Studies.

Magnus, Peter A. (1989). "The Canadian Antidumping System." In John H. Jackson and Edwin A. Vermulst (eds.), *Antidumping Law and Practice* (pp. 167–222). Ann Arbor: University of Michigan Press.

March, James G. and Johan P. Olsen. (1989). *Rediscovering Institutions: The Organizational Basis of Politics.* New York: Free Press.

Stone, Frank. (1984). *Canada, the GATT and the International Trade System.* Montreal: Institute for Research on Public Policy.

Woodside, Kenneth B. (1993). "Trade and Industrial Policy: Hard Choices." In Michael M. Atkinson (ed.), *Governing Canada: Institutions and Public Policy* (pp. 241–274). Toronto: Harcourt Brace Jovanovich Canada.

Yarbrough, Beth V. and Robert M. Yarbrough. (1992). *Cooperation and Governance in International Trade: The Strategic Organizational Approach.* Princeton, NJ: Princeton University Press.

7 THE TWO TRADITIONS OF INSTITUTIONAL DESIGNING: DIALOGUE VERSUS DECISION?

Stephen H. Linder
B. Guy Peters

1.0. Introduction

Practitioners of the arts of government, as well as their observers, have somewhat ambivalent views concerning the design of institutions within the public sector. On the one hand there is the "tireless tinkering" with institutions, ranging from the reform of a single institution or organization all the way to fundamental constitutional redesign. In practice, it appears that many people believe that structural reform is a worthy enterprise, given the amount of time and energy devoted to it. On the other hand, there is often profound skepticism about the real efficacy of conscious attempts at change. This skepticism is based in part on beliefs that institutions are highly resistant to change so that efforts at purposive transformation are likely to be thwarted by structural inertia. The skepticism may also be based on the belief that human capacities at understanding social structures and processes are sufficiently limited that attempts at imposing reforms may produce institutional outcomes worse than the problems they were intended to solve. In this view the best way to generate institutional change is to let it occur as an evolutionary process rather than imposing externally derived templates.

In addition to this fundamental question concerning the desirability and possibility of effective planned reform, there is also a very basic and often unstated question of "reform for what?" Different individuals may enter into a reform with very different goals and perhaps with rather different ideas of the acceptable means. The goal differences are closely associated with the diagnoses of the ills in the public sector requiring reform. Differences in diagnosis, in turn, often are functions of differences in political ideologies, professional training, or positions within the social and political system that cannot be bargained away in a political process. For example, political conservatives often argue that the public sector needs reform because it is inefficient, and consequently any reforms would be directed toward making the public sector function more like a market. On the other hand, lawyers may consider that there is inadequate accountability in the public sector so that they would suggest reforms directed toward improving popular control over politicians and civil servants. Ideological democrats would press for greater citizen involvement in identifying problems and framing policies. Thus, any analysis of institutional design must begin with the question of the desired end state of the reforms, as well as the criteria by which success would be judged.

Both the study of institutional design and the practice of designing institutions are complicated by a rivalry between two distinct traditions, each supporting a theory of design and a complementary depiction of institutions that are antithetical to the other's. While the intellectual support for these traditions draws on historical as well as philosophical currents, there is an internal coherence to each tradition that can clarify the ideas in contention and highlight what the stakes are in the designer's tacit commitment to one tradition over the other. Because one tradition — which we refer to as the *decisional tradition* — is relatively more conspicuous in the literature on institutional design, we emphasize its critique and illuminate its rival — the *dialogical tradition* (Bernstein, 1988; Handler, 1990). The former tradition tends to rely on analytical tools and formal (economic) criteria to determine the best "objective" choice, while the latter relies more on process values and politics as its criteria.

Our inquiry is also intended to separate assumptions about design from those about institutions, because some arguments over particular conceptions of design are more profitably viewed as arguments over the status and significance of institutions, and vice versa. Institutions, for example, may be defined in such a way that intrusions by an external designer are simply precluded (Denzin, 1990); conversely, design and designing may take on such conceptual prominence that the designation "institution" becomes little more than a label for an ensemble of design parameters (Hult and Walcott, 1990). Although much of the literature lies between these extremes, our intent is to counterpoise the two traditions as parallel, but competing, constructions responsible for the meanings assigned to both design and institutions. This approach permits us to attend to the tensions between these concepts while covering a great deal of intellectual ground in brief compass.

Rational choice theory is one contemporary referent for the decisional tradition, just as critical theory is for the dialogical. Elements of each find their way into our discussion. Yet it is useful to extend our treatment of decisional and dialogical themes beyond these referents in social theory, and to steer clear of the disagreements between the followers of James Coleman and of Jurgen Habermas, for example, as much of that ground is well trodden. Moreover, as this discussion is intended to analyze the basis of claims about institutional design, rather than to advance a full-blown philosophical argument, treatment of the decisional tradition by-passes much of the debate among social philosophers over modernity and loss of community. Similarly, our attention to the dialogical tradition slights its philosophical origins in antifoundationalism and the "linguistic turn" in the humanities. While these details are perhaps crucial to appreciating the depth of tension between the decisional and the dialogical, they can easily divert attention from design issues.

More is to be gained, at this point, from concentrating on design-relevant issues than either by expanding on them from a philosophical viewpoint or by introducing some new resolution, say, by advancing a postmodernist conception of institutional design. Accordingly, our treatment selects a small number of themes on which the contrast between traditions is high and relies on them for guidance in viewing and interpreting institutional design. We first consider the import of the decisional and dialogical traditions for the ways designs and designing are conceived and executed. Our attention then turns to institutions and finally to the different characterizations of institutional design under each tradition. As the conventional wisdom, approaches within the decisional tradition receive relatively closer scrutiny.

1.1. Examples

Although phrased in somewhat abstract terms, this contrast between the decisional and dialogical traditions is played out in practical politics. The decisional tradition appears more familiar to most people living in contemporary societies, but the dialogical tradition has deep roots. It is often so familiar that it is practiced without the observer being aware of its existence. If we take two characteristics – the creation of some "public space" and open deliberations about facts and values – as defining the dialogical tradition, then many self-defined communities draw on this tradition. Science, for example, functions as a community with an invisible but real public space and very open discourse about facts that entail value changes. Religious communities such as the Society of Friends and Congregationalists are governed in a manner requiring a great deal of communal "dialogue." Also some social movements, e.g. the ecology movement and countercultural movements, organize themselves in this way.

The dialogical tradition also manifests itself in government and policy making. For example, one frequent encounter between the decisional and dialogical traditions occurs in the siting of hazardous and undesirable facilities. The Department of Energy and its predecessors have invested millions of dollars determining the feasibility of nuclear power plants, attempting to maximize their safety, and promoting their use. Their advocacy has been based on the best available information and the commitment of experts. Despite this extensive rational analysis, the publics in several of the potentially affected areas have not been convinced. They have found ways to participate in the process and to divert the decisions away from their own areas (Goldstein and Schoor, 1991; Bedford, 1990). This was particularly true when the licensing proceedings were opened to new participants and began to search for consensus rather than choosing between winners and losers. Similarly, perceived failures in educational policy have provoked a variety of efforts at reform that involve the dialogical tradition. One set of these reforms have been "decisional," based on objective standards and professional expertise, such as competency testing or school choice programs. Another reform effort has been more "dialogical" relying on decentralized school management by parents and heavy community involvement in priority setting.

The two examples immediately above are perhaps at the margins of the dialogical tradition, given that the conflict is often between the public and authorities. At times community groups muster their own experts to contest the knowledge claims made by official actors. In other cases, however, expertise is simply rejected in favor of open dialogue over political values such as parental control and local autonomy. At whatever level the conflict may be occurring, these issues do demonstrate alternative conceptions of how different groups of actors believe "good" policy should be constructed.

The literature examining (and advocating) dialogical styles of policy making also contains a number of examples of the possible contrasts in policy styles. John Dryzek (1990) identifies a number of "incipient discursive designs" emerging in the mediation and alternative dispute resolution movements. Joel Handler (1990) provides four examples of the contrasting styles of policy making. In one example, there are marked contrasts in the style of education that educational experts want to provide for handicapped children and that which might best involve parents and the children themselves in the design of solutions. He points to the variety of efforts in one school district (Madison, Wisconsin) to involve parents and to provide informed advocacy for the children. His examples point to several other areas of social policy, but some of the same logic might apply to a range of other policy areas, such as the use of paid intervenors in regulatory proceedings (Gormley, 1989). Although regulatory reform of this sort has been criticized as returning economic regulation to "interest group liberalism" in which government merely validates the existing power relationships among interests (Harrington, 1988), these reforms do open the proceedings to a more active dialogue. In short, although most policy makers are accustomed to the technocratic style of making policy, there are meaningful alternatives and a whole alternative tradition that may require some consideration.

2. Concepts of Rationality and Designing

2.1. Global Versus Local

The recent challenges to epistemic claims of objectivity, appearing in some social sciences under the rubric of postpositivism, have led to a resurgence of interest in the meaning of rationality (Bernstein, 1976). Much of the current debate appears to turn on the viability of a distinction between local and global conceptions of rationality (Barnes and Bloor, 1982). Global conceptions support universal standards for judging authoritativeness of knowledge or method, while local conceptions argue for dependence of such standards on context and social setting. Under a global conception, judgments of authoritativeness have been increasingly professionalized, to the point where experts can lay claim in some matters to being the sole arbiters of what is rational, with the opinions of the lay public deemed sentimental or contradictory. Rationality under this conception is not so much a way of reasoning or a process, as an aesthetic that demands special training and admits only limited, individual access.

The global notion of rationality can be found at the core of Taylorism and the movement for technocratic planning and management in the public sector (Fischer, 1990). It prospered under the scientism of the late nineteenth and early twentieth centuries and to a large extent, as we argue below, remains central to both liberal moral theory and modernist views of human agency. Local conceptions, in contrast, are based, neither on generalizable principles nor fixed standards, but rely on adaptive forms of practical reasoning that are more immediately accessible to the nonexpert and are grounded in the values and collective experience of each community. In most of its appearances, the local conception has been adversarial: opposing Taylorism, for example, in the communal writings of Mary Parker Follett; opposing the centralized, social engineering of the Fabians in the organic planning of Patrick Geddes; and generally offering a vantage point for populist, communitarian, and romantic criticism of our modern technocratic culture and mass politics.

Although local versus global rationalities have been largely overlooked by the social sciences, notably excepting the recent "strong programme" in the sociology of science (Bloor, 1991), they have been a mainstay in anthropology, due in part to its preoccupation with cultural relativism (Marcus and Fischer, 1986). For our purposes, their presence can also be viewed as a function of anthropology's relative neglect of Weberian distinctions that cross-cut, and hence obscure, local versus global ones. Before considering Weberian conceptions, the parallel between local rationality and classical notions of politics remains to be drawn.

Global conceptions of rationality are typically averse to politics on at least three counts. First, in place of the play of contending meanings and categories that politics welcomes and that local rationality supports, global rationality depends on relatively invariant standards, objectively ascertained. This is not to suggest dogmatism on the part of the global view, so much as a commitment to a disciplined aesthetic whose application may well require inventiveness and adaptability by the expert, but without openly admitting subjectivity. Second, the communal basis of politics is eschewed in favor of the autonomous, and hence disinterested, expert whose judgment is impervious to any ties that bind. Fallibility in judgment is not denied; there are no illusions about synoptic capabilities. But when the prospects for error are high, they are better addressed through replication or critical reassessment than through a communal process of local deliberation. Conversely, local rationality incorporates the social and cultural context that helps constitute both the chooser and the choice. Deference is paid to the role of collective definition and shared discourse in bringing these socially constituted elements fully to bear on decisions. Third, to the extent that access to universal standards is framed as a technical problem demanding particular expertise, the usual political impetus to involve more rather than fewer people and to assume that each can contribute their own values or experience in defining standards, is stifled (Barber, 1984).

The reactions to the technocratic domination of policy by elites have taken at least two forms. These have been to some degree a function of ideology and to some degree a function of intellectual fashions of the times in which they were framed. One reaction was the advocacy of large-scale popular direct participation as the means of making public decisions. This is associated with the political left and was characteristic of the political debates of the 1960s and the 1970s, although it certainly has been reasserted more recently. The second reaction is more individualistic, and relies on individual consumer choices – for example, through voucher programs as an alternative to imposed policy choices. This stance is more associated with the political right and was characteristic of much of the political rhetoric of the 1980s. Although worlds apart ideologically these views converge around the idea of restricting the power of technical and political elites to dominate the policy-making process.

2.2. Technical Versus Social

The more traditional treatment of rationality, due largely to Max Weber, shifts attention from claims of universal standards and context to the connection between technique and values. Although Weber's original discussion considers both means and ends as proper candidates for careful reasoning and scrutiny, his term, instrumental rationality, has been narrowed over time to address only questions of means (Kloppenberg, 1986). This narrowing has set the stage for efforts to reintroduce the question of the rationality of ends into the conventional treatment of means. A rationality of means, or technical rationality, has become synonymous with calculations of relative performance for a given set of ends. While different criteria have been applied by different disciplines, the efficiency criterion of the neoclassical synthesis in economics is perhaps the most widely used, as it combines the rationality criteria of psychology with respect to preference orderings with those of sociology, with respect to social states. Further, the engineering and design sciences have placed technical rationality at the core of their efforts, not only for advantages in relative simplicity afforded by goal-directed, deterministic modeling, but also for the institutionalization of a principal-agent relationship that legitimates and rewards professional expertise through client service.

The alternative conception of rationality applied to ends, which John Friedmann terms *social rationality*, draws on the same intellectual tradition but speaks not to consistency or performance but to critical process (Friedmann, 1987). It appears in Dilthey and Weber, among the pragmatists and progressive era social planners, and later in Habermas. For most of its adherents, however, the pursuit of social rationality is either distinct from, or an alternative to, modern liberal politics. While efforts to infuse liberal politics with elements of social responsibility continue to draw on the public good as a touchstone for reform, they also tend to concentrate on the reform of our existing political institutions and to rely on advocacy as its principal vehicle (Bellah, 1991).

The essential difference between rationality as calculating means and as devising ends is that the latter is seen as a collective enterprise. Assuming diversity among individual ends — attributable, depending on whose account we follow, to differences in motivations, natural endowments, socialization, experience, or moral sensibilities — attaining a rationality of ends necessarily entails a collective process supporting deliberative, critical assessment and promoting convergence among individual ends. There is some divergence, however, among the proponents of social rationality that may account, at least in part, for its apparent diffuseness and ambiguity relative to the clarity and prominence afforded technical rationality.

For Progressive-era social planners, like Rexford Tugwell, social rationality is captured by the rubric of the public interest and could be imputed by an expert without recourse to any actual collective transformation of individual ends (Friedmann, 1987). For pragmatists, perhaps at the other extreme, individual ends are developed and refined in the pursuit of communal ones. Accordingly, without a collective, deliberative process there could be no rationality of ends for either the individual or the collectivity (West, 1987). For some historicists like Dilthey, the collective character of social rationality could best be served by a well-refined historical sensibility; an interpretive process of discovering the shared meaning of values serves as the vehicle for mutual understanding, and possibly convergence, rather than any formalized process of public deliberation (Kloppenberg, 1986). For others, like Habermas, social rationality only emerges from public dialogue that meets universal requirements for open discourse and equal participation (Dryzek, 1987). Here, the hermeneutical emphasis on sorting out meaningfulness of historically situated, collective values appears at odds with the formal dialogic requirements of recent critical theories. Both are compatible to some extent with pragmatic assumptions about interaction between individual and collective ends but share none of the elitism of technical expertise that animated New Deal social planners.

2.3. Contrasting the Conceptions: First Cut

The design implications of these differences and of the basic contrast between social and technical rationality can best be clarified by drawing on our earlier distinction between global and local conceptions. A summary display of the fourfold combinations that can result appears in Table 7.1. A global conception of technical rationality bases the assessment of means on the invocation of criteria and standards that are thought to transcend the problem setting as well as the critical judgment of the actors involved. These elements are not simply assumptions that can be added or dropped as the situation warrants. They represent a foundational commitment to principles whose justification has become self-evident in light of their rendering as both universal and certain. The entire scheme of assessment then becomes dependent on their presumed validity and unquestioned consignment to the background. As we will see, the rational choice approach to design typically is framed by technical rationality and the treatment of institutions as means. More important, it posits several key principles – one related to motivation (utility maximization) and another to the proper linkage between means and ends (efficiency) – that are taken as universals. Under a global conception of technical rationality, design activity becomes formalized and deterministic. Once a set of procedures can be specified, the logic can be followed uniformly and expected to yield designs of a given quality. Design itself becomes routinized and synonymous with other modeling tasks or familiar production processes.

A local conception of technical rationality retains the focus on means but abandons transcendent principles in favor of claims that are situationally specific and hence must be uniquely characterized through some actor's critical judgment. In contrast to the rational choice approach, the status of assumptions about motivation and the proper linkage of means to ends are left to depend on the context. Further, without the support of these assumptions, fixed ends give way to variable, local requirements. Means then are assessed with respect to how well they meet these requirements, with the normative status of "meet" in this instance derived from the

Table 7.1. Concepts of Rationality: The Basis of Designing

	Technical	Social
Global	Rational choice	Universal pragmatics
Local	Contingency models	Hermeneutical inquiry

setting and its interpretation. As applied to design, this local conception of technical rationality represents a contingency approach: the quality of design is predicated on an adequate depiction of the problem context rather than movement toward an efficiency standard (Bobrow and Dryzek, 1987). The assessment of means becomes complicated not only by the potential varieties of context but also by the resulting absence of any transcendent basis on which to judge the adequacy of their characterization. This indeterminacy is compounded by the demands of the technical side for a best-fitting design, often without a clear idea of what fit entails. The designer may have a blueprint of sorts, not unlike the one drawn under the global conception, but in the local instance she can never know ahead of time whether it is the right one. Asking people who share the context can sometimes help, but not always. And not every designer will feel the need to ask.

A global conception of social rationality subsumes the treatment of means under the assessment of ends. The typical assessment under this regime is structured by universal standards but, unlike the rational choice approach, consists of a collective deliberative process. To the extent that expert judgment plays a role, it is in the establishment and assurance of the basic conditions for effective deliberation, consistent with the dictates of the prevailing standards. For many critical theorists, these standards are based on Habermas's universal pragmatics – conditions requisite to undistorted and authentic communication in the public sphere. Intersubjective agreement coming out of this process is thought to combine the normative appeal of democratic participation with the critical and reflective capacity of open dialogue to validate truth claims and legitimate collective ends (see Forester, 1985). On one level, designs might simply replicate this kind of deliberative arena in other settings. Alternatively, the deliberations themselves might be taken up with fashioning means as a way of sorting out the implications of particular ends. This mode of discursive design is done without a blueprint, relying on procedural standards as the principal points of reference (Dryzek, 1990). There is a measure of indeterminacy here; however, it arises, not from the contextual dilemma of the contingency approach in resolving questions of fit, but from prospects for collective convergence on a particular ensemble of means and ends. This is design by multiple designers rather than by formula, absent the constraints of fixed ends and restricted access. And yet, even without a blueprint, there is reassurance in having a well-defined process fashioned according to universal principles that can bestow validity and legitimacy on whatever results. Moreover, in some instances, designing such a process may be enough. In the course of principled deliberation, problems may be solved and resolutions struck that obviate the need for new designs or new institutions.

The two traditions diverge in part over the nature of the crucial criteria for the selection of designs. For the *decisional* tradition the criteria are largely substantive and technical, and any process that enables these characteristics to be explored most fully and with the fewest barriers to objective "truth" emerging is acceptable and desirable. For the *dialogical* tradition, on the other hand, process considerations are the most important criteria for a "good" policy. In this latter tradition the actual technical quality of the decision is either assumed to be guaranteed by an open process or to be secondary to the inherent social value of that open process.[1]

A local conception of social rationality dispenses with such reassurance by abandoning claims of universality for its organizing principles. There is still confidence in the power of collective discourse, but the preconditions and contours of the process are left to local judgment. Again, designing is relatively free-wheeling, without benefit of structure (or constraints) imposed by technical treatments of fixed ends. In this instance, however, the process and, by extension, its products represent collective adaptations to context. Such adaptation might take the form of community-based designing, with multiple, citizen designers striving toward convergence on an ensemble of means and ends according to local conventions and traditions (Barber, 1984). The contingency approach's problem of finding the best fitting means is resolved by definition, as context effectively filters the means at issue and shapes their adjustment to local ends. This approach takes seriously the communitarian's confidence in the virtues of local democracy and is less concerned with the analytical requirements of an ideal speech situation, despite its warrant of quality in intersubjective communications (Handler, 1986).

The emphasis here is not on the best designs in a technical sense, or even on the best discourse around designing, but rather on the normative issues of appropriateness and meaningfulness. The most appropriate designs from this perspective will be those that best suit collective constructions of local purpose; that is, they will be socially rational. The most meaningful designs, however, will not only be appropriate in this sense, but will build on local experience and convey a sense of the community's identity and moral order. Nevertheless, whether meaningfulness and appropriateness are to be prized by the hypothetical designer uncommitted to one form of rationality over another, might well depend on the thing to be designed. To the extent that institutions, for example, are viewed as rule-based mechanisms serving externally defined ends, their design can be most directly accomplished through a rational choice approach based on global conceptions of technical rationality. Once the character of institutions is understood not as instrumental but as moral, this approach becomes too thin and the setting of ends and weighing of context moves to the foreground. The next section examines the relevance of moral premises to our understanding of institutions and their design.

3.0. Moral Premises and Institutions

3.1. Moral Versus Instrumental Definitions

The importance of moral premises to the designing of institutions rests on their central role in institutional definitions. Efforts to differentiate entities called "institutions" from everyday organizations generally involve an imputation of meaning and purpose inadequately conveyed in a simple depiction of skeletal structures and functions. Institutions are typically thought to *embody* particular values rather than merely serving them instrumentally and, as a result, have the potential to affirm or transform conceptions of the self and social practices that remain inaccessible to the regular functioning of most organizations (Dimaggio and Powell, 1991). Even in the rule-oriented conceptions of institutions (Ostrom, 1990) there is a strong element of moral claims on individual participants in the institution. Accordingly, even relatively thin definitions can be expected to engage certain normative claims by assumption. The claims may be utilitarian, for example, or may invoke implicit premises about persons as goal-directed or voluntaristic. Nonetheless, institutional status appears to carry with it expectations of cultural significance, varying in degree perhaps from some incidental, noninstrumental, purpose to the full reflection of a particular moral order, in addition to any presumptions of temporal continuity.

Designing institutions, as opposed to organizations, then is likely to entail more than structural manipulations alone. In the first place, institutional design will involve the structuring of the "logic of appropriateness" that will guide the institution and its members (March and Olsen, 1989). Likewise, attempts at institutional change through design will require conscious efforts at changing the cultural and ideational elements of the institution as well as its structural elements. When applied to the formation or reform of institutions, design-inspired manipulations should, by definition, have implications that extend well beyond institutional boundaries. Thus, institutional change will be at once more difficult than organizational change but, if successful, is likely to be enduring.

Anticipating these implications and factoring them into the design process are added burdens characterizing institutional design work. Further, one's commitment to a particular kind of definition or conception of an institution will set the focus of design activity. If, for example, we define institutions broadly to consist of socially embedded practices and frames, then design must be carried out, at least in part, at the level of symbolic forms, addressing modes of discourse and socially constructed meaning. By contrast, if institutions are viewed as historically contingent responses to collective action problems, then design must address modes of social learning and collective choice as a preface to any structural change. From this perspective, the more expansive the definition in terms of cultural significance, the more broadly focused the set of design considerations must be. In the extreme, institutions can become synonymous with cultural meanings and practices and thus beyond the reach of designers intent on reengineering an institution's organizational features. In these instances, the focus for design shifts to the broader canvass of cultural change as the medium of institutional reformation. Efforts by Bellah, Massen, Sullivan, Swidler, and Tipton (1985) to excavate "habits of the heart" as an indigenous cultural resource for enabling the structural reform of American institutions offer a prominent example of such premises.

For our consideration of intellectual traditions bearing on design, institutions will be understood as neither wholly immutable nor fully plastic. By this construction, design considerations are admissible and consequential, on the one hand, and are seen to involve something more than mechanical calculations, on the other. In short, the designer has a role to play, whether an endogenous or exogenous one, and the complexity of her script will vary with the normative assumptions behind her definition of institutions. Paralleling our earlier treatment of rationality and designing, we now turn to the connection between these normative assumptions grounded in moral theory and conceptions of design-susceptible institutions.

Once the character of institutions is understood not as instrumental but as moral, the rational choice approach becomes too thin, and setting purposes and weighing context move to the foreground. This is the view taken by the "new institutionalism" literature. The argument there is that organizations can best be understood as governed by the logic of appropriateness that is in essence a moral statement about purpose and that provides a meaning for other actions of the institution. Without understanding that embedded moral logic, it is not possible to understand the behavior of institutions or their occupants.

3.2. Concepts of Moral Agency and Institutions

As with the distinction between technical and social rationality, moral theory can also be cast in at least two countervailing traditions, one featuring decisional themes and the other dialogical ones. Additionally, we find that our second distinction between global and local conceptions translates easily into a contrast between the universal versus the particular (Selznick, 1992). Although in this case, the distinction applies to the presumed standing of moral claims, it also has a direct bearing on the relevance of context for designing institutions. Conceptions of local rationality, for example, prove to be most compatible with particularistic moral claims, and both defer to contextual sources, such as experience and tradition for validation.

The prevailing dichotomization of moral theory originates in the ongoing debate between Rawls, responsible for revitalizing liberal moral theory, and his neo-Aristotelean critics, many of whom have been lumped together as communitarians in deference to their anti-individualist sentiments (Mulhall and Swift, 1992). Earlier distinctions between utilitarian and deontological systems, despite their foothold in the social sciences, appear subsumed by the liberal camp as variations on the same individualist theme (Kymlicka, 1989). Similarly, emotivism, a perspective reasserting the fact-value separation through claims that moral judgment can only convey preferences, attitudes, or feelings without rational grounding, falls under a liberal aegis rather than a communitarian one (MacIntyre, 1981). Though practically a footnote to recent moral theory, this perspective looms large in contemporary accounts of institutions and will be dealt with later.

The label *communitarian* has lost much of its precision through overuse. It has been attached to writers both ancient and modern who champion the ideal of community, whether under the guise of reviving the polis or classical republic, realizing a democratic community, or fashioning a moral commonwealth (Lasch, 1988). It has also been extended to critics of modernity, of capitalist industrialization, and of our acquisitive, consumer culture. Feminists, populists, social democrats, civic republicans, and even traditional conservatives find common cause in opposing the atomism and autonomy of a liberal moral order in favor of a collective quest for mutuality and solidarity (Fraser, 1989; Glendon, 1991; Gray, 1986; Nisbet, 1986), but calling them all communitarians stretches the term beyond repair. As this is not the proper place to sort all of this out, we abandon the liberal-communitarian dichotomy for a simpler distinction between individualist and communal moral frameworks that more closely parallels our contrast between decisional and dialogical traditions.

For our purposes, the moral premises of relevance to institutional definition are principally ontological; they relate to assumptions about the self, its development, and its relation to others through social arrangements (Fay, 1987). We first consider the individualist and communal versions of the self and then refine them with a separation between claims of universal and of particularist standing. In so doing, we replicate analytically our fourfold depiction of rationality, and its import for designing, with a treatment of moral premises and their link to how we view institutions. The final task will be to bring these two pieces together to reassess the relative neglect in design work of the dialogical tradition in favor of the decisional one.

3.3. Individualist Versus Communal Values

Most depictions of the individualist view of the self trace their origins to Locke and its refinement by Kant and other Enlightenment figures (Arblaster, 1984). Two key ingredients of this conception are detachment and choice. The self exists prior to and is thus detached – conceptually – from social conventions, affiliations, or arrangements that might hinder the clarification of ends and interests. Choices for this "unencumbered self" then span the selection of social attachments that might be instrumental for the advancement of self-defined ends (Sandel, 1982). For some theorists, choice extends to the ends themselves, being revised and refined through empirical trial and error rather than simply intuited (Kymlicka, 1989). In either case, the self is morally autonomous, and the establishment and pursuit of ends can, and perhaps should, occur independently of the pursuits of others.

The communal view traces its origins to Aristotle, to the medieval revival of republicanism, and to Rousseau; in contrast to the individualist view, its basic version of the self warrants attachment rather than detachment, and a process of discovery rather than choice (MacIntyre, 1981). Here, the self both constitutes and is constituted by its culture and community. As a result, a better understanding of the self and its purposes becomes bound to a better understanding of these values and social arrangements; the roles, affiliations, and commitments of context provide a framework within which ends and purposes can best be discovered and critically assessed (Selznick, 1992). This process of discovery cannot be done in isolation but entails both reflection and dialogue with others who share, and hence mutually constitute, the same context. From this perspective, autonomous choice regarding ends is a misleading and potentially disabling fiction. Not only do choices invariably reflect a particular historically grounded setting — whether acknowledged or not — but, to express meaningful ends, they must first be discovered and validated through interaction with others.

The psychology implicit in the individualist view treats ends more as motives than as occasions for reflection; to the extent that refinements in ends are admitted, these are solitary ventures to accommodate shifting constraints or persistent failures. Moreover, this view poses a divided self whose multiple ends may be contradictory and subject to tradeoffs. For neo-Kantians, the divided self requires transcendent restraints, in the form of unconditional imperatives, because the indiscriminant pursuit of private ends may be harmful to the self or others. For utilitarians, the divided self serves as the ontological basis for their tolerant yet divided community; moral resolutions of conflicting ends follows the same formula, whether for individuals or for communities, of tallying prospective consequences and seeking protection from involuntary harms. Self-fulfillment is thought to depend on the freedom to define and pursue one's own ends. The burden for attaining these self-defined ends, however, falls to the proper choice of the necessary means. Accordingly, the primary function of knowledge in this scheme is to enable reasoning about means rather than to illuminate ends (Fay, 1987).

The communal assumptions about individual psychology, at least in their pragmatic version, pose a unified, growing self, whose ends and capabilities should be in balance rather than conflict (Westbrook, 1991). Appropriate ends must be discovered and validated, not privately, but in concert with others who share the traditions and social arrangements that help constitute the self. Socially defined obligations then become an essential part of an intersubjective process guiding one's reflection on ends. For critical theorists, the intersubjective process lies at the heart of true moral judgment; its adoption and operation are crucial to sorting out individual ends but, more important, to the rational direction of the community (Habermas, 1990). For the pragmatists and neo-Aristotelians alike, the development of the self appears more as a precondition for, rather than byproduct of, the moral betterment of the community. In effect, democratic participation in public deliberation — a grounded version of the intersubjective process — is thought to build the character necessary to harmonize one's ends and guide the community (Shalin, 1992; West, 1987).

From this perspective, self-fulfillment takes the form, not of satisfaction of personal wants, but of self-realization or the cultivation of certain qualities of character. To realize one's full potential, contrary to the individualist view, freedom of choice is not enough; it must be coupled with collective association and open, critical discourse. The source and expression of values then resides in the dialogical process itself rather than in choice making or its consequences. The purpose of knowledge from this angle is not to permit better control over means, for example, by identifying avenues for manipulating certain causal relations. Instead, the purpose is educative and potentially transformative, assisting in clarification of ends and their implications for social and institutional change (Fay, 1987).

From the individualist view, institutions are social arrangements that can be critically scrutinized with detachment and neutrality. As the self is thought to be constituted independently of particular institutions, one is permitted an external vantage point for judgment insulated from the sway of institutional values. Further, with self-development linked to choosing or fashioning appropriate means, institutions come to be valued instrumentally as vehicles for coordinating or multiplying efforts to attain particular ends. Institutions are thus judged for their performance with respect to these ends and not for their role in helping to form them. Now, consider how this view is qualified under universal and particularist conceptions.

3.4. Universal Versus Particularist Conceptions

The universal conception of the individualist view effectively magnifies the reach and significance of choice for social arrangements by assuming that a viable moral self exists apart from, or prior to, any such arrangements. From this perspective, human agency with regard to institutions knows few bounds. The attachments that might otherwise protect institutions through moral sentiments, such as empathy, gratitude, or involvement, are assumed not to operate. Moreover, in detaching the self from the institution, the individualist is assumedly removing the institution's moral content, leaving an empty shell. Most every institution then becomes subject to purposive change, and ones that are not can be replaced with new ones. The few bounds on agency that are recognized are self-imposed in conformity with either procedures or principles that have universal – that is, extrainstitutional – validity.

For utilitarians, the bounds are set by a confluence of individual ends. No matter how this confluence is formed, whether through aggregation, calculation, or thought experiment, collective ends emerge that narrow the range of morally sanctioned consequences. Consistent with the individualist view, however, these collective ends are afforded no special, moral status other than as a direct generalization of individual ends. Similarly, for the neo-Kantian, bounds are adduced from intuitively obvious principles that generalize, not from one individual to many, but from one situation to every situation (Kymlicka, 1989). And the narrowing that occurs is directed more to the character of permissible choices than to sanctioning particular consequences. Still, both utilitarians and neo-Kantians mirror the detachment of individuals from institutions in their claims of universality for bounds they set on individual choice. Ruling out a few purposes or avenues for attainment does little to alter the freedom of invention and manipulation that these views assign to individuals, essentially treating institutions as either morally neutral devices or vessels to be filled with generalized purposes of individuals.

The particularist conception, identified earlier with emotivism, eschews universal claims, as well as any procedures or principles that might reinforce their validity. Again, the institution appears as the product of individual choices. According to the particularist conception, however, the choices are neither aggregated nor generalized, but encoded as local, ongoing agreements – typically, of a contractual sort for improving coordination, resolving conflict, or responding to external conditions – that bind individuals to certain future behaviors. Detachment of the self from institutions, in this instance, connotes a decomposition of the institution into constituent selves rather than a moral separation. Institutions are composed of, and gain their identify from, the many selves that populate them, but the identity of the selves is limited a priori to the manifest components of ego psychology. This approach, referred to by Grafstein as "conventionalism" for its pervasiveness in the social science literature, not only embraces methodological individualism as an ordering principal for reducing wholes to component parts, but also "psychologizes" action as behaviors induced exclusively by cognitive and affective dispositions (Grafstein, 1991).

While these dispositions, including attitudes, beliefs, and motives, may bear certain similarities across individuals, the particularist neither assigns them moral import nor views them as a defensible product of reason or self-reflection. The moral aspect of the institution is left to reside in the character of the joint commitment by participants to forgo some ends to enhance the prospects of others. The strict detachment of the self under the universalist conception is mitigated by having commitments based on an idiosyncratic set of dispositions define the institution. The context for commitment in this instance is comprised both of the bundles of dispositions that others are seen to represent and to the historical and cultural influences that have shaped them. The atomism of private ends and the instrumental character of institutions largely remain. There is no intimation that the institution might have reciprocal influence on the development of dispositions or might support personal growth. And yet, the particularist conception acknowledges that the individual's role as participant is likely to delimit her choices. More important, basing these choices in psychological dispositions rather than rational calculation permits the contextual influences on these dispositions to influence the formation of the institution indirectly. From a design perspective, the institution becomes less plastic than the universalist would claim and subject to a larger measure of determinism, ultimately as a function of the biases and attachments of the participants involved.

3.5. Contrasting the Conceptions: Second Cut

The second set of contrasting conceptions, this time focusing on moral agency as the key premise in institutional definitions, is depicted in Table 7.2. From the communal as opposed to the individualist view, the appropriateness of locating the basis of institutions in individual dispositions depends in part on the source and character of these dispositions. To the extent that these dispositions reflect a more general context of traditions and values of an historically rooted community, then particularists within the communal view would agree up to this point with their brethren among the individualists. The communal particularists, however, would then extend the concept of negotiated agreement to take on a transformative potential as a process offering critical scrutiny of ends and capabilities, thereby contributing to self-realization (Selznick, 1992). In other words, we move from an ego psychology driven by private, closely held ends to a functional one featuring the contribution of collective processes to the development of the self and its ends. Further, these processes become more than multilateral negotiations over the placement of constraints; they must involve open discourse and a preoccupation with common rather than private ends. With these refinements, Grafstein's "conventionalists" evolve into communitarians who model their institutions after

Table 7.2. Concepts of Moral Agency: The Basis for Defining Institutions

	Individualist	Communal
Universalist	Utilitarian/neo-Kantian	Discourse ethics
Particularist	Emotivist/conventionalist	Communitarian ethics

diverse conceptions of a reflective, democratic community (Grafstein, 1991; Mulhall and Swift, 1992). From this perspective, the conventionalist portrayal of institutions as instrumental devices grossly understates their potential counterinfluence on the would-be (re-)designer. An institution that reflects the moral reference points of its context is positioned to draw on the strength and stability of that context. An encounter with an institution then becomes a special case of more general interchanges with the norms and conventions underpinning it. Devising new institutions or remaking old ones necessarily encounters all of the reflected elements of context and are thus best approached through a collective dialogue that simultaneously engages the broader context. Taking on the moral underpinnings of an institution, however, cannot be easily accomplished by an outsider insulated from the values she hopes to affect. In the process of remaking their institutions, communitarians – depicted here as communal particularists – fully expect to remake themselves.

The universalist version of this communal view not only formalizes what the appropriate collective process would look like, but also narrows the conceptions of its institutional expression. The most elaborate schema of this type is due to Habermas (1990). His "discourse ethics" is at home with the universality claimed by the neo-Kantians but is more particular about how such claims are validated. Critical self-reflection is not nearly enough; there must be an intersubjective process based, not in aggregation as the utilitarians would have it, but in structured dialogue. The interests of the particularists in bringing the richness of the context to bear on such determinations, while not entirely ignored, are relegated to the implementation phases. Here, the process is governed by relatively abstract criteria intended to assure full participation while guarding against manipulation for private ends. Unlike the utilitarians and neo-Kantians, the self is not taken as detached. On the contrary, the self must interact with others and is constituted in large part through such interaction; its moral relevance rests on the sharing of perspectives and resulting empathy that the dialogic process is intended to foster (Habermas, 1990). In a sense, however, the process itself becomes detached by invoking universal criteria that elevate it above the normative vagaries of any given setting. For Habermas, the most important criteria involve rules of argumentation, setting the proper conditions for collective reasoning and moral assessment.

By detaching the process of structured dialogue from local conditions, however, the sources of conscience and moral judgment favored by the particularists, including traditions, social conventions and practices, and the institutional forms that reflect and reinforce them, move to the foreground for critical scrutiny (Van Der Burg, 1990). Rather than building on these elements of context, the elements themselves must be justified by reasoned argument. In effect, each institution's moral standing comes to depend on whether it can survive a rule-governed process offering challenges to its form and rationale. Institutional status is effectively conferred on those entities that can pass this muster. Consequently, the choices or dispositions of a putative institution's participants matter only indirectly for its definition. What counts decisively, from this perspective, is a determination made by collective, but appropriately structured, deliberation. This amounts to an operational definition in a literal sense. Unlike utilitarian or neo-Kantian operations, however, the outcome is largely indeterminate; knowing the private interests of individuals ahead of time is of very little use in knowing how the process – one expected more to alter than to reflect such interests – will turn out. Further, the process is biased away from exclusively instrumental considerations. The institutions (or designs) that emerge from this process, by definition, are seen to embody moral expectations and convey collective purpose.

4.0. Two Traditions of Institutional Design

As we noted earlier, there is a larger ordering across our two families of concepts that further structures considerations in institutional design. Consider the left columns of both Tables 7.1 and 7.2, labeled "technical rationality" and "individualist moral agency," respectively. Both concepts have coincident attachments to choice making and instrumental logic; they are what some commentators would call manifestations of modernity. For our purposes, we need see them only as representative elements in an historically rooted intellectual tradition that features decisions by purposive actors as a central theme. As an intellectual tradition, the influence of these attachments becomes more pervasive and diffuse as the attachments themselves recede into the background. They become part of the conventional wisdom, or, to use a Lakatosian metaphor, they move from the provisional outer belt to the hard core of the research program. The significance of this decisional tradition in defining the appropriate pathways for design can best be appreciated from the vantage point of its countervailing alternative, the dialogical tradition.

The dialogical tradition subsumes the concepts appearing in the right columns of Tables 7.1 and 7.2. Attachments in this case are to public discourse and collective, as opposed to individual, agency; as a tradition, it draws on both premodern and postmodern themes. Although the two traditions have crossed paths on occasion, most recently in the Progressive era (Kloppenberg, 1986), they remain in tension as a part of our indigenous intellectual heritage and continue to serve as fresh sources for social and political movements (Selznick, 1992). While largely dormant through the cold war era, the dialogical tradition is enjoying a resurgence of interest not seen since the 1920s (Blake, 1990). Its basic appeal is to recast the governance of institutions as a democratic, communal task, repudiating rule by private interest, bureaucratic structures, or the authority of expertise.

The process of designing the institutions that reflect these commitments, and others based in Tables 7.1 and 7.2, are similarly bound by them. To the extent that the same assumptions underpin both designing and governance – designing's institutional outcome – their respective forms can be expected to resemble one another closely. Participatory forms of governance, for example, become the most likely progeny of participatory design. This connection is one of the key insights gained from tracing institutional design to its conceptual roots in a particular intellectual tradition. It is not uncommon, however, to move from the dialogical tradition to the conventional wisdom, representing the decisional tradition, when it comes to either designing or governance, but not necessarily both. Nonparticipatory designing, for example, may lead to participatory forms of governance, and vice versa. The problem with this opportunistic mixing is its contradictory premises.[2] In terms of our tables, the mixing effectively combines the right column of one table with the left column of the other.

One might well abandon concepts of social rationality or communal agency, for example, to make designing more efficient or more technically correct and thus less discursive (discourse-based), with the intent of fashioning a discursive form of institutional governance. As instrumental values, however, efficiency and technical precision have currency principally within the decisional tradition. Ironically, from within that tradition, discursive forms in general stand on very shaky ground. One is compelled then to return to the dialogical tradition to find value in discursive forms. Once there, given the tradition's high regard for discursive over instrumental forms, it becomes unclear how one would justify leaving in the first place. Either one is oblivious to the contradictions in premises, or there is some third, opportunistic tradition that values expediency over the commitments of the other two traditions. Given our attention to premises, obliviousness is the more central to our concerns.

Consistency within traditions appears as a recurring dilemma for reform-minded intellectuals anxious to transform institutions into less oppressive or more democratic forms but contented to employ nondemocratic means to do so. Design may be a centralized function, informed by technocratic rather than deliberative processes, even if the intended product is itself a deliberative process. Similarly, by crossing traditions, institutions could be designed to foster greater participation, without permitting any participation in the designing. Part of the impetus to cross traditions, effectively separating the premises of designing from those of the thing-designed, may simply be elitist, valorizing the role of the enlightened expert or bemoaning the apathy or false consciousness of nonexperts (Friedmann, 1991). More generally, the presumption that theory can be separated from practice gives one a stepping stone of sorts between the traditions; designing becomes the theory side and the resulting form of institutional governance, the practice. While the decisional tradition accepts this dichotomy, and thus may permit some opportunistic mixing of premises on the designer's part, the dialogical tradition, especially in its pragmatic version, explicitly rejects it (West, 1987). In effect, the dialogical tradition demands greater loyalty of its adherents and finds inconsistency among premises to weaken rather than strengthen its claims.

Table 7.3 summarizes the two traditions and their application to designing and institutional governance. Note that in crossing traditions, one moves along either diagonal rather than down a given column of the table. Further, each column in Table 7.3 is based on the premises listed in the respective columns of Tables 7.1 and 7.2, the decisional tradition drawing on the left columns and the dialogical on the right ones. Global (local) conceptions of rationality will generally accompany universalist (particularist) views of moral agency and constitute a coherent emphasis within one tradition or the other; accordingly, the first row of Tables 7.1 and 7.2 go together, as do the second rows. Finally, the entries in Table 7.3 are intended as a sample of the possible characterizations of institutional governance and designing under each tradition; they should be viewed as suggestive rather than definitive and might easily be replaced with different characterizations drawn from the literatures of each tradition. The important elements of difference highlighted in this sample of entries include

Table 7.3. Traditions and Institutional Design

	Decision Tradition	Dialogic Tradition
Governance	Elite choice-making	Discursive steering
Designing	Expert formulation	Forums for reasoned arguments

greater emphasis on selective rather than inclusive participation within the decisional tradition and a process focus on language and argument in the dialogical tradition. Translating these into concrete examples would entail a return to the premises of Tables 7.1 and 7.2 to consider the import of global-universalist conceptions as compared to local-particularist ones.

While a full elaboration of the possible forms of designing and institutional governance that might emerge from these conceptions cannot be undertaken here, a few comments on the kinds of forms that have recently emerged under the dialogical tradition might be suggestive. Within some oppositional social movements tied to feminism and ecologism, there is an emphasis on democratic over bureaucratic organization, on discourse rooted in context over formalized rules, and on the transformative character of involvement in the movement (Young, 1990). There is a growing literature on the formation and accommodation of these movements that seems to parallel the literature on industrial democracy and labor history of a generation ago. Perhaps more relevant to the task of institutional design, is the neofunctionalist work of Niklaus Luhmann, Gunther Teubner, and other continental sociologists of law on the juridification of the modern welfare state (see Teubner, 1986). Their appeal to the dialogical tradition takes the form of "reflexive law," advocating informal procedures for resolving conflicts and facilitating communication in lieu of formal rules and regulated relationships. The development in the U.S. of alternative dispute resolution methods, private orderings, and mediation would appear to follow the same logic.

Given the relative prominence of the decisional tradition and its compatibility with liberalism, and modernity more generally, the dialogical tradition offers and alternative set of premises that provides a coherent focal point for dissent and social criticism. Whether in search of community, *Gemeinschaft*, or social justice, dialogical premises appear to promise a sufficiently different social and moral order to support the claims of a wide variety of critics and reformers. Further, for American intellectuals, the tradition is both familiar, given its resonance in Jeffersonian republicaism and American pragmatism (Blake, 1990), and novel, in view of its appeal to the affirmative postmoderns (Rosenau, 1992).

5.0. Conclusion

The design of institutions is usually considered an exercise in structural manipulation and, perhaps, changes of rules. We hope that this discussion has emphasized the fundamental normative element of institutions and with that the normative element of institutional design. This normative component makes the task of design all the more difficult because it requires structuring a set of value premises to guide the institution and its role occupants. Further, these normative elements within institutions are not transient but often are linked to fundamental philosophical and ideological traditions within political systems. This means that any design choice may involve the choice of whole systems of thought, not just the simple choice of a structure or organization.

We have outlined two alternative viewpoints of institutions and their design that can be seen as dividing much of our thought about institutions and about governance more generally. The dichotomy between these views is perhaps drawn overly sharply, but that is done in order to highlight the tensions that exist in our collective thinking about governance, and the implications of the commitment to one or the other perspective. These alternative traditions are also linked to a variety of ethical and theoretical systems that influence the management of governments, and the process of making decisions in liberal, democratic states. Unless the very basic issues involved in the designer's commitment to one or the other of these systems is understood adequately, there is the possibility of attempting to act on contradictory normative premises while designing and the misdirection of public effort.

Recognition of these alternative traditions also raises questions about the role of the analyst as designer. The dialogical tradition questions the legitimacy of designer as detached outsider bringing "objective knowledge" to bear on others' institutions. In its stead, the designer is cast in a minor role, setting a larger process into motion rather than controlling it. Rather than engineer, the designer is animateur.

Notes

1. For a discussion of the importance of procedural criteria as opposed to utilitarian considerations of process see Chan and Miller (1991).

2. There ultimately will be a need to establish in some metatheoretic manner, the conditions most conducive to the operation of one or the other of these paradigms (Linder and Peters, 1991; 1992).

References

Arblaster, Anthony. (1984). *The Rise and Decline of Western Liberalism.* New York: Basil Blackwell.

Barber, Benjamin. (1984). *Strong Democracy*. Berkeley: University of California Press.

Barnes, B. and David Bloor. (1982). "Relativism, Rationalism, and the Sociology of Knowledge." In M. Hollis and S. Lukes. (eds.), *Rationality and Relativism* (pp. 21–47). Oxford: Blackwell.

Bedford, Henry F. (1990). *Seabrook Station: Citizen Politics and Nuclear Power*. Amherst: University of Massachusetts Press.

Bellah, Robert, Richard Massen, William Sullivan, Ann Swidler, and Steven Tipton. (1985). *Habits of the Heart: Individualism and Commitment in American Life*. Berkeley: University of California Press.

Bellah, Robert, et al. (1991). *The Good Society*. Berkeley: University of California Press.

Bernstein, Richard. (1976). *The Restructuring of Social and Political Theory*. Philadelphia: University of Pennsylvania Press.

———. (1988). *Beyond Objectivism and Relativism*. Philadelphia: University of Pennsylvania Press.

Blake, Casey. (1990). *Beloved Community*. Chapel Hill: University of North Carolina Press.

Bloor, David. (1991). *Knowledge and Social Imagery* (2nd ed.). Chicago: University of Chicago Press.

Bobrow, Davis and John Dryzek. (1989). *Policy Analysis by Design*. Pittsburgh: University of Pittsburgh Press.

Chan, Joseph and David Miller. (1991). "Elster on Self-Realization in Politics: A Critical Note." *Ethics* 102(1): 96–102.

DiMaggio, Paul and Walter Powell. (1991). "Introduction." In Walter Powell and Paul DiMaggio (eds.), *The New Institutionalism in Organizational Analysis* (pp. 1–38). Chicago: University of Chicago Press.

Denzin, Norman. (1990). "Reading Rational Choice Theory." *Rationality and Society* 2(2): 172–189.

Dryzek, John. (1987). "Discursive Designs: Critical Theory and Political Institutions." *American Journal of Political Science* 31(3): 656–679.

———. (1990). *Discursive Democracy*. New York: Cambridge University Press.

Fay, Brian. (1987). *Critical Social Science*. Ithaca, NY: Cornell University Press.

Fischer, Frank. (1990). *Technocracy and the Politics of Expertise*. Newbury Park, CA: Sage.

Forester, John (ed.). (1985). *Critical Theory and Public Life*. Cambridge, MA: MIT Press.

Fraser, Nancy. (1989). *Unruly Practices*. Minneapolis: University of Minnesota Press.

Friedmann, John. (1987). *Planning in the Public Domain*. Princeton, NJ: Princeton University Press.

———. (1991). *Empowerment*. Cambridge, MA: Blackwell.

Glendon, Mary Ann. (1991). *Rights Talk*. New York: Free Press.

Goldstein, Raymond L. and John K. Schoor. (1991). *Demanding Democracy after Three Mile Island*. Gainesville: University of Florida Press.

Gormley, William T. (1989). *Taming the Bureaucracy: Muscles, Prayers and Other Strategies*. Princeton, NJ: Princeton University Press.
Grafstein, Robert. (1991). *Institutional Realism*. New Haven, CT: Yale University Press.
Gray, John. (1986). *Liberalism*. Minneapolis: University of Minnesota Press.
Habermas, Jurgen. (1990). *Moral Consciousness and Communicative Action*. Translated by Christian Lenhardt and Shierry Weber Nicholsen. Cambridge, MA: MIT Press.
Handler, Joel. (1986). "Dependent People, the State, and the Modern/Postmodern Search for the Dialogic Community." *UCLA Law Review* 35(6): 999–1113.
———. (1990). *Law and the Search for Community*. Philadelphia: University of Pennsylvania Press.
Harrington, Christine. (1988). "Regulatory Reform: Creating Gaps and Creating Markets." *Law and Policy* 10(2): 291–316.
Hult, Karen and Charles Walcott. (1990). *Governing Public Organizations: Politics, Structure, and Institutional Design*. Pacific Grove, CA: Brooks/Cole.
Kloppenberg, James. (1986). *Uncertain Victory: Social Democracy and Progressivism in European and American Thought, 1870–1920*. New York: Oxford University Press.
Kymlicka, Will. (1989). *Liberalism, Community, and Culture*. New York: Oxford University Press.
Lasch, Christopher. (1988). "The Communitarian Critique of Liberalism." In Charles Reynolds and Ralph Norman (eds.), *Community in America* (pp. 173–184). Berkeley: University of California Press.
Linder, Stephen and B. Guy Peters. (1991). "The Logic of Public Policy Design: Linking Policy Actors and Plausible Instruments." *Knowledge and Policy* 4(1&2): 125–151.
———. (1992). "A Metatheoretic Analysis of Policy Design." In William N. Dunn and Rita Mae Kelly (eds.), *Advances in the Policy Sciences Since 1950* (pp. 201–237). New Brunswick, NJ: Transaction.
MacIntyre, Alisdair. (1981). *After Virtue: A Study in Moral Theory*. Notre Dame, IN: University of Notre Dame Press.
March, James G. and Johan P. Oslen. (1989). *Rediscovering Institutions: The Organizational Basis of Politics*. New York: Free Press.
Marcus, George and Michael M.J. Fischer. (1986). *Anthropology as Cultural Critique*. Chicago: University of Chicago Press.
Mulhall, Stephen and Adam Swift. (1992). *Liberals and Communitarians*. Cambridge, MA: Blackwell.
Nisbet, Robert. (1986). *Conservatism*. Minneapolis: University of Minnesota Press.
Ostrom, Elinor. (1990). *Managing the Commons*. New York: Cambridge University Press.
Rosenau, Pauline V. (1992). *Post-Modernism and the Social Sciences*. Princeton, NJ: Princeton University Press.
Sandel, Michael. (1982). *Liberalism and the Limits of Justice*. New York: Cam-

bridge University Press.
Selznick, Philip. (1992). *The Moral Commonwealth*. Berkeley: University of California Press.
Shalin, Dmitri. (1992). "Critical Theory and the Pragmatist Challenge." *American Journal of Sociology* 98(2): 237–279.
Teubner, Gunther (ed.). (1986). *Dilemmas of Law in the Welfare State*. New York: Walter de Gruyter.
Van Der Burg, Wibren. (1990). "Jurgen Habermas on Law and Morality: Some Critical Comments." *Theory, Culture and Society* 7(4): 105–112.
West, Cornel. (1987). *The American Evasion of Philosophy*. Madison: University of Wisconsin Press.
Westbrook, Robert. (1991). *John Dewey and American Democracy*. Ithaca, NY: Cornell University Press.
Young, Iris. (1990). *Justice and the Politics of Difference*. Princeton, NJ: Princeton University Press.

8 POLICY NETWORKS AND GOVERNANCE

Johan A. de Bruijn
Ernst F. ten Heuvelhof

1.0. Introduction: Institutionalism and Networks

In this chapter we focus on the management and the restructuring of networks, two themes that have recently attracted interest within the fields of public administration and policy analysis. Network approaches are in part a response to models in which policy making is seen as a more or less rational and sequential process from problem definition through policy intervention to evaluation and feedback. In network approaches, policy is seen as the result of interaction among corporate actors (Marin and Mayntz, 1991). These actors depend on each other for the realization of their aims and for this reason maintain ongoing relations with each other. This mutual dependency is often long-lived, leading to networks of relations that can be viewed as institutions. The policy networks evolve structures consisting of sets of values, norms, and rules. From a network perspective, institutional design can be viewed as efforts to alter these structures to achieve more desired outcomes.

Network approaches have their roots in, among other things, the literature on interorganizational relations, policy communities, "iron triangles," and policy subsystems (Rhodes, 1990; Klijn, 1992). These approaches have developed generally within European public administration, but especially in England (Rhodes, 1990), Germany (Marin and Mayntz, 1991), and the Netherlands (Hufen and Ringeling, 1990). The network perspective is a response to a number of scholarly and social developments (Kenis and Schneider, 1991; Willke, 1989: 236): First, modern Western societies have a high degree of functional differentiation. Society is divided into a large number of sectors, most of which possess a high degree of professionalism. Second, partly as a result of this process, the government itself is also highly fragmented. Many social problems require the involvement of several levels or units of government, which leads automatically to network-like situations. Third, the boundaries between the public and private sectors have become very blurred. There are corporate public actors who possess some of the characteristics of private firms and private actors who promote social goals. Fourth, many projects require involvement of both governments and private actors. The resultant entanglement brings into question the neat distinction between a government and a society to be governed; both public and private actors have ambitions for governance. Fifth, because many sectors of society have a high degree of professionalism, the possibilities for governance interventions by outside actors (including governments) are often highly dependent on professionals. Finally, internationalization involves governments in many policy processes that transcend the national level. Thus, national governments must increasingly make policy in circumstances involving nonhierarchic relations.

It is only very recently that much attention has been given to the question of how change occurs in networks. If one views governments as parts of networks, then the question has obvious relevance for understanding how governmental actors can realize their governance ambitions. In many European countries, where governments play a major role in the welfare state, this is an especially relevant question. Consequently, an interest among European scholars in network approaches arose not only out of a desire to describe but also to prescribe. The key question in terms of prescription is: How can a government realize its objectives in networks? This is often referred to as the issue of governance in policy networks.

In this chapter we first give a more detalied definition of a policy network. We then consider the question of how change processes can be shaped within networks. More particularly: How can governance take place in a network? In order to answer this question, we demonstrate that governance can be analyzed on three levels: the instrumental level (the use of policy instruments), the network management level (the change in relations among actors), and the network restructuring level (change in the cast of actors in a network). In subsequent sections, we explore the more strategic concepts of network management and network restructuring in greater depth.

2.0. Policy Networks: Main Characteristics

A consequence of the disparate origins of network theories is the absence of widely accepted and clearly defined concepts. We offer here what we believe to be useful elements of a theory of policy networks. We begin by defining a network as an entity consisting of public, quasi-public, or private actors who are dependent on each other and, as a consequence of this dependence, maintain relations with each other. In the following subsections, we identify four important characteristics of policy networks that are relevant to governance.

2.1. Interdependence

Actors in a network are dependent on each other in order to realize their goals. Consider, for example, an infrastructure project. It will almost certainly involve a number of actors (various governments, private firms, and pressure groups), who have various resources at their disposal (statutory powers and democratic legitimation; information and funds; and public support, respectively). If all these resources are essential to realize a particular project, then these actors are mutually dependent. These interdependent relations among actors constitute the defining characteristic of networks.

Interdependencies can be usefully described in terms of several dimensions: the number of actors who are mutually dependent (bilateral or multilateral relations); the relative stakes of the actors in the relations (symmetrical or asymmetrical stakes); the relative importance of their contributions to desired collective outcomes (essential or nonessential contributions); the timing of the contributions (simultaneous or sequential); the recurrence of the relationship (one-time or repeated); the stability of the characteristics of repeated relations (static or dynamic); and the complexity of the contributions exchanged in the relations (single-valued or multivalued).[1]

Interdependencies mean that actors often cannot further their goals without cooperation. Government actors, in particular, generally must seek cooperation to achieve effective governance because, first and foremost, the government is dependent on nongovernmental actors in the network. These other actors can use this dependence to realize their interests, perhaps adversely affecting the effectiveness of government action. Further, governance may be difficult because the overall picture of the interdependencies in a network can be complex and uncertain and therefore difficult to comprehend. For example, when a situation arises in which two governments and a dozen nongovernmental actors form a network, various interdependencies may manifest themselves simultaneously. Actors can, for example, be asynchronously, multilaterally, and recurrently dependent on each other. The resultant complexity can lead to frequent deadlocks in a network and, when government can act, to unpredictable and unintended side effects.

2.2. Pluriformity

Pluriformity describes the extent to which corporate actors in networks behave as if they were individuals with stable preferences: low pluriformity means that an actor can be reasonably treated as a individual; high pluriformity means that the actor behaves as a coalition of individuals.[2] Large organizations often consist of units that differ widely from each other. Anyone wishing to use policy instruments in a large organization must often deal with units of that organization. The nominal governing unit within the organization is sometimes as little capable as a government of governing the organization as a whole (Stone, 1975).

Limiting the number of actors during policy formation to facilitate negotiation and agreement risks confronting the problem of pluriformity during implementation. For example, a regulatory instrument developed in a network consisting of government agencies and a few peak organizations representing general business interests may actually result in a great variety of responses from firms in different sectors and of different sizes during implementation. Students of implementation recognize this problem as that of variability in the targets of policy intervention (Bardach, 1977: 129–132).

2.3. Self-Containment

The many actors and relations in a network generate a turbulent and complex environment. In response to this, organizations in a network can attempt to close themselves off from it (Willke, 1989). For example, state enterprises in the former Soviet Union often responded to uncertainty in supply of inputs by attempting to produce intermediate products, food, housing, and other services for their workers. Self-containment alters the frame of reference and norms that these organizations apply to issues in the policy network (Katz and Kahn, 1966). Laws and regulations may have little chance of success if their effectiveness depends on norms that do not fit within the frames of reference of the relevant actors.

The combination of interdependence and self-containment gives rise to a paradoxical image. Interdependencies require some form of cooperation between actors in a network. The uncertainty created by the large number of interdependencies, however, can lead to organizations closing themselves off from their environment and, consequently, making it harder to induce their cooperation. This is a well-known phenomenon that occurs in numerous policy fields: an "objective" analysis demonstrates that every actor in a network benefits from cooperation, but the actors are not receptive to cooperation because either they fear others will not make necessary contributions or they expect to receive some benefits even if they do not contribute (in other words, they "free ride").

2.4. *Instability*

Positions and relations in policy networks are continually undergoing change. The resources available to actors may change. New actors may join the network, while others may leave. Exogenous developments in the environment of a network can greatly change the relations among the actors in it. Previously independent networks can come into contact with each other with respect to particular policy issues such as might occur, for example, when the environmental consequences of agricultural policy become apparent. Networks can break up into independent parts as, for example, when a profession is granted authority for self-regulation by a government that previously regulated directly. Such instability implies that a previously effective policy instrument may, within a very short time, become inappropriate for a network. Flexibility in terms of changing policy may thus appear to be desirable. Ironically, however, the capacity for flexibility may make it difficult for actors to make credible commitments necessary to secure cooperation (Rodrik and Zeckhauser, 1988).

3.0. Strategic Governance

The characteristics of policy networks have important implications for governance. Interdependence, plurifomity, self-containment, and instability often impede the effectiveness of the standard sorts of policy instruments, such as prohibitions, direct regulation, taxes, and subsides, that suggest themselves in a hierarchical framework with strong governmental authority and plentiful governmental resources. In other words, the perspective of network theory brings into question the feasibility, and therefore the desirability, of instrumental governance. At the same time, network theory suggests two important strategic approaches to governance: network management and network restructuring. They are strategic in the sense that they anticipate the reactions of actors to changes in the characteristics of networks so as to make instrumental governance unnecessary or more effective. In contrast, instrumental governance is tactical in that it takes the network as given and attempts to alter behavior within it.

The characteristics of networks suggest approaches for their strategic governance. Interdependencies can be altered by such approaches as changes in liability rules or the avaliability of information. The degree of pluriformity can be changed by facilitating the organization of interests. Self-containment can be changed by making it more or less costly, say, by changing the nature of public discussion to shift the boundary between the publicly held views of the appropriate separation between the public and private spheres. Regulatory policies that attenuate international economic changes, for example, can be altered to change the level of network stability, perhaps to increase it in an effort to overcome entrenched interests or to decrease it in an effort to preserve cooperative coalitions.

As an illustration of the difference between instrumental governance and strategic governance, consider responses to the problem of the high social cost of disposal of the large quantities of domestic refuse that burden most developed economies. The use of disposable packaging contributes to these large quantities of refuse. Were reusable packaging to be employed, these quantities would be considerably reduced. A government that wishes to promote reusable packaging finds itself in a network of actors. These include, among others, the various suppliers of raw materials, the manufacturers of packaging materials, the packagers, distributors, retailers of products, and the consumers of the products.

Complicated patterns of interdependencies exist among these actors. The network is pluriform (for example, the consumers' movement may consist of various sections; there are major differences between the manufacturers of cardboard and those of glass; and there are numerous products and many packagers). Some actors are self-contained or might close themselves off in response to the implementation to specific policy instruments (international trading partners may set contradictory packaging standards). Finally, in a complicated network like this there is a good deal of instability (product innovations may change packaging patterns).

An instrumental governance approach might involve the government simply bringing a policy instrument into play. It could, for example, attempt to prescribe the adoption of reusable packaging through legislation. In view of the characteristics of the network, however, the consequences of such an approach would be difficult to predict.

A network management approach would involve the government altering the relations among actors. It could strengthen the position of the consumer movement and so enable it to exert more pressure on industry to favor recycling. Or it could, within the packagers' trade, find out which are the most important companies and strive to maintain strong ties with them to secure their cooperation in gradual movement toward greater use of recycled packaging. It could perhaps trade access to regulatory decision making in return for proprietary information to coopt industry leaders.

The network restructuring approach involves changing the number of actors. A government can, for example, make an effort to establish a number of organizations that specialize in setting up return systems. Once these have been set up, they can be expected to be a significant factor in promoting reusable packaging systems. Network management and network restructuring together can be used to provide a favorable climate for instrumental governance. A government may, in time, decide to impose regulations on the packagers' requiring the use of reusable packaging (instrumental governance). If done in cooperation with the coopted firms, then there is a chance that other firms will follow, especially if all firms are under pressure from the consumer's movement, while, due to the entry of new actors (the return specialists), reusable packaging has become a more attractive option.

We develop the strategies of network managment and restructuring further in the following section where we outline the specific activities that can be used to implement them. First, however, two general points are worthy of note.

First, network management and restructuring are very closely associated with each other. Network restructuring provides opportunities for network management; by adding actors to a network, relations among existing actors can change. An example of network restructuring that will have this effect is the breakup of the range of activities engaged in by public rail transportation companies. This topic is currently being discussed in several West European countries. The present situation is that the construction of the rail infrastructure, the operation of it, and transportation activities are all in one hand – that of the public transportation company. Consequently, it is a monopolistic organization. It is the intention that these three types of activities be disentangled from each other and transferred to different organizations. Transportation could then be provided by several companies. As a result, the monopoly in this area will cease to exist, which will drastically change the relations between the users and providers of transportation. The connection between network management and network restructuring may also go in the other direction. Network management may take shape in such a way that opportunities for network restructuring are created: relations among actors are reworked so as to attract new actors to join the network. A government may impose an obligation on the packaging industry to take back part of the packagings supplied to the retail trade. It thus changes relations among actors in the packaging chain (the network management). At the same time, it creates for various types of actors (recycling firms, transportation companies and the like) possibilities to acquire a position in the network (network restructuring).

Second, the changes in interdependencies, pluriformity, self-containment, and instability may interact. For example, a change in interdependencies can lead to a change in the self-containment of actors, or reducing pluriformity by facilitating more coherent internal organization of an actor can lead to the actor having more favorable interdependencies. Thus, strategic governance does not necessarily avoid the complexity that plagues instrumental governance. Rather, it attempts to take account of the complexity more explicity.

4.0. Approaches to Network Management and Restructuring

In this section we explore approaches to network management and restructuring: developing redundant relations among actors, changing perceptions of actors, balancing relations, altering network stability, and generating symbiotic relations.

4.1. Developing Redundancy

Governance in networks is, first and foremost, a highly information-sensitive process. Effectiveness usually requires governments to kept informed of the relations and contact patterns of the actors in the network. The less stable a network, the more important it is for governments to update their information frequently.

In practice, governments usually must maintain ongoing contacts with the other actors in the network to gather timely information. A number of scholars have drawn attention to the importance of redundant contacts (Landau, 1969; Bendor, 1985), which, in the network context, can be thought of as establishing channels through which information reaches actors. Redundancy allows governments to extract more information out of a network. It also makes it more difficult for actors to manipulate information for strategic purposes because discrepancies with information from alternative sources can alert the recipient to the manipulation. A redundant system of information streams increases the chance of governments "accidentally" receiving useful information (Rosenthal, 1988).

More generally, maintaining redundant relations is a form of network management and restructuring because these relations ("linkages," Gage and Mandell, 1989) can function as a means of reducing or utilizing the dependencies of certain actors (Emerson, 1962).

A government can develop "bypasses": in conjunction with the existing relation, a new relation is developed (the bypass) with an actor who intends to be more cooperative (Gilmore and Krantz, 1991). Bilateral dependencies are thus turned into multilateral ones. The additional relations reduce inflexibility. They may also reduce the problem of "odd man out" whereby the actor holding the last essential contribution to a collective effort can extra returns from those who have already agreed to contribute (Bardach, 1977: 163–167).

A government can strive to convert a one-time or irregular relation with a certain actor to one that is recurrent. If the actor in question anticipates important dealings with the government not only in the present but also in the future, then a higher level of cooperation may result.[3] The possibilities for creating recurrent relations range from subjecting some aspect of the actor's behavior to ongoing regulation to the creation of consultative bodies.

A government can often increase its opportunities for governance by better understanding the relations in the network. For example, actors can sometimes be clearly identified as "leaders" in a target group: should they decide to change their bahavior, the remaining members of a network tend to follow. A government can use this information to strengthen relations with the leaders. Close relations with the leaders not only open up potential avenues for intervening in the network but can also strengthen the leadership position of these actors. Thus a government can maintain close relations with a "leader" (network management), so that specific policies (instrumental governance) will be more effective. For example, subsidies for innovation given to leaders may result in adoption of the innovations throughout the targeted network (De Bruijn, 1990).

When there is no clear leader, a government may be able to create a leadership group by establishing close relations with several actors, thus upsetting the equal position of the actors in the network. If the selected group is favored by the government through the use of preferential instruments, then the remaining actors in the network may be forced to adapt their bahavior in desirable ways. A similar form of network management has been used with regard to innovations in Dutch universities (Maassen and Potman, 1990).

Finally, recognizing that many networks are very unstable, there is one more significant point to be made here. Maintaining relations is certainly vital with regard to actors who occupy strategically important positions in a network. Ongoing relations with actors who have a less strategic positions, however, are often no less important. These are often known as "weak ties." Relations are not very intensive but are kept alive, as it were, for occasional use. Maintaining "weak ties" can be crucial to good network management because instability may make previously unimportant actors strategic. "Weak ties" increase the changes that effective relations can be established quickly with the newly strategic actors (Granovetter, 19973).

4.2. Changing Perceptions

Within networks, opinions and value systems become institutionalized as self-reinforcing expectations. It is important for governance how varied the opinions and value systems are in the network, and what the perceptions of the actors belonging to the network are of these various opinions and value systems. Katrien Termeer describes the problems of the overproduction of manure in the Netherlands in these terms. Within the livestock industry network, reducing the number of livestock is an idea that has been unacceptable for a long time. In the network of environmentalist groups and certain government agencies, there is an image of agriculture as a major polluter and consumer of endless subsides (Termeer, 1993). The relevant network for policy making can greatly influence the reception received by certain policy instruments. This may mean, for example, that the use of policy instruments geared toward reducing the number of livestock would receive a much less favorable reception from the target group than from the environmentalist network.

Institutionalized opinions and value systems have a function within networks. They facilitate contact and communication between actors, which is often not easy owing to the complex structure of the network. On the other hand, this institutionalization can also be obstructive: certain reality and problem definitions are systematically excluded from the network. As a result of this, the effectiveness of policy instruments may be radically reduced.

In such situations it is important that the government strive to overturn the institutionalized opinions. In general terms this means convincing the actors in a network of the dysfunctionality of their reality definitions. Such a "reframing" can be attempted on the instrumental level by bringing communicative instruments into play. The effectiveness of these instruments appears from a great deal of research to be limited (de Bruijn and ten Heuvelhof, 1991). It is, indeed, a characteristic of institutionalized norms that they do not allow themselves to be changed by a small-scale transfer of information. Thus "reframing" through network management and restructuring may be necessary to alter the norms.

Network management may involve generating uncertainty in the network; uncertainty implies, indeed, that existing definitions are called into question. An example of this might be announcements that a radical stepping up of regulatory stringency is in the offing. The actors who think they might fall under these regulations may reinforce their mutual contacts and those with the government, whereby opportunities may arise for the exchange of ideas about problems, perhaps creating an opportunity to achieve a greater convergence of views. Environmental policy in Holland provides an example of such convergence. Issues are described in increasingly strident terms and the threat of draconic international measures is raised. As a consequence, industry draws together and initiates research, often in collaboration with the government, that increases the chance of agreement on national policy.

Adding actors to a network (network restructuring) can help weaken institutionalized opinions and value systems. These actors bring with them different perceptions that they employ in relations with other actors who are already present. This can lead to reflection by the original actors in the network that may change opinions and value systems.

Network restructuring and management can take shape in innumerable ways. The government can set up a new organization and equip it with certain powers, so that actors in the network must interact with it. Or the government can make use of market mechanisms. It can create a demand for goods or services that induces the entry of new actors. Thus, for example, by prescribing that municipal refuse be collected in separate categories, it may be able to induce the entry of recycling firms whose existence alters the entire network of refuse processing. The government also can add new actors to a network through regulation that induces the introduction of new actors. Requiring that certain industrial processes be subjected to independent professional review, for instance, might induce the formation of firms that offer such review services. It can be thought of as "restructuring regulation," which is distinct from "instrumental regulation" (Van Der Doelen, 1989).

It is worth noting that actors almost always operate in several networks simultaneously. From the perspective of any particular network, they have internal and external relations. The external relations that actors maintain influence their behavior in the network: actors take perceptions along with them from one network to the other.

Perceptions and insights acquired in one network can lead to unfreezing of entrenched perceptions and relations in the other network (Termeer and Van Twist, 1991: 189–190; Klijn and Teisman, 1991), thereby changing opportunities for governance. Here, again, the importance of redundant relations is evident: by entering into a number of relations, a government may be able to employ insights gained in one network to another network. It also may be able to influence an actor who has set up blocks in one network by changing the nature of a relations with this actor in some other network.

4.3. Balancing Relations: Cooperation and Conflict

Network management and restructuring are activities in which the balance of cooperation and conflict is crucial. A government can display cooperative behavior such as consulation, negotiation, coalition formation, and conciliation of divergent aims or problem definitions (Klijn and Teisman, 1992). Moreover, various techniques can be employed, such as negotiating package deals, splitting the difference, securing concurrent consent, and agreeing to disagree (Streeck and Schmitter, 1991: 228). At the same time, the government can initiate conflict through the use of its various coercive powers.

These processes can sometimes be executed in such a way that certain actors are effectively eliminated from the network. Elimination can be achieved through the removal of actors (for example: withdrawing a subsidy to an advisory body), through market mechanisms (for example, causing the demand for an actor's products or services to fall), or through constitutive regulation (for example, by building barriers to entry in restructuring regulation).

Striking a balance between cooperation and conflict is an important aspect of effective network management. The government must be able to send both negative and positive signals in response to the behaviors of those in the network. In the international arena, a network-type situation, countries may be in conflict, but simultaneously maintain (informal) cooperative relations because they anticipate that in the future they may again wish to have "normal" relations.

Alternating, or simultaneously maintaining, relations of cooperation and conflict can become counterproductive in circumstances of imperfect information. Actors may not be able to relate fully their perceptions of their own actions to the government responses. Actors observing these interactions are likely to be even less able to see the connection between actions and responses. The government thus runs the risk of developing a reputation for being unreliable (ten Heuvelhof, 1993).

A government may be able to take advantage of its own pluriformity in balancing relations of cooperation and conflict. For example, several of its agencies can enter into contact with the actors in a network simultaneously. Conflicts initiated by some agencies may induce agents to cooperate with other agencies that can intervene on their behalf. A government imposing environmental measures on industry will be able to induce intense conflicts. Nevertheless, it must remain on speaking terms with this very industry. Industry in turn will wish to maintain constructive relations on other issues, in spite of conflicts about environmental issues. A government that channels its environmental signals through a department for the environment and its other signals through a department of economic affairs is able to take advantage of its pluriformity and maintain at the same time relations of cooperation and conflict.

4.4. Altering Stability: A "Negotiated Environment"

Instability in a network generally creates demand for greater certainty and predictability. Some instability is unavoidable, in view of the many actors and interests; some instability is desirable, if deadlocks are to be avoided in responding to changing environments. Moreover, if there occurs much movement in a network, in which actors and the relations among them are changing frequently and rapidly, then there arise possibilities for alert actors to strengthen their respective positions. The entry of new actors and the disappearance of linkages will increase the need for new relations and coalitions. An actor capable of dealing with this instability will have possibilities to present itself as a new coalition partner.

Yet if there is too much instability, actors have difficulty advancing their own interests and cooperating because they cannot anticipate the bahavior of others.

In addition, however, there is also need for stability. Actors that try to govern are doing so on the basis of a so-called governance theory: the connection between their interventions and the bahavior of the actors to be governed. As the movement of the relations in the network intensifies, it becomes increasingly problematic to formulate and test such a theory. Instability may eventually reach a point at which an actor can no longer form an idea about the consequences of its interventions. Instability then becomes an obstacle to the formulation of a governance theory.

Creating stability and points of reference in a network is considered in the literature as a important aspect of network management (Termeer, 1993). One approach to reducing instability and the uncertainty it produces is for organizations to develop more credible relations by sharing members (Lang and Lockhart, 1990: 106–128). These members, as in interlocking directorates, can convey reliable information between organizations to facilitate coordination. Other devices, such as memoranda of understanding, formalized agreements, and agreed-upon decision-making procedures and structures can also contribute to greater stability.

Government can play a role in facilitating greater stability by providing a negotiated environment. Consider, for example, the many advisory bodies that are set up by governments. They provide a negotiated environment for nongovernment actors who know that government interventions will take shape only after the advisory bodies have issued their reports. Sometimes these actors can contribute indirectly to the reports through their relations to members of these bodies.

The demand for stabilization from members in a network varies over time. It is particularly at such times that a government has many opportunities for structuring a network in a way favorable to itself. Indeed, this suggests that a government may at times find it useful to generate uncertainty, thereby generating a demand for stability and the opportunities that arise in satisfying it. For example, threatening to use draconian measures in the battle against environmental pollution, or conducting a publicity offensive about the economic consequences of a single European market, can generate uncertainty and with it a demand for stability. Rob Van Es points out that some forms of behavior that might appear on the surface to be irrational may actually be quite rational if they generate a demand for stability and thus provide opportunities for restructuring the network (Van Es, 1991).

Interventions to restructure networks may lead to changes that are deeper and more permanent than those typically obtained through the use of ordinary governance instruments. Thus, they are both attractive and risky. The attraction is that entrenched relations, which would otherwise leave no room for change, can be unfrozen. The risk is that the resulting movement may put in motion changes that grow sufficiently large so as to produce a net degradation of governance.

Network management and restructuring are brought into play with a view to mitigating problems. Perhaps even specific goals are formulated. The complexity of the network structures involved, and of the current and new processes within them, however, may be far too great to be able to make reliable predictions about the changes that will actually result. With network management and restructuring, new opportunities may arise that, on account of their complexity and interrelated nature, are difficult to predict in advance. It may be productive, therefore, to consider such processes as "garbage cans" – that is, "highly contextual combinations of people, choice opportunities, problems and solutions" (March and Olsen, 1989: 80; Kingdon, 1984; Cohen, March, and Olsen, 1972). From this perspective, governance is to only a limited extent a process that lends itself to ex ante planning. To use Mintzberg's terminology, network management will consist partly of "intended strategies" and partly of "emergent strategies" (Mintzberg, 1978). Emergent strategies are not planned beforehand but manifest themselves during the process of network management as a consequence of unexpected developments.

4.5. Generating Symbiosis

In oder to promote cooperative behavior, a network should be structured in such a way that actors, with their interests and dependencies, perceive a need for each other's cooperation to further their interests. The expectation of net benefits from being in the network motivates actors to remain willingly in it. Network management can be viewed as the reworking of relations in such a way that the goals of individual actors and those of the governing actor are sufficiently congruent to offer mutual benefits from cooperation.

For all actors, the search for net benefits makes two key demands on those attempting to manage the network. First of all, a "cooperative surplus" must be generated for each actor. It must be evident to all actors that the potential net benefits in the case of uncooperative behavior will be smaller than the net benefits in the case of cooperative bahavior. Second, actors must be prevented from displaying opportunistic behavior (on opportunism, see Williamson, 1985). Russell Johnston and Paul Lorenz indicate the significant risk of ex post opportunism: actors have already realized their own gains and pull out of the network to avoid costs, thereby endangering realization of aggregate net benefits for the rest of the network (Johnston and Lorenz, 1991).

How may this kind of network management be executed? The point of departure for governance lies in the way in which the interactions are perceived and how mutual relations are seen to work. It is important for a government to offer to actors the prospect of net benefits. The least complex situation is one in which the government promises to reward certain kinds of behavior directly. The government can prohibit actors from displaying certain kinds of behavior by means of legal measures, through financial incentives, or by offering other things of value to actors such as information. Ensuring net benefits may also be attempted through lowering the net benefits from noncooperation. For example, cooperating firms might be exempted from costly new regulations. The perception of such threats is often more important than the question of whether and how these threats are actually carried out.

5.0. Conclusion

In this chapter we focused attention on networks and, in particular, on the question of how governance in networks can be accomplished. Governments should not limit their attention to particular instruments. Rather, it is important that they also create a favorable climate in which these instruments can be used with the greatest chance of success if they are to achieve effective governance. Managing and restructuring networks are the processes by which more favorable environments can be created. Yet because networks are complex, these processes involve considerable uncertainty. Consequently, effective governance in networks requires establishing relations for the gathering of information and flexibility in the use of strategies.

Notes

1. To make a connection to game theory, a nonrepeated prisoner's dilemma would be described as bilateral, symmetric, essential, simultaneous, single valued, and one-time.

2. Theories of international relations, for example, usually treat the network of countries as having low pluriformity. Theories that attempt to incorporate domestic politics assume a

high level of pluriformity. For tests of these competing theories of international relations, see Bueno de Mesquita and Lalman (1992).

3. In game theoretic terms, the repetition of the game may support cooperative equilibria that would not be supportable in one-time play.

References

Bardach, Eugene. (1977). *The Implementation Game: What Happens After a Bill Becomes a Law*. Cambridge, MA: MIT Press.

Bendor, Jonathan. (1985). *Parallel Systmes: Redundancy in Government*. Berkeley: University of California Press.

Bueno de Mesquita, Bruce and David Lalman. (1992). *War and Reason: Domestic and International Imperatives*. New Haven, CT: Yale University Press.

Cohen, Michael D., James G. March, and Johan P. Olsen. (1972). "A Garbage Can Model of Organizational Choice." *Administrative Science Quarterly* 17(1): 1–25.

de Bruijn, Johan A. (1990). *Economische zaken en economische subsidies*. 's-Gravenhage: VUGA Uitgeverij.

de Bruijn, Johan A. and Ernst F. Ten Heuvelhof. (1991). *Sturingsinstrumenten voor de overheid*. Leiden/Antwerpen: Stenfert Kroese Uitgevers.

Emerson, Richard M. (1962). "Power-Dependance Relations." *American Sociological Review* 27(1): 31–41.

Gage, Robert W. and Myrna P. Mandell. (1989). *Strategies for Managing Intergovernmental Policies and Networks*. New York: Praeger.

Gilmore, Thomas N. and James Krantz. (1991). "Innovation in the Public Sector, Dilemmas in the Use of Ad Hoc Processes." *Journal of Policy Analysis and Management* 10(3): 455–468.

Granovetter, Mark S. (1973). "The Strength of Weak Ties." *American Journal of Sociology* 78(6): 1360–1380.

Hufen, Hans A.M. and Arthur B. Ringeling (eds.). (1990). *Beleidsnetwerken. Overheids-, semi-overheids- en particuliere organisaties in wisselwerking*. 's-Gravenhage: VUGA Uitgeverij.

Johnston, Russell and Paul R. Lorenz. (1991). "Beyond Vertical Integration. The Rise of the Value Adding Partnership." In Grahame Thompson, Jennifer Frances, Rosalind Levačić and Jeremy Mitchell (eds.), *Markets, Hierarchies and Networks: The Coordination of Social Life* (pp. 193–202). London: Sage.

Katz, Daniel and Robert L. Kahn. (1966). *The Social Psychology of Organizations*. New York: Willey.

Kenis, Patrick and Volker Schneider. (1991). "Policy Networks and Policy Analysis: Scrutinizing a New Analytical Toolbox." In Bernd Marin and Renate Mayntz (eds.), *Policy Networks: Empirical Evidence and Theoretical Considerations* (pp. 26–59). Frankfurt am Main: Campus Verlag.

Kingdon, John W. (1989). *Agendas, Alternatives, and Public Policies*. Boston: Little, Brown.

Klijn, Erik-Hans. (1992). *Policy Communities, Subsystems and Networks: An Examination and Reformulation of Some Concepts for Analyzing Complex Policy Processes*. Rotterdam: Erasmus University.

Klijn, Erik-Hans and Geert R. Teisman. (1992). "Besluitvorming in beleidsnetwerken: een theoretische beschouwing over het analyseren en verbeteren van beleidsprocessen in complexe beleidsstelsels (Decision Making in Policy Networks: A Theoretical Study on Analysing and Improving Policy Processes in Complex Policy Systems)." *Beleidswetenschap* 6(1): 32–51.

Landau, Martin. (1969). "Redundancy, Rationality and the Problem of Duplication and Overlap." *Public Administration Review* 29(4): 346–350.

Lang, James R. and Daniel E. Lockhart. (1990). "Increased Environmental Uncertainty and Changes in Board Linkage Patterns." *Academy of Management Journal* 39(1): 106–128.

Maassen, Peter A.M. and Henry P. Potman. (1990). "Strategievorming in het hoger onderwijs." *Beleidswetenschap* 4(2): 112–130.

March, James G. and Johan P. Olsen. (1989). *Rediscovering Institutions: The Organizational Basis of Politics*. New York: Free Press.

Marin, Bernd. (1990). *Generalized Political Exchange*. Frankfurt am Main: Campus Verlag.

Marin, Bernd and Renate Mayntz (eds.). (1991). *Policy Networks, Empirical Evidence and Theoretical Considerations*. Frankfurt am Main: Campus Verlag.

Mintzberg, Henry. (1978). "Patterns in Strategy Formation." *Management Science* 24(9): 934–948.

Rhodes, Richard A.W. (1990). "Policy Networks, A British Perspective." *Journal of Theoretical Politics* 2(3): 293–317.

Rodrik, Dani and Richard J. Zeckhauser. (1988). "The Dilemma of Government Responsiveness." *Journal of Policy Analysis and Management* 7(4): 601–620.

Rosenthal, Uri. (1988). "Van sturing tot toeval (From Governance to Coincidence)." In W.C.M. van Lieshout et al. (eds.), *Bestuur en meesterschap: opstellen over samenleving, staat en sturing* (pp. 19–27). 's-Gravenhage: Staatsuitgeverij.

Stone, Christopher D. (1975). *Where the Law Ends: The Social Control of Corporate Behavior*. New York: Harper & Row.

Streeck, Wolfgang and Philippe C. Schmitter. (1991). "Community, Market, State – and Associations? The Prospective Contribution of Interest Governance to Social Order." In Grahame Thompson, Jennifer Frances, Rosalind Levačić and Jeremy Mitchell (eds.), *Markets, Hierarchies and Networks: The Coordination of Social Life* (pp. 227–241). London: Sage.

ten Heuvelhof, Ernst F. (1993). *Gedragsnormen voor overheden in horizontale structuren*. 's-Gravenhage: VUGA Uitgeverij.

Termeer, Katrien J.A.M. (1993). *Dynamiek en inertie rondom mestbeleid*. 's-Gravenhage: VUGA Uitgeverij.

Termeer, Katrien J.A.M. and Mark J.W. Van Twist. (1991). "De configuratiebenadering: een procestheorie over sturingvraagstukken (The Configuration Approach: A Process Theory of Governance Issues)." *Beleid & Maatschappij* 6(4): 185–195.

Van Der Doelen, Frans C.J. (1989). *Beleidsinstrumenten en energiebesparing: de toepassing en effectiviteit van voorlichting en subsidies, gericht op energiebesparing in de industrie van 1977 tot 1987*. Enschede: Universiteit Twente.

Van Es, Rob. (1991). *Een ethiek van belangen: moreel handelen door onderhandelen over belangen*. Groningen: Wolters Noordhoff.

Williamson, Oliver E. (1985). *The Economic Institutions of Capitalism*. New York: Free Press.

Willke, Helmut. (1989). *Systemtheorie entwickelter Gesellschaften: Dynamik und Riskanz moderner gesellschaftlicher Selbstorganisation*. Weinheim: Juventa.

AUTHOR INDEX

SUBJECT INDEX